THE FIRST TEN
K R NARAYANAN ORATIONS

Essays by Eminent Persons on the
Rapidly Transforming Indian Economy

THE FIRST TEN
K R NARAYANAN ORATIONS

Essays by Eminent Persons on the
Rapidly Transforming Indian Economy

RAGHBENDRA JHA (EDITOR)

ANU
THE AUSTRALIAN NATIONAL UNIVERSITY

E PRESS

ANU

E PRESS

Published by ANU E Press
The Australian National University
Canberra ACT 0200, Australia
Email: anuepress@anu.edu.au
Web: http://epress.anu.edu.au

National Library of Australia
Cataloguing-in-Publication entry

The first ten K R Narayanan orations : essays by eminent
persons on the rapidly transforming Indian economy.

Bibliography
ISBN 1 920942 71 8 (pbk)
ISBN 1 920942 72 6 (online)

1. India - Economic conditions - 1947- . 2. India -
Economic policy - 1947- . 3. India - Politics and
government - 1947- . I. Jha, Raghbendra.

330.954

Cover design by ANU E Press

To the memory of Dr K R Narayanan

Contents

An Introduction to the Volume

The Australia South Asia Research Centre (henceforth ASARC) was established in 1994 in one of the premier universities of the world — The Australian National University. ASARC was inaugurated by His Excellency Dr K R Narayanan, then Vice President of India and was given the broad mandate of pursuing research into the economics and politics of the South Asia region taking into account Australia's national interests, and the dynamics of economic cooperation and interaction in the Asia–Pacific and Indian Ocean regions.

Whereas such research would be pursued by the faculty and graduate students associated with the centre, ASARC needed a public forum with a truly global reach, to involve the best minds working on the problem of economic development in India as well as to honour its founder, Dr K R Narayanan. The K R Narayanan Oration (henceforth the Oration) series was conceived in response to these twin needs.

The first Oration was held in 1994 and the tenth in 2006. ASARC has decided to collect the texts of these ten lectures in a commemorative volume as a mark of its contribution to the debate on the nascent process of economic reforms in India. This volume contains reflections on several dimensions of this process by eminent economists and policymakers. The topics covered include broad perspectives on tax reforms, India's space program and its role in economic development, prospects for the Indian economy, democratisation of India's reforms, the transformation of India's monetary policy regime from one of excessive control to one guided by market principles, political economy issues, the recent acceleration in India's growth rate and the role of science in shaping India's agricultural future.

These topics cover a very wide canvas and the orators themselves are not just among the leading experts in their respective fields, but have contributed significantly to policymaking in India in general and the reforms in particular and are also household names in India. This has led to widespread recognition of the Narayanan Oration series as one of the very best 'India' oration series anywhere in the world.

This overview of the lectures is organized around five broad themes that the oration has pursued rather than chronologically. I first consider contributions in the economics area by four orators who have played important roles in the formulation of India's economic reforms program. I then consider other contributions in the economics area, the political economy of India's development and two other scientific areas closely related to India's economic development — science and food security and space research. I now briefly discuss the orations organized around these themes.

Although the current phase of India's economic reforms program began in earnest in 1991 when the current Prime Minister, Dr Manmohan Singh, was Minister of Finance, background work for the reforms program had begun earlier, in particular during the period when Mr Rajiv Gandhi was India's Prime Minister. Under his visionary leadership a significant amount of preparatory work for the reforms program was done. Four of the most significant contributors to this work, as well as outstanding articulators of the reforms program, have since delivered the Narayanan Oration. Thus Dr Raja Chelliah, one of the leading experts on public finance and chair of an important government committee constituted by Mr Gandhi to institute tax reforms in India, delivered the first Oration in 1994. Dr Chelliah gave a lucid account of the tax reforms that had taken place in India and laid down a roadmap for subsequent reform. Various governments since then have broadly followed the Chelliah Committee's recommendations in respect of tax reforms. This has not only led to a degree of fiscal consolidation, but also a more harmonised tax structure and an improved revenue performance, among several other benefits.

Professor Jagdish Bhagwati had been a staunch advocate pf pro-market reform even in the 1960s when most economists in India were inclined to favour central planning. When Manmohan Singh's reforms were initiated in 1991, Bhagwati (along with T.N. Srinivasan) provided a robust intellectual backdrop and a roadmap for these reforms. In the 1996 Oration Bhagwati gave a succinct account of the reforms program India had embarked upon and the tasks that lay ahead. Although the reforms program had yielded some dividends much remained to be done, he argued.

The 1999 Oration was delivered by Mr P. Chidambaram who, as Minister in Rajiv Gandhi's cabinet and in several subsequent cabinets, had a ringside view and an important direct role in the reforms program. Mr Chidambaram made important contributions to India's tariff reforms program (as Minister of Commerce) as well as to tax and expenditure policies (as Finance Minister, which he is now as well) and to administrative reforms (as Minister of Personnel Affairs). In his oration Mr Chidambaram emphasized the needs for democratisation of the Indian reforms program since, in a democratic country such as India, political support was essential for the success of any reforms program.

Another major policy initiative during Rajiv Gandhi's tenure as Prime Minister was the constitution of a committee to advise on the transition to a monetary policy regime characterised by market-based instruments with the Reserve Bank of India (India's central bank) progressively becoming more independent of the Ministry of Finance. Some of the most significant steps in this direction were begun when Dr C. Rangarajan was Deputy Governor and then Governor of the Reserve Bank of India. Among his many lasting contributions to monetary policy-making in India are the breaking of the, till then, automatic link between central government deficits and changes in the money supply, the devising of several market-based instruments as well as designing an appropriate monetary policy response to the balance of payments crisis in the early 1990s. In his 2001 Narayanan Oration Dr Rangarajan gave a lucid account of monetary policy reforms in India and the tasks that lay ahead.

The 2004 Narayanan Oration was delivered by Dr Vijay Kelkar who, as a distinguished economist and policymaker, has contributed much to sustaining the economic reforms program. For instance he chaired a recent influential tax reforms committee and worked as Minister of State in the Ministry of Finance until 2004. Dr Kelkar's oration sought to underscore the strengths that the Indian economy has been amassing since the reforms program began as well as the supply side dividends that are expected to last for at least a couple of decades. He emphasized that the role of deep reforms in a number of areas including foreign trade, taxation, financial markets and policy, investment and budgetary consolidation along with important supply side changes such as India's demographic dividend have placed the economy on a path of sustainable higher growth which could well accelerate in the future.

In the 2002 Narayanan Oration Lord Meghnad Desai gave a vivid account of the political dimensions of economic reforms in India. The pro-reform political space in India is small and political parties in opposition have sometimes taken a populist or anti-reforms stance whereas the same political parties may have been pro-reform when in power. Lord Desai pointed out the significance of timing in the reforms strategy and argued that political consensus in favour of reforms needs to be consolidated rapidly in order to ensure that rapid growth is sustained and fruits of reforms percolate to the poor. He argued that only the formation of a German style grand coalition between the Congress and the Bharatiya Janata Party could deliver this.

In his 2003 Oration Professor Pranab Bardhan argued that democracy in India had empowered many marginal groups and had made them assertive partners in the decision-making process. In this transition, however, several disjunctures have appeared. In particular the state has, at the margin, been abdicating its responsibilities in relation to the provision of many basic services like quality education. Addressing these junctures should be a matter of the highest priority for Indian policymakers because in the absence of such efforts it would be difficult to sustain any program of economic reforms. Consequently any reduction in poverty and/or inequality that would attend these reforms would also be hard to achieve.

Apart from these contributions on the economics and political economy aspects of India's economic development the Narayanan Oration has featured the highest quality speakers in two areas intimately linked to sustaining rapid economic growth — science and food security and space research. In the 2005 Oration the distinguished agricultural scientist Dr M.S. Swaminathan, often known as the father of the Indian Green Revolution, presented an overview of the many difficulties on the food security front that India had successfully faced. He also outlined the emerging challenges in regard to food security as well as to making agricultural growth sustainable with respect to, among other factors, its impact on the environment. Dr Swaminathan outlined the contours of a policy of an evergreen revolution and sketched the implications of this policy for the Indian government as well as global arrangements and agreements.

In the 1995 Oration Professor U R Rao, one of India's foremost space scientists who was then a member of the Space Commission of India gave an account of the role that space research had already played in India's economic development. Indeed applications of space research had revolutionised many critical areas of infrastructure such as weather forecasting, satellite communication and imaging, food security, distance education and the like. Solutions to the ever growing and changing problems faced by Indians, indeed the entire humankind, could not be sought in resources available on earth alone. In fact it was more economical and efficient to address many of these problems by harnessing space research.

In the 2006 Oration Dr K. Kasturirangan, another of India's top space scientists, traced the growth of India's space program over the past forty-five years and argued that this program has distinguished itself through its focus on societal applications of advanced technology, unbroken chain of innovations in the organization of a multidisciplinary venture of high risk nature, and accomplishments of multidimensional character engaging industry, academia and international bodies. The program successfully met the myriads of challenges emanating from difficulties in the creation of scientific organizational culture in a bureaucratic set up; from forging linkages between creators and users of technologies to coping with geopolitical vicissitudes of technology denials; and from sustaining confidence of multi-party democratic political systems to maintaining a conscious drive for cost efficiency, autonomy and the ethic of social responsibility. Dr Kasturirangan also outlined a conceptual model as to how space achievements of India could be shared with neighboring countries.

This collection of the Narayanan Orations is thus at once both an expert account of key aspects of the economic development process in India and a peek into India's potential in the future. As such, the publication of these essays marks a watershed in the intellectual debate on India's economic reforms program and should be welcomed by all those interested in the economic development of India.

Apart from the orators themselves a number of individuals have contributed to the success of the Narayanan Oration series. Dr K R Narayanan sent messages of introduction for the 1994, 1995, 1996, 1999 and 2001 orations and remained a supporter of the oration almost until his passing away in November 2005. Dr Narayanan was Vice President of India during the 1994, 1995, and 1996 orations and President during the 1999 and 2001 orations. His successor as President of India, His Excellency Dr A.P.J. Abdul Kalam, sent kind messages for the 2002, 2004, 2005 and 2006 orations. These messages are printed along with the respective accompanying orations. ASARC is honoured to have the high office of the President of India continue to be associated with the oration.

We are much obliged to the Australia–India Council (AIC) for its consistent and unflinching financial support for this oration. Members of AIC have participated generously and enthusiastically in the oration series and, additionally, AIC has financially supported the publication of this commemorative volume.

We are also grateful to our other funding agencies over the years: Australian Bureau of Statistics (ABS) (2001), Network Economics Consulting Group (NECG now CRA International) (2001–2003), ANU's National Institute for Asia & the Pacific (2004), National Institute of Economics & Business (2003–2005) and the Research School of Pacific & Asian Studies (2004 & 2006), as well as the Australian Centre for International Agricultural Research (ACIAR) (2005).

In Canberra the office of the High Commissioner of India has been very helpful in organising the oration. The High Commissioner of India has traditionally read out the message sent by Dr Narayanan to the oration, when he was, first, Vice President and, subsequently, President of India. Since 2002 the Indian High Commissioner has read out the message sent to the oration by the current President of India — Dr A.P.J. Abdul Kalam. We are grateful to Their Excellencies Mr A.M. Khaleeli (1994), Mr G.S. Parthasarathy (1995 & 1996), Mrs Jordana Pavel (Acting 1999), Mr R.S. Rathore (2001–2003) and Mr P.P. Shukla (2004–2006) for reading out these messages.

I would like to thank the previous organizers of the Narayanan Oration, particularly Richard Shand, Kaliappa Kalirajan and Prema-chandra Athukorala, for initiating and sustaining this lecture series in its early years. The oration series in its present form builds upon their hard work.

Over the years a number of ASARC administrators have organized the details of the oration and helped ensure that each oration was a success. Carolyn Sweeney managed the 1994, 1995, 1996, 1999 orations whereas Hilda Heidemanns, Loan Dao-Czezowski and Bonny Allen were associated with the 2001 oration. ASARC is grateful to all of them for their contributions. Stephanie Hancock has worked tirelessly and efficiently in organizing the minutest detail of each of the last five Narayanan Orations. She has also helped the editing and publication of this volume. I would like to thank her for these efforts.

At ANU E Press Vic Elliott and Lorena Kanellopoulos have been supportive throughout and have seen the book through from conception to final product with efficiency and good humor. My thanks to them and the other staff at ANU E Press involved in the production, storage and distribution of this book.

Raghbendra Jha,
Executive Director
Australia South Asia Research Centre
The Australian National University
Canberra ACT
August 2006

About the Australia–India Council

The Australia–India Council (AIC) was established on 21 May 1992, in response to a recommendation by the Senate Standing Committee on Foreign Affairs, Defence and Trade, following an inquiry into Australia's relations with India.

The Council's purpose is to broaden the relationship between Australia and India by encouraging and supporting contacts and increasing levels of knowledge and understanding between the peoples and institutions of the two countries. The Council initiates or supports a range of activities designed to promote a greater awareness of Australia in India and a greater awareness of India in Australia, including visits and exchanges between the two countries, development of institutional links, and support of studies in each country of the other. The Council offers support, in the form of funding, for projects likely to contribute to the development of the relationship, within the context of AIC objectives and guidelines.

By initiating and supporting a range of activities that have put it on the map, the Council has played a recognised and respected role in promoting the relationship between Australia and India. It has informed and educated Australians about India, and it has informed persons interested in the bilateral relationship about the way it is developing. It has furthered the Government's foreign policy and trade objectives and added value to Australia–India relations.

Australian Government

AIC
AUSTRALIA–INDIA COUNCIL

K R Narayanan Orators 1994 to 2006[1]

1994 — **Dr Raja J. Chelliah** is Professor Emeritus, National Institute of Public Finance and Policy, New Delhi, and Chairperson, Madras School of Economics. (In 1994 he was Fiscal Adviser, Ministry of Finance, Government of India.) He has been a highly influential policy economist and has held several important positions in the Government of India and world bodies. As one of India's leading fiscal experts, Dr Chelliah has exerted the foremost important influence in fiscal policy reforms in India. After completing his post-graduate degree from Madras University, Dr Chelliah obtained his doctorate from the University of Pittsburgh, USA, as a Fullbright Scholar. He worked as a Senior Economist at the National Council of Applied Economic Research, New Delhi before becoming Professor of Economics at the University of Rajasthan, Jaipur and later at Osmania University, Hyderabad. He joined the International Monetary Fund and headed the Fiscal Analysis Division of the Fiscal Affairs Department from 1969 to 1975. After his return to India in 1975, Dr Chelliah played a very active role in the design and reform of fiscal policy in the country. He founded the National Institute of Public Finance and Policy in 1976 which became a premier research institute for work on fiscal policy. He served as: Honorary Consultant to the Ministry of Finance; Member of the Economic Administration Reforms Commission, New Delhi (1982–83); Member of the Planning Commission (1985–89); Member of the Ninth Finance Commission and Fiscal Adviser with the rank of Minister of State, Ministry of Finance, Government of India (1992–95). He was invited to become the Chairman of the Tax Reforms Commission by the Government of Zimbabwe (1984–85). In his capacities as Chairman, Consultant and Member of various taxation enquiry committees, study groups and tax missions, he made significant contributions and gave policy directions not only to the Central and State governments of India but also to the Governments of Papua New Guinea, Peru and Zimbabwe. During his illustrious career, Dr Chelliah worked on several UN sponsored research projects and carried out and supervised research work in public economics extensively. He has authored several books and research papers. He was elected as the President of the Indian Economic Association in 1994.

1995 — **Professor U R Rao,** a Member of the Space Commission of India is a world renowned space scientist known for his original contributions to space science, for the establishment and development of space technology in India and for its extensive application to development problems in India. He has worked tirelessly towards the use of space technology for the development of India, in particular to benefit weaker groups in society. Satellites have initiated a total communications revolution in India, providing human connectivity to the remotest areas. They have had a dramatic impact in the expansion of TV

with a talk-back facility. Perhaps his most significant contribution has been in evolving a highly innovative integrated resource management strategy leading to the development of sustainable management of the micro level to meet present and future needs without affecting ecological balance. As Vice-President of the International Astronautical Association he has taken strong initiatives in promoting the use of space technology in developing countries.

1996 — **Professor Jagdish Bhagwati** is the Arthur Lehman Professor of Economics and Professor of Political Science at Columbia University, New York. He is regarded as one of the foremost international trade theorists of his generation and he recently served as Economic Policy Adviser to the Director-General, GATT (1991–93). He has also made major contributions to development theory and policy, public finance, and to the new theory of political economy. His early books are acknowledged to have provided the intellectual case for the major economic reforms now under way in India. He was recently an adviser to India's Finance Minister on India's recent economic reforms. His most recent book *India in Transition* is highly regarded for its contribution to the ongoing reform process.

1999 — **Mr P Chidambaram** is from Tamil Nadu where he graduated with Science and Law degrees before receiving an MBA at Harvard. He is the Minister of Finance in the Government of India. (In 1999 he was a senior advocate in the Chennai High Court and has established a successful law practice in the Supreme Court of India and in various High Courts.) Mr Chidambaram was first elected to the Lok Sabha (Lower House) of the Indian Parliament in 1984 and was re-elected in the four subsequent general elections through to 1998. He was inducted in 1985 as a Deputy Minister in the Ministry of Commerce and of Personnel. He was elevated to Minister of State of Personnel, Public Grievances and Pensions, and of Home Affairs in 1986 until elections in 1989. Following general elections in 1991, he was Minister of State (Independent Charge) for Commerce and Chairman, Board of Trade in 1991–92, and again in 1995–96. He held the portfolio of Finance Minister from June 1996 until March 1998. He is a founder-member of the Tamil Maanila Congress and was leader of the regional Tamil Maanila Group in the Lok Sabha from 1998. Mr Chidambaram was one of the architects of the New Economic Policy initiated by the Narasimha Rao government in 1991. He was also a member of the United Front Sub-Committee which drafted the UF's Common Minimum Programme in June 1996. Mr Chidambaram was rated as Asia's best Finance Minister in 1997 by the London-based 'Euromoney' publication. He has attended the annual sessions of the World Economic Forum in Switzerland. He was leader of the Indian Delegation to the India–Australia Joint Ministerial Meetings in New Delhi in 1992 and 1995.

2001 — **Dr C Rangarajan** is Chairman of the Prime Minister's Economic Advisory Council. He was Governor of Andhra Pradesh and Chair of the National Statistical Commission designed to oversee a review of India's statistical infrastructure since November 1997 to 2003. From 1992 to 1997, he was Governor of the Reserve Bank of India and guided the reforms through its comprehensive program of economic liberalisation and reforms. During his tenure as Governor, he was responsible for initiating widespread reforms in India's financial and monetary sector including the current account convertibility of the rupee. The rapid economic growth (almost double the average rate achieved during 1950 to 1990) and macroeconomic stability enjoyed by the country earned him the respect of the international financial community, which, in 1997, earned him one of the best central bankers in the world. Dr Rangarajan has a PhD in economics from the University of Pennsylvania, he has taught at Wharton School of Finance, University of Pennsylvania; Graduate School of Business, New York University and Indian Institute of Management, Ahmedabad — India's premier business school.

2002 — **Lord Meghnad J. Desai** is Professor Emeritus of Economics at the LSE. He is founder of the Centre for the Study of Global Governance. From 1990 to 1995 he was Director of LSE's Development Studies Institute and has been at the LSE for over 30 years. His latest book is *Marx's Revenge: The Resurgence of Capitalism and the Death of Statist Socialism*. He was born in Baroda, India in 1940. He is a British subject, but Indian by origin and was created Lord Desai of St Clement Danes in April 1991. He has a BA (Hons) from the University of Bombay (1958), a MA from the University of Bombay (1960) and a PhD from the University of Pennsylvania (1964) as well as honorary doctorates from the University of Kingston, Duniv University of Middlesex, Duniv University of East London, and London Guildhall University. Recent publications include: 'Seattle: A Tragi-comedy', in *After Seattle: Globalisation and its discontents*, Gunnell, B & D Timms (eds) Catalyst, Aldgate Press, 2000; 'Communalism, Secularism and the Dilemma of Indian Nationhood', in *Asian Nationalism*, M Leifer (ed.), Routledge, 2000; 'Globalisation: Neither Ideology nor Utopia', *Cambridge Review of International Affairs*, autumn/winter 2000 volume XIV/1; 'Well being or Welfare?' in *Public Policy for the 21st Century: Social and Economic Essays in Memory of Henry Neuberger*, Fraser, N & J Hills (eds) Policy Press; London, 2001; *Marx's Revenge; The Resurgence of Capitalism and the Death of Statist Socialism* (Verso; London, New York), 2002

2003 — **Professor Pranab Bardhan** is Professor of Economics in the University of California at Berkeley. He has been at the faculty at MIT, Delhi School of Economics and Indian Statistical Institute. He is the Chief Editor of the Journal of Development Economics, and co-chair of the MacArthur Foundation Research Network on Inequality and Economic Performance. He is the author of nine books and numerous journal articles in the areas of political economy, agrarian institutions, economic development, and international trade. Two collections of his selected articles have been published in early 2003: *International Trade, Growth, and Development* (Blackwell) and *Poverty, Agrarian Structure, and Political Economy in India* (Oxford University Press).

2004 — Dr Vijay Kelkar is Advisor to the Minister of Finance in the rank of a Minister of State, Ministry of Finance, New Delhi. He has more than 30 years of post-PhD experience at high level economic policy-making relating to both national and international economic policy issues, and in disseminating experiences through seminars and teaching at graduate level on development economics, international trade and finance and globalization. Dr Kelkar has served with the Tariff Commission; the Ministry of Petroleum & Natural Gas; Economic Advisory Council to the Prime Minister; Economic Policy & Planning, Ministry of Petroleum & Natural Gas; Ministry of Commerce; and Planning Division, in the Planning Commission. He was Chairman of the Bureau of Industrial Costs & Prices and Secretary to the Government of India; Director and Coordinator of the International Trade Division, UNCTAD, Geneva, and a consultant at the Office of the Secretary General, United Nations, UNCTAD, Geneva. Educated at the University of Pune, India; the University of Minnesota; and the University of California at Berkeley, USA, his publications include: 'South Asia in 2020: Economic Outlook', in Chambers (ed.), *South Asia in 2020: Future Strategic Balances and Alliances*; 'India's Reforms Agenda: Micro, Meso and Macro Economic Reforms', Annual Fellows Lecture, University of Pennsylvania, 2001; 'Transforming India's Oil Industry — The Agenda Beyond Pricing Reforms', Second Vasant J. Sheth Memorial Lecture, 1997; *India: Development Policy Imperatives*, Vijay Kelkar & Bhanoji Rao (eds), Tata Mcgraw-Hill, New Delhi, 1996; 'Strategies of Privatisation: An Approach to the Oil Industry', in Rothermund (ed.), *Liberalising India — Progress and Problems*, New Delhi, 1996; India's Oil Policy in the Coming Century', 3rd Lovraj Kuma Memorial Lecture, Indian Society for chemicals Engineers, 1996; and 'Efficiency of Public Sector Enterprises', the Eighth Dr Deepak K Marchant Memorial Lecture, Bombay, 1991.

2005 — Professor M S Swaminathan has been acclaimed by *TIME* magazine as one of the twenty most influential Asians of the 20th century and one of only three from India, the other two being Mahatma Gandhi and Rabindranath Tagore. He has been described by the United Nations Environment Programme as 'the Father of Economic Ecology' and by Javier Perez de Cuellar, Secretary General of the United Nations, as 'a living legend who will go into the annals of history as a world scientist of rare distinction'. He was Chairman of the UN Science Advisory Committee set up in1980 to take follow-up action on the Vienna Plan of Action. He has also served as Independent Chairman of the FAO Council and

President of the International Union for the Conservation of Nature and Natural Resources. He is the current President of the Pugwash Conferences on Science and World Affairs. Professor Swaminathan's contributions to the agricultural renaissance of India have led to his being widely referred to as the scientific leader of the green revolution movement. His advocacy of sustainable agriculture leading to an evergreen revolution makes him an acknowledged world leader in the field of sustainable food security. The International Association of Women and Development conferred on him the first international award for significant contributions to promoting the knowledge, skill, and technological empowerment of women in agriculture and for his pioneering role in mainstreaming gender considerations in agriculture and rural development. Professor Swaminathan was awarded the Ramon Magsaysay Award for Community Leadership in 1971, the Albert Einstein World Science Award in 1986, and the first World Food Prize in 1987. Professor Swaminathan is a Fellow of many of the leading scientific academies of India and the world, including the Royal Society of London and the US National Academy of Sciences. He has received 46 honorary doctorate degrees from universities around the world.

2006 — Dr K. Kasturirangan, in 1976–83 was Project Director, Bhaskar-I and II, Indian Space Research Organisation (ISRO) Satellite Centre, Bangalore. In 1980–89 was Project Director, IRS-1A, ISRO Satellite Centre, Bangalore. From 1984–86 was Deputy Director, ISRO Satellite Centre, Bangalore. From 1986–89, Associate Director, ISRO Satellite Centre, Bangalore. 1990 to March 1994 Director, ISRO Satellite Centre, Bangalore. From April 1994 to Aug. 2003, Secretary, Department of Space, Government of India/Chairman, ISRO Chairman, Space Commission Chairman, Governing Body, National Remote Sensing Agency, Hyderabad Chairman, Antrix Corporation Limited, Bangalore. Aug. 2003 Nominated to Rajya Sabha. Jan.–Feb. and Oct. 2004 onwards Member, Consultative Committee for the Ministry of Human Resource Development. Jan. 2004–Feb. 2004 Member, Committee on Energy and Aug. 2004 onwards Member, Library Committee. Oct. 2005 onwards Member, Parliamentary Forum on Water Conservation and Management. Dr Kasturirangan has a B.Sc. (Hons.) in Physics, M.Sc. (Physics) with specialization in Electronics, and a Ph.D. (Astronomy and Astrophysics). He was educated at Bombay University, Mumbai and Physical Research Laboratory, Gujarat University, Ahmedabad.

Endnotes

[1] These profiles are taken from the year of the Orator's presentation.

The K R Narayanan Orations
1994 to 2006

1994 K R Narayanan Oration

Message from the Vice-President

I am honoured to learn that the Australia South Asia Research Centre (ASARC) of The Australian National University (ANU) has instituted a 'K R Narayanan Oration' and that the inaugural Oration is being given by Dr Raja J Chelliah, Minister of State and Fiscal Adviser, Ministry of Finance, Government of India.

I have very pleasant memory of inaugurating the Australia South Asia Research Centre (ASARC) of The Australian National University in April 1994. I believe that it was one of the significant events that took place during my official visit to Australia. That a Centre for the study of the economic development of South Asia as a whole has been established at a reputed University like ANU is important in itself. South Asia is a sub-continent constituting nearly one-sixth of the world population. Endowed with rich natural and human resources it occupies a strategic position on the world map. From ancient times to our own it has been open to influences from and has influenced the rest of the world particularly Africa, West Africa, South East Asia, East Asia and the Asia Pacific. Today South Asia is going through a new phase of economic development and far-reaching liberalisation. It has created an objectively favourable environment for promoting regional cooperation among South Asia nations and for expanding cooperation with Australia and the wider circle of the Asia Pacific. In this context I am happy that the Australia South Asia Research Centre has taken the initiative to hold a Conference on Economic Liberalisation in South Asia. I congratulate ASARC for this very constructive initiative and wish it every success.

I am particularly glad that on this occasion Dr Raja Chelliah is delivering the 'K R Narayanan Oration' on the subject of 'Reforming the Tax Base for Economic Development in India'. Dr Chelliah is a distinguished friend and an eminent economist who is part of the fundamental intellectual brain-work behind India's liberalisation policy. I am sure that his oration and his participation in the Conference will throw light on the new economic policy that is transforming India into a dynamic economy and an active player in the evolving Asian and the global economic system.

K R Narayanan
New Delhi 1994

Reforming India's Tax Base for Economic Development

Raja J. Chelliah

Introduction

I deem it a great honour and privilege to be invited to deliver the first K R Narayanan Oration under the auspices of the Australia South Asia Research Centre of the prestigious Australian National University. It is an honour to be invited by such a prestigious educational centre and a privilege to deliver a lecture named after a national leader of my country, Mr K R Narayanan, who is now the Vice-President of India. Both as an academician and as a political leader, he is held in great respect in India. I am happy that this oration has been named after him and will be delivered every year.

Great challenges are taking place in India. The wide-ranging economic reform programme encompasses every major sector of the economy. One of the important sectors of reform is the tax system. Since I have been associated with the work of reforms in this area, I have chosen to speak on the subject of *Reforming the Tax Base for Economic Development*.

Tax reform has been an integral part of the economic reforms of most countries that have undertaken structural adjustment programmes. Even in the developed countries, tax reforms have been a prominent feature during the 1980s. One of the important reasons impelling governments of the developing countries embarking on economic reform programmes to undertake tax reform has been the need to cut the fiscal deficit through higher growth of revenues. That is perhaps also the reason why multilateral agencies supporting structural adjustment programmes have usually insisted on tax reform. But in most developing countries including India thoroughgoing tax reform was needed in order to improve the efficiency of resource allocation, to remove obstacles to the smooth flow of business activities, to minimise costs and to improve the equity of the system. Improvement in equity was needed not merely for its own sake, but also for encouraging tax compliance.

The need for reforms and the nature of reforms in other important areas such as industrial policy, the financial sector, trade policy and foreign exchange regime, as a prerequisite for improving efficiency and accelerating growth has been widely discussed and understood. The need for tax reform exactly for the same reasons has not been fully appreciated or understood by the general public and by policy makers. Even economists in general in India have only stressed the need for higher tax revenues and better enforcement to ensure vertical equity. The economic aspects of taxation were neglected in India by economists themselves, which is one of the reasons why we ended up by having a complicated and irrational tax system.

Taxation was thus an area of darkness. It was, therefore, especially difficult to make people understand the serious shortcomings of the system and the nature of the reforms needed. However, the task had to be undertaken because the tax system was one of the major contributory factors to the inefficient functioning of the economy and the distortions in resource allocation.

The Pre-Reform Structure

A brief description of the pre-reform structure of direct and indirect taxes in India may be given as a prelude to a discussion of tax reform.

Direct Taxes

Although direct taxes formed less than 3 per cent of GDP on the eve of reform (about 20 per cent of total tax revenues), they exerted a profound influence on economic decisions, the generation and availability of savings for the private sector and the pattern of investment. The impact of the direct taxes on the economy was disproportionate to their relatively small share in total tax revenues.

The system of direct taxes was unnecessarily complicated, deficient in terms of horizontal equity and destructive of incentives because of high combined marginal rates of personal income and wealth taxation as well as high rates of taxation of corporate profits. Erosion of horizontal equity arose through unjustified concessions, provision of tax shelters in the form of untaxed perquisites and weak enforcement which made it possible for a large section of the tax payable population to get away with no or little payment of tax. The top marginal rate of income tax including surcharge was 56 per cent and the top marginal rate of wealth tax was 2 per cent. Thus with a marginal rate of return of 10 per cent on wealth, the combined marginal rate of income and wealth taxes on capital income worked out to 76 per cent. As there was no automatic indexation of inflation and as the average rate of inflation was around 8 per cent during the 80s, the real rate of return after tax was negative if the nominal rate of return before tax was 10 per cent. This was so even if no wealth tax was payable.

The rate of corporate profit tax for widely held companies was 45 per cent whereas for closely held companies the rate was 50 per cent. On this there was a surcharge of 15 per cent (the rate of profits tax for foreign companies was 65 per cent). Such high rates of corporate profits tax combined with a tax on dividend as part of regular income in the hands of the shareholders led naturally to a low rate of return to equity holders, besides leaving very little in the hands of companies, which are the main engine of industrial growth, for investment.

Such high rates could continue only because of large-scale evasion and because of the provision of adequate tax shelters for those who advocated and introduced the high rates of tax. Members of Parliament and Central government Ministers receive relatively low salaries but then they are granted a sitting allowance which is exempt from tax. A proportion of government servants as well as Ministers and Members of Parliament were and are provided with living accommodation for which they are charged very nominal rates while the market rent for the accommodation would be several times higher. If the fortunate occupant of government accommodation paid 10 per cent of his salary as rent, no perquisite value is deemed to arise. Similarly, senior civil servants and top personnel in the organised private sector receive perquisites, which are not subject to tax fully; for example, use of telephones provided by the employer, leave travel concession, use of passenger cars given by the employer for private purposes on payment of relatively low charges. In a similar fashion very liberal rules for the valuation of house property for wealth tax purposes made possible for some groups of people to pay very little wealth tax. The tax law was unnecessarily complicated partly because of the provision of several concessions and deductions, but also because the Tax Department wanted to provide safeguards against every possible attempt at tax avoidance and tax evasion. The result was the generation of a plethora of disputes, growing litigation, with the Tribunals and High Courts coming to have such a large volume of pending cases that one could not hope to get a decision on an income tax case from the High Court within a period of 10 years. Most of the disputes related to minor points of interpretation involving insignificant amounts of money were taking up enormous time and effort, which was totally meaningless in view of the large-scale evasion of direct taxes.

Indirect Taxes

We had built up a totally irrational structure of indirect taxes. The Constitution provides for the imposition of a number of indirect taxes. But the major ones are customs and excise duties leviable by the Central government and the sales tax other than inter-State sales tax leviable by the State governments (the inter-State sales tax is levied under Central legislation). The irrationality in the indirect tax structure arose partly because of the nature of the Constitutional provisions but mainly because, in developing the indirect tax structure after independence, no attention was paid to the economic consequences of different ways of levying indirect taxes.

Prior to 1986, the indirect taxes levied by the Centre — customs, Union excise and Central sales tax — taken by themselves or the Central indirect taxes and the major indirect taxes levied by the States and the local authorities — taxes on intra-State sales, the passengers and goods tax, the electricity duty and the octroi[1] taken together did not constitute an integrated and rational system. There were levies that have been developed independently with no coordination, and acted and reacted on one another with little government intervention. They were all cascading type taxes, except for the limited operation of a rule under the Central excise which provided credit for tax paid on inputs and the similarly limited concessional treatment granted to inputs in the sales tax laws in some States. The taxes were levied at widely different rates and the total impact on relative prices or on the pattern of expenditure of households could not be easily known; nor did the government bother about such matters although they swore by the commitment to progression and equity in the distribution of tax burden. To quote the Tax Reforms Committee (1991):

> It was a truly irrational system from the economic as well as equity point of view; and the misallocation of resources and the loss of welfare caused by the high and desperate import duties and the multi-rated cascading type excise and sales taxes was palpable. While the unduly large number of rates resulted in classification disputes, the high rates spawned evasion abetted by corruption (p. 98).

In 1986 a system called MODVAT was introduced in the Central excise under which excise paid on many important inputs became eligible for credit against tax payable on output. This represented a major step in the reform of the Central indirect tax system. However, under the MODVAT system only tax paid on inputs that physically get incorporated in output or those that get consumed in the process of production qualified for set-off. Capital goods were not covered by MODVAT. Also three important sectors, namely, petroleum products, tobacco products and textile products were kept outside this system. After the changes introduced in 1986, there was hardly any progress towards a full-fledged value added tax.

While there had been some sincere attempt to reform the Central excise, there was no attempt to reform the import duty structure. In fact, in pursuit of the revenue objective, duty rates were considerably raised in the late 80s. At the beginning of the 90s, the Indian import duty structure

> presented a bewildering picture of combination of 'basic' and 'auxiliary' duties with combined rates on different goods varying widely and often consisting of double application of *ad valorem* and specific duties. (Interim Report, p. 38)

The duty rates ranged from over 400 per cent *ad valorem* to 0 per cent. With the bulk of the imports falling in the range of 50 to 150 per cent, the average effective rate worked out to 85 per cent excluding exempted items (around 50 per cent if they are included). Furthermore, the statute gave only the maximum rates. The actual rates applied to different products or their varieties were fixed through numerous executive notifications. The notifications gave exemptions or concessional treatment to particular classes of users or sub-categories of goods, introducing further rate differentiation.

The special treatment given to the small scale sector under the excise taxation system represented and still represents another distortion. The concessional tax system extended to this sector has been a source of substantial tax evasion. The exemption of a substantial part of the industrial sector from excise taxation represents an obstacle to the introduction of a full-fledged value added tax.

As can be easily imagined, the application of many rates of excises led to numerous classification disputes. Much time, effort and money was expended by the department and the assessees in relation to disputes regarding classification. Of course, if the tax is limited to the manufacturing stage, there is always a temptation for the producers to under-estimate the values of the products. Apart from this, there have been problems arising from the difficulty in unambiguously defining the manufacturer's price.

On the irrational and complicated structure of central indirect taxes represented by import and excise duties, was imposed the State sales taxes. The State sales taxes are levied on industrial as well as agricultural products; however, numerous exemptions are granted. the sales tax is imposed on prices inclusive of excise. Various types of sales taxes were experimented with by the different States, but most of them have shifted, in the main, to a first-stage, single-point tax, although in some States this is supplemented by a low rate turnover tax or an additional tax payable by the larger dealers.[2]

The sales taxes in the different States are also levied at many rates and the rates of tax on particular commodities vary between States. As already noted, in general the sales taxes levied by the States are of the cascading type. To quote a recent report by the National Institute of Public Finance and Policy (1994), *Reform of Domestic Trade Taxes in India*

> Neither the structures nor the procedures are, however, simple in any State. Also, with the shift in the point of levy to the first point, the problems in excise taxation associated with the definition of manufacturing, under valuation and commodity classification, are revisited when one looks at the sales tax system. In sheer complexity and irrationality, the sales tax systems, as they are structured and implemented at present, surpass the excise even at their worst (p. 12).

This is not all. In 1956 the Central government enacted the Central Sales Tax Act authorising the States to impose a tax on inter-State sales emanating from within their respective territories. The tax was imposed on the recommendation of the Taxation Enquiry Commission, 1953–54, which argued that the producing State (i.e., state of origin) should get a small part of the total sales tax burden that could be imposed on a commodity. That Commission recommended that the rate of the inter-State sales tax (CST) should be fixed by the Central government and suggested a 1 per cent rate of tax, presumably believing that such a low rate of tax would not be a serious barrier to inter-State trade nor lead to any significant cascading. In course of time, the rate of Central sales tax was raised by the Central government in stages to 4 per cent which taken together with the unremitted sales tax on inputs not only became an effective barrier to inter-State trade but also added significantly to the total cascading effect. Incidentally, the 4 per cent inter-State sales tax combined with the unremitted sales tax on inputs made possible substantial tax exportation by the industrially more advanced States. It is obvious that the rate of Central sales tax was raised with connivance of the Central planners in the mistaken belief that such increases would enable the States as a whole to raise more resources, whereas in fact the taxable capacity of the States to which there was net exportation of inter-State sales tax was reduced.

The Logic of Tax Reform

The complicated structure and deficiencies of the Indian tax system and the way in which the taxes were administered were mind boggling. But the shortcomings were so prominent that it was easy to lay down the basic lines of reform and suggest the ultimate structure that the government should aim to bring into existence. The problem was to initiate the first steps and then recommend other measures in proper sequence so as to reach the final goal. In practice, the tax reform process encounters much opposition because of ignorance and inertia. Also, there are always losers and gainers when changes are to be effected and long-term gains are often overlooked because of fear of short-term losses. But the job had to be done because, as was pointed out earlier, the irrational and totally antiquated tax structure in the country was a stumbling block to accelerating the growth of the economy. It is to be said to the credit of the Central government of India that within a period of 3 years they have brought about very substantial reform of the structure of the Central taxes, although even in the Central sphere much remains to be done in the field of administration. Tax reform has barely started in the realm of the State governments.

The principles that have guided tax reform in India may be briefly stated as follows:

a. economic rationality which involves (i) removal or avoidance of distortions in economic decision making as well as of unnecessary cost escalation and (ii) ensuring that economic incentives will not be affected to any significant extent by the tax structure and tax rates.

b. horizontal equity is as important as vertical equity. Hence a satisfactory definition of income (if that is chosen as the index of ability) and a tax system that would enable one to move close to the fulfilment of horizontal equity were called for.

c. broad bases with limited concessions. This would mean simplicity of structure and make possible the reduction in rates.

d. Reduction of the high rates prevailing particularly marginal rates, both to preserve incentives and to encourage compliance.

e. Ensuring that the well-to-do sections will pay proportionately more taxes. This should be ensured not through high marginal rates of income and wealth taxes but through a proper combination of taxes on income and wealth and taxes on expenditure. A steep degree of progression was undesirable and was in any case unenforceable.

f. Considerable improvement in tax administration and enforcement.

The above-mentioned principles or criteria laid down by the Tax Reform Committee were broadly accepted by the government. These principles have been generally applied in the reform of tax systems in many other countries. In the context of globalisation of Indian economy which the government wanted to promote, it was necessary to align the Indian tax system in important respects with those of our trading partners; and if India wanted to attract foreign investment, the rate of corporate profits tax could not be far out of line with those in countries competing for the same capital flows. Thus a regime of moderate rates had to be brought into existence for several important reasons. However, it must be pointed out that if the reforms suggested were fully implemented, there would not only be greater horizontal equity — which should be a great gain — but also a sufficient degree of vertical equity. In fact, if enforcement was strengthened, the actual degree of progression would perhaps be greater than under the previous regime. This assumes much more effective tax enforcement which would become possible due to the reform.

Reform Carried Out To-Date

Import Duties

The import duty structure has been simplified by the amalgamation of the basic and auxiliary duties. On the eve of reform the combined duty rates ranged from 250 per cent to zero per cent and the number of statutory rates, which were many, were effectively multiplied by special or concessional rates brought about through notifications. By now the peak rate has been reduced to 65 per cent and the total number of statutory rates has come down to 14. With the reduction of the peak rate, there has been general reduction in the level of rates and with such reduction a large number of notifications have been abolished. The import duty structure has become much simpler and less irrational, although several anomalies exist and the rates on raw materials such as metals and certain intermediate products particularly chemicals still remain high. The Tax Reforms Committee suggested that by 1997–78 (at the latest) the rates of import duty should range between 30 and 10 per cent (There should be no zero duty items). The only exception was to be consumer goods whose imports are now banned. When they are allowed in, the Committee suggested that, the rate of duty initially should be 50 per cent to give time for the domestic industry to adjust itself. It is clear that we still have a long way to go to arrive at the structure recommended by the Tax Reforms Committee which itself has been criticised for not going far enough.

Union Excise Duty

Here again there has been progress in terms of reform towards a full-fledged value added tax. A major reform has been to make capital goods eligible for MODVAT credit. Additionally, the rates of duty have been unified and the number of rates has been brought down to 10 apart from the rate of tax on tobacco products. Another major change is the switch over from specific duties to *ad valorem* duties which would facilitate the introduction of the value added tax and also would make revenue more responsive to increases in nominal income. With the reduction in import duties, almost all imports have been made subject to countervailing duty and the countervailing duty in turn has been made eligible for MODVAT credit like the excise duty. There have also been several procedural improvements and subject to certain limitations the invoice has been made the basis of tax assessment. Some attempt has also been made to broaden the base through the removal of exemptions, although here the fear of political opposition and the strong pressures exerted by the affected groups have prevented the inclusion of many commodities within the tax net whose exemptions are clearly unjustified (for example, umbrellas and bicycles). But there is no denying the fact that the excise tax system is a much more rational and simpler system today than it was in 1991.

Direct Taxes

The direct tax structure has been greatly simplified. There is now only one rate of corporate profits tax for all domestic companies at 40 per cent. The personal income tax is levied at three rates: 20, 30 and 40 per cent and the surcharge on personal income tax has been removed, while the surcharge on the corporate profits tax (retained for revenue reasons) is expected to be abolished shortly. The rate of tax on branches of foreign companies has been brought down from 65 to 55 per cent.

Government has not found it possible to bring under tax all perquisites wholly or partially and thus remove tax shelters. Also, many tax concessions for industry continue such as partial tax holiday for a specified period of time for new industries or those located in backward States. Since the several perquisites of government employees, public sector employees and Ministers have not been brought under tax, it is difficult to justify strict taxation of all perquisites in the private sector. The real solution is, of course, to raise the salaries of senior government officials and Ministers and subject all their incomes in money and kind to tax. But this would demand a major change in the salary structure and is not likely to take place soon. Meanwhile, some broadening of the income tax base has been accomplished. For example, the property incomes of minor children is now included in the income of the parents. Again, all capital gains are now subject to tax provided taxable income including capital gains rises beyond the exemption level. Long-term capital gains which are worked out after proper indexation are taxable at a separate lower rate. Now there is no possibility of avoiding the tax on long-term capital gains by investing the proceeds in approved securities as could be done in the past. An attempt has also been made to broaden the base through the introduction of a presumptive tax in the form of a fixed sum payment by small businesses, and for certain classes of businesses an estimated income scheme has been introduced according to which the net taxable income is simply taken to be a given percentage of gross receipts, so that the assessee is freed of the necessity to produce detailed accounts and claim deductions and allowances. Lastly, efforts are under way to introduce comprehensive computerisation of the operations of the income tax department, which the in course of time would lead to the broadening of the base. However, it must be pointed out that the existence of several untaxed perquisites constitutes a violation of the principles of horizontal equity. This problem remains on the agenda of further tax reform.

The wealth tax on all assets other than what are termed as unproductive assets has been abolished. Unproductive assets which include jewellery, bullion, real estate (excluding one house where the assessee resides), passenger automobiles, yachts, aeroplanes, and urban land are subject to a flat 1 per cent tax on the excess of their value over Rs 1.5 million. This tax together with the marginal rate of income tax at 40 per cent represents in our view a sufficient degree of progression. In fact, with buoyancy in revenues it should be possible to reduce the marginal rate of personal income tax as well as the rate of corporate profits tax to 30 per cent which in the Indian context would lead to substantial improvement in tax compliance.

As noted earlier, one of the major shortcomings of the indirect tax system in India was the absence of any tax on the service sector, i.e., the value added by the service sector has been left untouched. It is clear that if a comprehensive value added tax is to be introduced, the tax on services must become an integral part of the system. A beginning has been made in this respect. Recently, tax at 5 per cent has been introduced on telephone services, on the services of stock brokers, and on premia for insurance of jewellery, real estate and passenger automobiles. There is also a so-called expenditure tax which is a tax to be paid on hotel bills whether for food or accommodation (cheaper hotels are exempt). The idea is that more and more services will be brought under tax and after a sufficient number of services are included, the services tax will be merged with the Union excise, in terms of eligibility for obtaining set-off for taxes paid on services by the manufacturers of goods and for getting set-off for taxes paid on goods by the producers of services. The regime of indirect taxes levied by the State governments still remains basically unreformed and quite unsatisfactory. The State indirect taxes, of which the sales tax forms the major component, are a source of distortion and cause hindrance to the smooth flow of trade and economic activity. The main sources of distortion are the sales tax and the octroi.

The major shortcomings of the existing system of State and local indirect taxes may be summarised briefly:

a.   The sales tax is levied on the price inclusive of excise at every stage of manufacture.

b.   In most States, there is no complete set off for the sales tax paid on inputs; however, the cascading is to some extent mitigated by the lower rate of tax for inputs bought by manufacturers. The administration of the special rate creates problems.

c.   The inter-State sales tax (or the Central sales tax) levied by most State governments at the maximum rate of 4 per cent (except where reduced for reasons of competition) acts as a hindrance to inter-State trade and also adds to the total cascading effect.

d.   The octroi levied by local authorities in several States not only leads to physical obstacles to the smooth flow of trade but acts as an additional trade barrier in the economic sense. By the same token it adds to the cascading effect.

e.   The sales tax in general is levied at multiple rates creating compliance problems and leading to classification disputes. There is unnecessary inter-ference with consumer preferences.

f.   Most State governments rely on the so called first-point tax, that is, they levy the tax on the first sale in the State effected by the manufacturers and importers. As the first-point tax does not cover the value added at sub-sequent stages, the rates have to be higher than otherwise and there is temptation and attempt to undervalue commodities at the stage of taxation.

g.   In their quest for revenue some States have levied a low rate, multi-point tax or turnover tax in addition to the first-point tax, thus further complicating the structure and adding to cascading.

h.   States indulge in intense tax competition: the rates of tax on particular commodities are reduced from time to time in order to divert trade and industry from other States. This competition has sometimes led to the bizarre situation in which taxes on motor vehicles become lower than those on foodgrains.

i.   The States also offer tax incentives under the sales tax to attract industries. Such offers by several States tend to become a zero sum game which leads to the erosion of the tax base and artificial diversion of trade.

j.   The administration of State taxes leaves much to be desired. The whole system needs to be modernised and computerised. As things stand now, assessments are kept pending too long and there is much prolonged litigation.

The State governments have become aware that their tax systems should be rationalised and tax administration modernised. They are now making efforts to bring about greater uniformity in their sales tax systems. A committee of State Finance Ministers has been appointed by the Finance Minister of India. Under the auspices of this Committee, work is being done to fix floor rates for particular groups of commodities (to prevent tax competition) to rationalise the systems of incentives and to evolve uniform procedures. With only three or four rates besides zero, it should be possible for the State governments to adopt a State value added tax. This would essentially involve two steps:

The first is to give full credit for tax paid on inputs by manufacturers against the tax payable by them; and the second is to convert the single point tax into a multi-point tax with a set-off for tax paid at the earlier stage. Before these steps are taken, there would have to be a fairly wide-spread educational programme and training of the officers. The Government of India is expected to provide assistance in respect of these matters.

Conclusion

Several critics of the tax reform programme in India have tended to judge the success or failure of the programme in terms of increases in revenue that the reform has brought about. Adequacy of increase is measured in terms of revenue to GDP ratio. To be sure, one of the objectives of tax reform is to improve revenue elasticity and the tax ratio. However, it should be remembered that the impact of the reform on revenue increase will not be immediate; tax compliance will increase with reduction in rates only gradually. Similarly, improvements in tax enforcement will take time. It has been emphasised in the Report of the Tax Reforms Committee that mere reduction in rates would not lead to an increase in compliance and that stricter enforcement, which becomes easier with rate reduction, is a necessary complementary step. Secondly, the growth in revenue is not to be measured only by the tax ratio. A major objective of the tax reform is to facilitate and promote faster growth of the economy. What is needed is not an immediate increase in the tax ratio but a faster growth in revenue arising from a higher growth rate of the economy. With an elasticity greater than one, in course of time, the tax ratio will rise. It could be said with some confidence that the tax system has been reformed in India significantly enough to facilitate a higher rate of growth.

It must be admitted, however, that the structural reform is far from complete, although quite a bit of ground has been covered in a short period of three years. Again, there has been only slow progress in the reform of the tax administration. Tax policy makers and tax administrators will have their hands full in the coming years.

Endnotes

[1] Defined as a tax on the entry of goods into a local area for consumption or use therein.

[2] Most interestingly, the additional sales tax is not to be passed on to the buyers according to law which has been upheld by the courts. Of course, nothing can prevent the dealers from altering the price if they can.

1995 K R Narayanan Oration

Message from the Vice-President

In April 1994 I had the pleasure of inaugurating the Australia South Asia Research Centre at The Australian National University. I have vivid memories of the occasion. A distinguished audience was present along with the Foreign Minister of Australia, Senator Gareth Evans and the former Prime Minister of Australia Mr Gough Whitlam and representatives of the South Asian Missions in Canberra.

The Establishment of an annual lecture to commemorate that occasion was a significant step. The first lecture in the series was given by Dr Raja J Chelliah. I am glad that the second oration this year will be given by Professor U R Rao on 'Space Technology for Sustainable Development in Asia'. Professor Rao is one of the pioneers of India's space programme to the present stage. He is taking it to the threshold of self-reliance in designing and building satellites and in achieving launch capability.

Space explorations and the practical applications for space technology have opened up exciting vistas for human knowledge and the progress of mankind. It has already conferred great benefits on humanity through the development of telecommunications, television broadcasting, meteorology, disaster warning and natural resources survey and management. India has developed these capabilities in the mainstream of international cooperation. The significance of space science and technology for sustainable development in Asia is self-evident. Large parts of this ancient continent are still afflicted by poverty, illiteracy and general underdevelopment and therefore co-operation in this field among the countries of the Asian region is of great importance. I am sure that Professor Rao and his wide experience of expertise will throw light on the prospects of such co-operation in Asia.

K R Narayanan
New Delhi 1995

Space Technology for Sustainable Development in Asia

U R Rao

I am indeed honoured at being invited to deliver the prestigious second K R Narayanan Oration of the Australia South Asia Research Centre at The Australian National University, Canberra. My pleasure is all the more since I have intimately known and closely worked with Dr Narayanan, Vice President of India who is an unique combination of an outstanding journalist, successful diplomat, honest politician and above all a self-effacing, humble and exemplary human being. He firmly believed that the welfare of the world depends on creating a new world order guided by the spirit of sharing and cooperation at the international level involving politics, economics, social engineering and all the resources of science and technology. Quoting his own words, 'The development of the awesome power of the science and technology has to be animated by the spirit of humanism for the good of mankind and not for purposes of exploitation or destruction'. In tune with his philosophy, I have chosen the topic 'Space Technology for Sustainable Development' for this lecture.

The spectacular achievements in the last three decades have firmly established the capability of space technology for bringing out a socio-economic revolution in the world because of its immense potential to transform even stagnant societies in a most cost effective and timely manner. While the ability to view in entire electromagnetic spectrum enabled space exploration to unveil the magnificent panorama of the vast cosmos, satellites from their vantage point in space have been able to provide a synoptic, repetitive and instantaneous access to any point on our planet, virtually shrinking time and distance. The vast and unlimited potential benefits of space technology have already extended to communication, meteorology, TV broadcast, education, agriculture, industrial growth, resource management, environmental pollution, disaster mitigation, flood and drought management, health and entertainment, virtually touching every facet of human endeavour (Rao 1995a).

In spite of these spectacular advances, as Smt. Indira Gandhi stated at the UNISPACE '82 conference 'It is pertinent to ask if such spectacular advances, which in some way have brought the world together have also contributed to reducing the glaring disparities which divide people, the rich and the poor, the haves and the have-nots. The promise of gains from advanced technologies elude the majority of peoples, whose aspirations for a better and richer life remain unfulfilled'. Developing countries, in particular, which account for over 75 per cent of the world population, suffering from serious shortage of resources and capital, lack of trained man power, large scale illiteracy, low agricultural productivity, industrial backwardness and exploding population, have become the target of the pollution of rampant poverty. In spite of the food grain production increasing at an average rate of about 3 per cent per year, the food productivity in the developing countries continues to remain very low varying between 0.5 to 2.5 ton/ha. as against the world average of 2.6 tons/ha. leave alone the productivity of over 4.5 ton/ha. in the developed nations (Fig. 1). With the steadily increasing population in these countries more than offsetting the increased food production, over 65 countries are today facing serious food deficit and acute famine conditions (Rao 1991). The Asia-Pacific region alone accounts for a staggering 65 per cent of world's extremely poor population, sustaining on less than 2000 calories/day. The gap between the total food grain production in the world and the demand is expected to reach 140 million tons by 2000 and with the projected increase in population from the present 5.7 billion to 8.5 billion by the year 2025 and 11 billion by 2100, the situation is bound to become explosive.

The term sustainable development coined several years ago has now become a common currency. The World Commission on Environment in its report 'Our Common Future' (1987) defined sustainable development as:

> ... development that meets the needs of the present without compromising the ability of the future generations to meet their own needs. It is not a fixed state of harmony, but rather a process of change in which the exploitation of resources, the direction of investments, the orientation of technological development and institutional changes are made consistent with future as well as present needs.

Unless sustainable development to overcome poverty alleviation concurrently addresses food, economic and health security for achieving substantial improvement in the quality of life across the world, we will surely fail in our attempt to reverse the prevalent state of scarcity and social structure of inequity in our society.

Serious concern for the well being of humanity has led to the definition of more appropriate indices, such as sustainable livelihood security index (SLSI), for providing a realistic and accurate representation of the quality of life. Fundamentally, assessment of quality of life must encompass four basic components namely food sufficiency, ecological integrity, economic security and social equity. While ecological security covers environmental degradation over land, forest and water, economic efficiency deals with input/output ratio of productivity in monetary terms. The social equity factor essentially deals with human aspects in a given region in terms of their statistics below the poverty line, literacy rate, nutritional status, health care aspects and employment opportunities. It is only through the adoption of a holistic approach involving sustainable development strategies that we can ensure a reasonable quality of life to meet the basic requirements of the present as well as future generations. Considering that each one per cent growth in population would require at least 2.5 per cent growth in GNP as demographic investment, providing food, economic and health security to all the people in the world becomes our greatest challenge.

Social Dimensions of the Pollution of Poverty

The rampant pollution of poverty in the developing nations is further being severely stretched on an elastic scale due to the explosive growth in population. Even with the assumption of reaching the replacement fertility rate of 21 per thousand by 2025 based on an optimistic extrapolation of reduction in crude birth rate during the last two decades, the present level of population of 4.3 billion in the developing countries will cross 7.2 billion by 2025 and reach 9.4 billion in 2100 as compared to the total population of the affluent societies, expected to stabilise below 2 billion (UN 1994). Asian regions, which accounted for 3.1 billion or 59 per cent of the global population of 5.4 billion in 1990, will cross 5.9 billion by 2100 (Fig. 2) of which the share of India alone is likely to be around 1.8 billion. It is clear that the only choice we have is to appeal to science and technology for rapidly building up the necessary carrying capacity to meet the basic demands of the population projected by the realistic scenario. The impressive economic breakthrough achieved by the East Asian Tiger countries[5] is a good example of the impact of rapid industrial development and massive literacy programme in substantially improving their GNP.

An immediate consequence of the population growth is the decrease in the available per capita arable land from 0.17 ha. to just about 0.1 ha (Rao 1991; World Resources Institute 1992), which will inevitably force large scale migration of rural people into urban areas in search of gainful employment. Globally the urban population has increased from 1.4 billion in 1970 to 2.6 billion in 1992 and is expected to cross 3.5 billion by 2000, which means almost 55 per cent of the global population will reside in cities by the turn of this century. The developing countries in Asia, Africa and Latin America are witnessing exactly the same phenomena of urbanisation which occurred in the developed west 50 years ago. Urban population in Asia which has already crossed 1 billion is increasing at the phenomenal rate of almost 4 per cent per year as compared to less than 1.2 per cent in America and Europe (World Bank 1994). In India, the urban population has dramatically increased from a mere 30 million in 1900 to over 260 million and is expected to cross 400 million by 2000. Inadequate public transportation, scarcity of safe drinking water and poor sanitation have turned all our major cities into sources of concentrated hazard instead of engines of growth. The solid waste generated each day by the megacities in Asia is over 80 to 100 tons per million, almost twice that in the western cities, turning them into breeding grounds of all communicable diseases. The city of Calcutta alone produces over half a million ton of solid waste every year, half of which is not even collected, let alone recycled.

Despite of the exponential growth in communication capabilities all across the world in the last 50 years, the glaring differences in the development of communication infrastructure between developed and developing nations is very striking. Communication infrastructure like many other social parameters such as energy consumption and literacy, is traditionally considered as an indicator of the level of economic development. Even with the impact of satellite communication revolution, the availability of telephones in the metropolitan cities of the developing countries is less than one for every 100 persons as against one for every two persons in the developed societies. The picture in the rural developing areas is even more dismal with over 2000 persons having to compete for access to a single telephone (Rao 1993). While practically all the developing countries have taken some advantage of satellite communication, only just about 20 out of the 170 geostationary satellites in orbit today, belong to the developing nations and at the present rate of growth, the share of the developing countries either in leased transponders or in terms of dedicated satellites is unlikely to exceed 15 per cent of the global usage even by the year 2000.

The close organic linkage between development and education is abundantly clear from the existence of the powerful functional relationship between the literacy index of a country and its gross national product. Analysis indicates that least developed countries with 70–80 per cent illiteracy have only a per capita income of about $200 per year whereas middle income group of nations with illiteracy rates of 35–50 per cent have an annual per capita income of about $600 as against over $10,000 annual per capita income enjoyed by the citizens of developed nations having less than 5 per cent illiterates (Gao and Rao 1992) (Fig. 3). According to UNESCO 1985 statistics, almost 30 per cent of the global population were illiterates, 98 per cent of whom belonged to the developing countries. The geographical distribution of illiterate population indicates that Asia alone accounted for 75 per cent of the total illiterates, in the world, Africa coming a close second with 18 per cent and the rest 7 per cent being distributed in Latin America and other parts of the world (Rao 1995; World Bank 1994), most of them being in dispersed and remote rural areas. Unless eradication of illiteracy is tackled on a war footing and not by mere slogan adoption, over 2.5 billion or about 30 per cent out of an estimated 7.2 billion population in the developing countries will continue to remain illiterate even by the year 2025 (Rao 1988).

In spite of the wide recognition that the existing socio-economic imbalance between developed and developing nations is directly attributable to the significant difference in their levels of educational advancement, lack of adequate resources continues to prevent the developing countries from overcoming their fundamental disadvantage. In 1986 alone, out of a total investment of about $800 billion on education, 40 developed nations accounted for 80 per cent of this expenditure while the total share of the 161 developing nations (Rao 1995; Gao and Rao 1992) was just 14 per cent. The annual per capita investment in all forms of education including higher education in the third world countries is hardly $ 25 per year compared to over $500 per year in the developed world. Many of the rural areas of the third world countries do not even possess an elementary education facility and where schools exist, they seldom have more than a single qualified teacher and are often run without even a black board. Typical is the example of China, where most of the teachers employed in the primary schools, are those who graduated from the same schools under poorly qualified teachers, resulting in massive inbreeding which has perpetuated the vicious circle. It is estimated that over 3 million poorly qualified teachers in China comprising of 40 per cent of teacher population in primary schools and 72 per cent in junior schools are continuing to cater to the educational growth of that country (Liu 1994). Statistics clearly indicate that the birth rate as well as infant mortality of children drastically gets reduced with the increase in female literacy level. Considering that education of women is most crucial for achieving social equilibrium, through population control and health care (Fig. 4), the task of eradicating illiteracy among women who constitute over 60 per cent of the total illiterates in a developing society, becomes the single most important goal for promoting cultural growth and socio-economic prosperity of any rural society. The answer clearly lies in the wide spread utilisation of distance education involving satellite based TV and radio broadcasting media, which are most ideally suited to provide basic education as well as continuing education to the vast, inaccessible and sparsely distributed population of the world.

State of Agriculture and Environment

A dramatic increase in the global food grain production since the 1960s occurred with the initiation of the green revolution, which was primarily based on the high technology package involving large scale use of chemical fertilisers, pesticides, high response better seeds and extensive irrigation. The increase in India's annual food grain production from just about 55 million tons in 1947 to about 180 million tons in the 1990s is clearly a result of the emphasis given to large scale irrigation which has risen from less than 20 per cent to over 35 per cent of total arable land of 160 million ha. during this period. Ironically however, the negative repercussions of the very practice of irrigation due to water logging, inadequate drainage and indiscriminate use of chemical fertilisers have resulted in making the soil in the irrigated areas highly saline and unproductive. It is estimated that over one third of the approximately 200 million ha. of irrigated cultivable land in the world is already salt affected (Swaminathan 1980). Almost 40 per cent of the highly fertile Indo-gangetic plain in India, which was once the cradle of civilisation, suffers from intense salinity making it unfavourable for crop growth. Almost 25 per cent of the arable land area in every continent has become problem land with another 25 per cent having very low productivity.

The extreme pressure of population and industrialisation particularly in the developing countries has resulted in the annual rate of deforestation of 17 million ha including almost 4 million ha. in Asia (Fig. 5). An imperative consequence of deforestation is increased run off of rain water and severe soil erosion resulting in the deterioration of the top soil, degradation of land and sedimentation of water bases. The high rate of soil erosion in deforested areas in India, China and elsewhere ranges from 10 t/ha. in the plains to almost 30 t/ha. in the north-eastern hilly regions, as against just 1 t/ha in the forested area. World wide soil erosion has reached the limit of 100 million tons per year as against 45 million tons in 1860 and less than 16 million tons three hundred years ago. Extensive deforestation has resulted in increased carbon dioxide in the atmosphere, increased rain precipitation run off from 20 per cent to almost 50 per cent, frequent flooding and a gradual extinction of biodiversity (Khoshoo 1990; Brown 1992). Overgrazing, deforestation, encroachment by agricultural crops and general mismanagement of land and water resources have resulted in increasing desertification in Asia, Africa and Latin America. About 3000 million ha, a quarter earth's land surface has now turned out as desert or damaged by factors that contribute to desertification. On a global scale the desertification is increasing almost by 1 million ha. per year. The changes in climatic and rain patterns gradually setting in because of deforestation are yet to be fully understood due to our inadequate understanding of the phenomena, particularly the energy exchange between the surface aerodynamic roughness over the forest and the atmosphere above it.

Management of water resources particularly in the developing countries, has been even more pathetic. Optimal management of water becomes crucial in the dry land tracts of tropical countries where most of the precipitation occurs in less than 100 days as compared to mid and high latitude countries where snow and rain precipitation continue to keep the soil moisture in tact for almost 8 months in a year. With the added problems of higher temperature regimes and higher evapo-transpiration rates, need for optimal harvesting of run off and recharging of underground aquifers in tropical countries assumes paramount importance. Although major irrigation projects and big dams have contributed to improved agricultural production in the last few decades, the problem of water-logging, salinization and loss of valuable bio-resources have led to gradual degradation of land in many areas in the developing world. Intensive use of chemical fertilizers and pesticides combined with poor management of water-sheds and highly fragmented land holdings have resulted in severe water stress, pesticide contamination not only in the water but also in the agricultural crops, resulting in the severe degradation of over 1.2 billion ha. across the world, in the last 45 years alone (Fig. 6). The material delivery from rivers to the oceans which was just 9.3 billion tons 50 years ago has now increased to 25 billion tons a year, with the largest discharge of over 15 billion tons per year coming from Asia alone.

Superimposed on these seemingly insurmountable difficulties is the real prospect of the widely accepted global warming scenario due to the unprecedented anthropogenic intervention causing a rapid increase in the green house gases, upsetting the delicate greenhouse equilibrium which could lead to irreversible climatic changes (Ramanathan 1985). Particularly since the beginning of the industrial revolution, CO_2 concentration in the atmosphere has steadily increased from 280 ppmv to 350 ppmv and at the present rate of increase is expected to reach 450 ppmv by 2050. Concentration of methane in the atmosphere has also been increasing steadily at the rate of about 0.9 per cent per year and has now already reached 1.7 ppmv. Detailed rigorous analysis of surface temperature over the last century indicates an average increase in global temperature of about 0.5° K. While the primary cause of the global temperature increase in the past has been the increasing atmospheric concentration of CO_2 due to industrialisation, fossil fuel burning and extensive deforestation, the rapid increase of CFCs in the last decade which has large residence time of over 100 years in the atmosphere has further added to the global environmental problem. In spite of the universal adoption of the Montreal Protocol the spectre of global warming, which can cause depletion of ozone, rise in sea level, inundation of highly populated coastal areas and severe modification of climatic and rain pattern, continues to pose a real threat unless all countries, both developed and developing, make appropriate structural adjustments in their life style and consumption pattern.

Communication Revolution

The remarkable developments in space communication in just three decades since the successful relay of TV signals across the Atlantic in 1962 using TELSTAR, have brought us to the threshold of achieving the capability of establishing human connectivity anywhere in the world, on land, air or sea. The superior quality and reliability of satellite links in combination with their high percentage of availability, distance insensitivity, high degree of flexibility for rapid reconfiguration and their ability to aggregate small requirements to provide cost effective specialised services across vast territories have made satellite communication the most vital link for establishing human connectivity promoting a new perspective of our planet, that of a global village. The evolutionary nature of satellite communication is reflected in their capacity increase, from just 240 voice channels in 1965 to the present day satellites which on an average can easily carry over 20,000 voice circuits, in addition to several TV channels (Pant 1994). Practically all the developing nations in the world today including Asian countries have taken advantage of satellite communication by either leasing transponders from international systems like INTELSAT, INMARSAT and INTER SPUTNIK or by establishing regional systems like Arabsat.

Recognising the paramount need of the Governments, societies and institutions to quickly respond to fast changing situations in a demassified society where niche markets, customised services and rapid transactions are essential to successfully compete in the liberalised global market place, a few Asian countries like India (INSAT), Indonesia (PALAPA), China (CHINASAT), Japan (JCSAT) and Australia (AUSSAT) have already established their own satellite communication systems. Other Asian countries like Korea (KOREASAT), Thailand (THAICOM) and Malaysia (MEASAT) are in the process of establishing their own communication systems to meet their growing requirements of telecommunication and TV distribution services.

Unlike most of the countries, India decided to build its own indigenous technology base and use space technology for solving its national problems on a self reliant basis. Establishing the feasibility of using satellite medium for imparting education in health, hygiene, family planning and better agricultural practices to over 2400 remote rural villages through the year long Satellite Instructional Television Experiment (SITE) conducted using NASA's ATS satellite during 1975, India successfully launched and operated its own three axis stabilised experimental satellite APPLE in 1981 followed by the introduction of the unique, multipurpose INSAT series of communication satellites to provide operational services on a continuing basis. INSAT system, with over 5000 two way speech circuits covering 140 routes amounting to 150,000 route kms initiated a communication revolution in the country (Fig. 7) connecting for the first time, even remote rural areas and off shore islands with the main stream of the nation using Low Cost Terminals (LCT). The nation wide geographic reach of INSAT satellite has been advantageously used for a variety of applications such as administrative, business and computer communications through a number of captive networks using small terminals. New specialised services such as rural telegraphy to remote areas, news service, facsimile transmission and emergency communication for post disaster relief operations have been commissioned. The

National Information Center's Network (NICNET) using VSATs and spread-spectrum techniques with over 700 micro-terminals provides reliable data communication links interconnecting district headquarters, state capitals, and central government departments. The Remote Area Business and Message Network (RABMN), to provide data communication between city-based industries and construction projects located in remote areas is already operational with over 450 micro terminals and with a registered demand for more than 2000 terminals (Rao 1995b).

Similar expansion of telecommunication to provide low cost VSAT services in addition to point to point communication has been achieved in China, Australia, Indonesia and other countries in Asia either through satellites procured from abroad or through leased transponders. Increasingly all over the world the future trends in communication is towards establishing personalised communication services to meet the needs of the people at individual and group levels. Remarkable developments in digital compression techniques, use of advanced modulation systems for optimal utilisation of space segment and innovative use of low cost VSAT's to provide several value added services have initiated the new age of information super-highway making it possible to have information on demand. The merging of large computation and communication capabilities through technological innovations are paving the way for the establishment of seamless networks to provide personalised communication and multimedia services including audio, video and data transmission, thus creating a world where communication, information, entertainment and motivation are literally at the will of one's finger tips. The imminent introduction of mobile communication services in the next three years will surely make the dream of every communication engineer of establishing human connectivity anywhere in the world, on land, air or sea come true.

Space Technology for Universal Education

The phenomenal success of the Satellite Instructional Television Experiment (SITE) conducted in India followed by similar experiments conducted elsewhere in the Appalachian Region, Rocky Mountains, Alaska, Canada, China and Latin America in the mid seventies and early eighties, clearly established the tremendous potential of using satellite TV for educational purposes (Rao 1987). It is very satisfying to note that operational beginning of satellite based distance education facility is already making a significant impact in Indonesia, providing an effective educational system to the sparsely distributed population in 14,000 individual islands stretching across a distance of over 5000 Km, many of which are inaccessible mountainous or jungle terrain. Successful use of PALAPA satellite in Indonesia, INSAT in India and AUSSAT in Australia have prompted other developing countries like Brazil, China and Mexico also to develop their own satellite based educational system. Extensive use of satellite medium in China provides 31 hour adult educational programmes every day to 30 million people annually through 6300 TVRO earth stations and more than 50,000 learning centres.

Most dramatic impact of INSAT has been in the rapid expansion of TV dissemination in the country through installation of more than 600 TV transmitters and use of a large number of direct reception community sets in sparsely populated areas, for providing access to over 80 per cent of India's population, through national and regional transmissions. INSAT is being extensively used for Educational TV broadcasting with about 100 hours of programme per month to over 4000 schools and colleges. An effective educational system requires not just a one way system of instruction but a two way interactive communication system enabling the target audience to ask questions and obtain clarifications from experts, in real time. Special inexpensive talk back facilities have been developed within ISRO to promote this activity in the country and a number of selected large scale experiments aimed at improving the level of understanding of rural people, providing refresher courses to industrial workers in cities and specialised education to schools and colleges were conducted to demonstrate the effectiveness of the satellite media for imparting interactive education (Rao 1995b). Recognising the acute need for eradication of illiteracy, particularly in the rural areas, ISRO has conceived of dedicated GRAMSAT satellites (Rao 1993) (Fig. 8), carrying six to eight high powered C-band and Ku-band transponders which together with video compression techniques can disseminate region and culture specific audio visual programmes of relevance in each of the regional languages through rebroadcast mode on to an ordinary TV set.

Vast improvements in technology have made it possible to reach millions of homes with antenna dish sizes as small as 90 to 45cm in ku-band. The recent upsurge in video compression technology now enables several TV channels to be carried on a single transponder. Availability of about 150 channels from a single satellite location can entirely change the complexion of home entertainment through direct to home television broadcast. Video-on-demand which includes specific group interest programmes in addition to general entertainment programmes, allows individuals to choose and even manipulate programmes of their choice. What was cost prohibitive yesterday has suddenly become affordable today with the availability of TV using only a small space segment resource in an economic way which can have a dramatic impact on educational and developmental services.

Management of Natural Disasters

The enormous havoc and dislocation caused by natural and man made disasters have become a great burden particularly on the highly populated and poverty stricken developing countries causing perpetual misery to thousands of lives and livestock. Over the past 20 years alone, these extreme natural disasters have resulted in the loss of life of more than 3 million people and have affected over 800 million people all over the world, causing damage to property to the tune of 50–100 billion dollars, 50 per cent of which is due to floods and cyclones. Over 60 per cent of all the major disasters have occurred in the developing countries, two-thirds of which have been in the developing Asian regions (Rao 1995a; World Resources Institute 1992). Even though extreme natural events such as floods, drought, cyclones and earthquakes are not totally under human control, prediction of occurrence of some of these events with a good degree of certainty is possible, thanks to the developments in space technology. Instead of collectively taking up the challenge of preventing or at least mitigating the effects of such disasters, providing aids after the events which are both inadequate and untimely has only resulted in perpetuating the misery of the worst affected, silently suffering victims of disasters.

An effective disaster management system consists of four main components — disaster prediction, disaster warning, disaster management and disaster relief. Disaster warning is a basic prerequisite for ensuring disaster preparedness and in some cases to help in the prevention of disaster itself. Clearly the most important application of satellites is in detecting, predicting and delivering early warning of impending disasters such as flood, drought, cyclone and even forest fires (Rao et al. 1987; Heath 1994). Continuous monitoring by both geostationary and low earth orbiting weather satellites like GOES, INSAT, METEOSAT and NOAA is capable of providing early warning on cyclones and floods. Forest fires, environmental hazards, volcanic eruptions and even propagation of desert locust phenomena can be detected well in time by remote sensing satellites like, LANDSAT, SPOT and IRS. Sustainable development strategy must address this important issue in order to provide stability and reasonable security to the vulnerable rural population in these countries. Remote sensing information are now operationally used to regularly monitor flood conditions, volume of water flow and damage assessment. From such a database collected over years, it is possible to identify different risk zones in the flood prone area based on the severity index for flood proneness of each zone. Optimal treatment of each zone on a long term basis, depending on the severity, can then be attempted to achieve reduction in flood damage without impairing environmental integrity (Rao 1993) (Fig. 9).

Data relay and communication satellites have the ability not only to deliver early warnings on various disasters but also in disseminating requisite information on hazard awareness and educating the local people in preparing themselves to face such hazards. Locale specific unattended Disaster Warning Systems (DWS) installed by India along the vulnerable eastern coast of the country, using communication and meteorological capability of INSAT multipurpose satellites, have proven their immense value in providing timely warning on cyclone and flood disasters over the last 10 years. Most dramatic use of DWS, consisting of over 150 disaster warning receivers was during the cyclone that hit the eastern coast of India in May 1990, enabling the civic authorities to evacuate over 170,000 people from the cyclone affected area, which saved thousands of lives and livestock. But for the operation of DWS, analysis of cyclone events which occurred in the pre INSAT era indicates that the total human death toll would have been at least 20,000 during this event, as against only 800 deaths recorded (Rao 1995a; 1995b).

Drought is a complex phenomena, the causes for which are many involving both natural and induced factors such as atmospheric perturbation, climatic variability, sea surface temperature changes and human intervention, ranging from deforestation and poor land management to destabilization of green house effect. While it is difficult to identify the exact onset and the end of drought because of its slow creeping nature, remote sensing derived Vegetation Index (VI) has been very effective in monitoring drought conditions on a real time basis, often helping the decision makers to initiate appropriate strategies for recovery by changing crop patterns and practices. The use of meteorological satellite data to assess spatial and temporal inadequacies of rainfall at critical crop stages and subsequent assessment of the crop condition status based on VI analysis provide an excellent drought monitoring mechanism. Comparison of the temporal changes in the bi-weekly VI indices with the corresponding figures in a normal year can easily provide advance information on the onset of drought conditions in any given region (Fig. 10). Under the National Agricultural Drought Assessment and Monitoring System (NADAMS), bi-weekly drought bulletins are issued, almost on real time, to all the drought prone districts in India to enable decision makers to assess the severity of drought and take appropriate remedial measures (Rao 1995c).

Food Security

The solution for providing food security to the world without affecting ecological balance lies in the adoption of new scientific tools available, particularly the use of vital inputs from space remote sensing and bio-technological advances. While India and China have built an impressive capability in space technology by developing their own launch vehicles, communication and remote sensing satellites and application programmes, other countries in Asia have also successfully used space imageries available from International satellites for monitoring and management of their natural resources through cooperative arrangements. India for example, has effectively used its own IRS series of remote sensing satellites to establish and continuously monitor its national forest inventory and to prevent further encroachment of its forest wealth. Extensive use of satellite imageries for mapping soil characteristics, land-use in terms of single crop, double crop, fallow and residual land areas, meteorological parameters and water resources have led to the identification of agro-climatically coherent regions having homogeneous characteristics such as slope, soil depth, texture and water holding capacity, which are vital for developing locale specific and agro-climatically suitable cropping patterns. The ability to identify saline/alkaline soils at micro levels using space imageries have enabled the application of suitable measures to reduce soil salinity and adoption of alternate crops or cropping patterns to restore the fertility of the land to the original level. Country wide mapping of wasteland at micro-level has been able to identify 54 million ha. of wasteland (Fig. 11), about half of which can be reclaimed for productive agricultural usage with appropriate corrective actions (Rao 1995a; 1995c).

Repetitive coverage provided by satellites has been widely used for mapping the temporal changes in water bodies and reservoirs in addition to providing a reliable estimate of water storage in the reservoirs thereby facilitating optimal scheduling of irrigation. A classic example is the country wide hydrogeomorphological mapping from space showing ground water prospect areas which has improved the rate of success of finding underground water to 92 per cent compared to 45 per cent achieved using purely conventional methods. Models based on the area extent of seasonal snow fall have been developed to predict snow-melt runoff into the reservoirs. Identification of waterlogged pockets in the command areas of irrigation projects and inventory of crop lands and cropping patterns have facilitated efficient water use, thereby increasing the cropping intensity. Remote sensing data are being extensively used to predict the acreage and yield of all major crops and also to identify degraded watersheds for initiating appropriate conservation measures for soil and water (Rao 1995c). Space imageries have fully established their ability for substantially improving the marine fish catch by identifying areas of rich fish shoals based on ocean temperatures and phyto-plankton density measurements.

Doubling or in some cases tripling of food grain productivity is required to meet the basic minimal requirements of the projected population growth in many of the developing countries in Asia, Africa and Latin America. Even though the global cultivable land area can in principle be increased from the present 1500 million ha. to about 2150 million ha. through reclamation of culturable wasteland, the prospect of such increase is limited to less than 10 per cent, or about 60 million ha. over the presently cultivated crop land of 820 million ha. in Asian continent. Historically, it is recognised that increase in the area of cultivation in the recent past has in fact only contributed to less than 10 per cent increase in the food grain output. Even with the possible reclamation of about 25 million ha. of wasteland and exploitation of the full irrigation potential by doubling the presently irrigated area of 40 million ha., the annual food grain output in India can at best be increased to 250 million tons as against the requirement of 450 million tons by 2050. Analysis by the world bank and FAO have clearly pointed out that countries like India and China cannot support beyond 1.5 times their present population (FIAO 1988; Murai et al. 1990) using the present agricultural technology.

The challenge of providing adequate food security to the growing population can only be solved by achieving substantially higher yields through initiation of sustainable integrated development strategies. Significant advances in biotechnology have resulted in a variety of new genetic breeds, early maturing dwarf varieties of crops, pest resistant hybrid varieties and suitable cultivation strategies. Combined with integrated pest management strategy, use of bio-pesticides and conservation of top soil and water resources, these bio-technological advances have led to a substantial increase in the genetic potential up to 8–10 ton/ha. under controlled conditions, which implies that achieving an average yield of 4–5 ton/ha even in field conditions is well within our technological capability. Practical realisation on nationwide scales however must take into account the boundary conditions imposed by ecological, environmental, social and cultural factors in each country to ensure long term sustainability. This requires a clear understanding of land capability, continuous monitoring and optimal management of natural resources, and use appropriate agricultural practices.

Sustainable development of natural resources is obviously dependent on maintaining the fragile balance between productivity functions and conservation practices through monitoring and identification of problem areas requiring application of energy intensive agricultural practices, crop rotation, bio-fertilisers and reclamation of underutilised lands.[24] It calls for the integration of various renewable and non-renewable resources, characterisation of coherent zones of agricultural identities and identification of physical constraints as well as ecological problems at the micro-level of each watershed. Combining space derived vital inputs on soil characteristics, agricultural practices, underground and surface water resources, forest cover, environmental status and meteorological information with collateral data on socio-economic factors it is possible to subdivide each watershed into 400–500 micro-level homogeneous units for identifying suitable conservation measures and appropriate bio-technological practices to significantly enhance the production on a sustainable basis (Fig 12). In the few selected watersheds where sustainable integrated development strategy has been implemented, as in the cases of drought prone districts of Anantapur and Ahmednagar in India, two healthy crops are now grown and the water table has gone up by almost 3–5 meters in the last three years as against non-availability of even drinking water in summer months (Rao 1995a; Rao, Chandrasekhar and Jayaraman 1995).

International Cooperation and Policy Issues

While the spectacular advances in science and technology and space technology in particular, can provide appropriate solutions to meet the basic requirements of all the nations, the success of meeting the global challenges of the next century clearly depends on the ability of both North and South in making wise choices concerning the future path of progress. Despite of the fact that space exploration, for the first time, has given us a new perspective of our own beautiful planet, true appreciation of this global view is yet to percolate into the conflicting minds concerned solely with immediate national interests and artificial geographical boundaries. The concept of oneness of humankind has been an integral part of the Indian heritage which was enunciated in our great epic Mahabharata

This is mine that is another's
Such reckonings are for the narrow minded
For the noble hearted
The whole world is one family'.

The last few decades of inadequate efforts to bridge the inequities between the developed and the developing societies have been primarily through aids and soft loans, largely due to moral dictates of guilt complex. It is essential that we clearly realise that the prevalent extensive deforestation, illiteracy, lack of basic resources such as food and water, non availability of technological know-how will drive the developing world through the same suicidal pathway followed earlier by the developed world, in their anxiety to achieve rapid development. While the developed countries which have contributed maximally to the deterioration of the global environment in the past will discover alternate environment friendly technological solutions, rapid deterioration of the ecological state cannot be stopped unless such technologies are made available to the 75 per cent of the world's population. In other words, the betterment of human society as a whole has to be viewed as an implicit requirement for the very survival of this planet.

The emerging independent nations of the South, on the other hand, have to create a new social order which starts recognising that not only the quantitative transformation but the very survival of their society depends on the optimal utilisation of science and technology. The socio political system in most of the developing countries, which is self serving, near sighted and devoid of scientific temper, still regards science and technology only as an embroidery and not the main social fabric of their culture. There is an urgent need for the developing countries to replace the widespread political opportunism with a healthy scientific attitude and seriously tackle the problem of rapid rural development, eradication of illiteracy, establishment of basic communication infrastructure and industrialisation not through vote catching, populist schemes but by purposeful action oriented approach. Accomplishment of these tasks needs the total involvement of highly skilled and fully committed scientists, massive education at the grass root levels and widespread dissemination of scientific culture, in other words, the 'greening' of the human mind.

Despite of the creation of a conducive atmosphere for promotion of international cooperation with the end of the cold war, agreements reached during the Rio summit, general acceptance of Montreal Protocol for the preservation of the environment and signing of the GATT agreement, the technological gap between the developed and the developing nations is continuing to grow. While GATT has introduced a few concessions to the developing nations for a limited period of time to enable them to compete in the global market place on equal footing, the possibility of invoking highly subjective criteria to apply trade sanctions and restrictions on newly industrialised countries continues to pose a threat to the third world nations. Even the so called free market trade in reality has been adroitly used for commercial exploitation. Exploitation of global market by fixing prices based on opportunity cost and not on production economics, till the competition builds up has been followed throughout history while at the same time propagating ethical approaches to market demand. Instead of providing preferential access to developing countries for selling their products and services in the global market, attempts are made to restrict the competition in the name of fair geographical returns policy, application of quota system and equally dubious arguments based on level playing field and human rights (Rao 1995a).

Security concerns as perceived by developed nations have greatly influenced the level and nature of international cooperation. One of the major regimes impinging on the transfer of components, equipment, information and technologies particularly related to space programmes is the Missile Technology Control Regime (MTCR). Although at the beginning, MTCR had the laudable objective of restricting the proliferation of only missile related technologies and not peaceful space programmes, slowly over the years, high technology components and equipment required even for peaceful programmes have been denied as a part of the implementation strategy. The release of the same components for sale immediately after such components are either indigenously developed or become available from alternate sources has left a strong impression that such technology regimes have been turned into a strong weapon in the armour of the developed countries for commercial and political gains. Philosophical statements, such as 'if we are to lead the world towards a hopeful future, we must understand that technology is part of the planetary environment, to be shared like air and water with the rest of the mankind', are pronounced in every conceivable international forum. The reality, however, is that science and technology has become the most powerful currency of power, monopolized and zealously guarded by a minority of few advanced nations, who have employed technological hegemonism — as a means of influencing and controlling the developing world.

The key to the development of a proper strategy for survival clearly depends on achieving integrated sustainable development through both national and international cooperation. It calls for the initiation of a new sustainable green revolution, taking into account the lessons learnt from past experience, to meet the basic needs of the present and future generations through adoption of environment friendly scientific and technological approach aimed at achieving rapid progress without sacrificing the 'owl'. As beautifully summarised at the 1992 Rio Summit (UN 1992):

> Humanity stands at a defining moment in history. We are confronted with a perpetuation of disparities between and within nations, a worsening of poverty, hunger, ill health and illiteracy, and the continuing deterioration of the eco-systems on which we depend for our well being. However, integration of environment and development concerns and greater attention to them will lead to the fulfillment of basic needs, improved living standard for all, better protected and managed eco-systems and a safe, more prosperous future. No nation can achieve this on its own; but together we can in a global partnership for sustainable development.

Conclusion

Interconnectivity of both natural and anthropogenic phenomena occurring anywhere on the earth, through weather, climate, geosphere and biosphere have inextricably linked the fate of each country with that of the world as a whole. The fact that the increase in green house gases, deforestation and depletion of ozone result in global warming affecting the entire global climate, disturbances in EL Nino and ENSO off the coast of Peru can result in severe drought across Asia, Australia and Africa, or volcanic eruptions and industrial activity can change pattern of rain precipitation across the world clearly emphasise the necessity to take a global view for the survival of humankind, as a whole.

The fundamental aspect of long term sustainable development strategy is based on the paradigm of technological innovations, economic determinism and physical constraints arising out of the need to strike a judicious balance between ultimate exploitability and regenerative capacity. This essentially means that all nations must think globally and act locally, because the survival of the planet as a whole depends on the restoration of equity and assurance of minimal needs to all the people in the world. With his remarkable insight, President Kennedy stated over thirty years ago that:

> Never before has man had such capacity to control his own environment, to end thirst and hunger, to conquer poverty and disease, to banish illiteracy and massive human misery. We have the power to make this the best generation of mankind or to make it the last.

We hope that the human kind will have the wisdom to choose the former and strive ceaselessly towards achieving sustainable integrated development of our planet as a whole to enable all peoples of the world, both in the developed and the developing countries, to live a reasonably good quality of life. It is only then we can make Isiah's prophecy come true that

> The desert shall rejoice
> and blossom as the rose....
> The parched ground shall become a pool
> and the thirsty land springs of water.

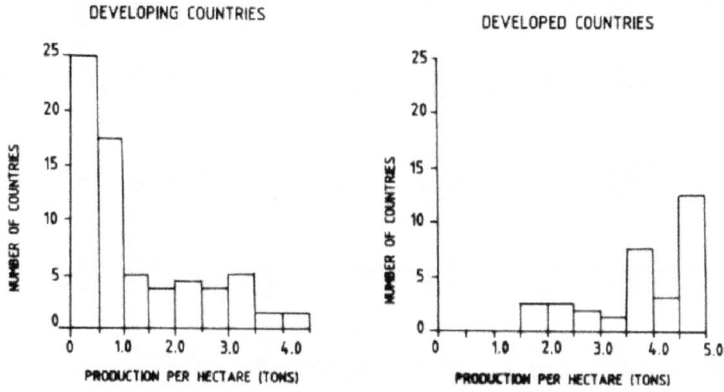

Fig. 1 : Foodgrain productivity in developed and developing countries

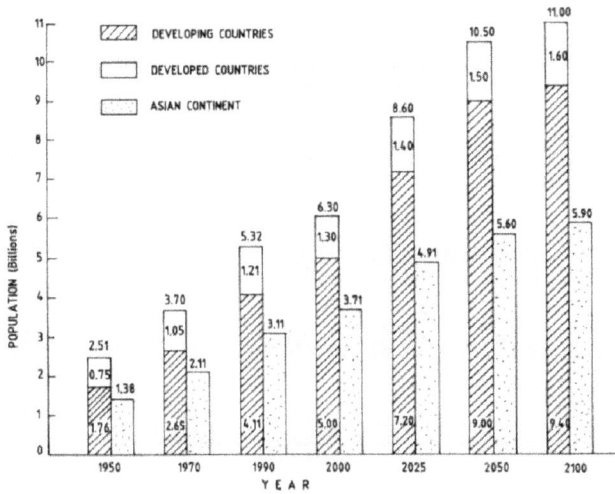

Fig. 2 : Growth of population in the developed an
developing countries of the world

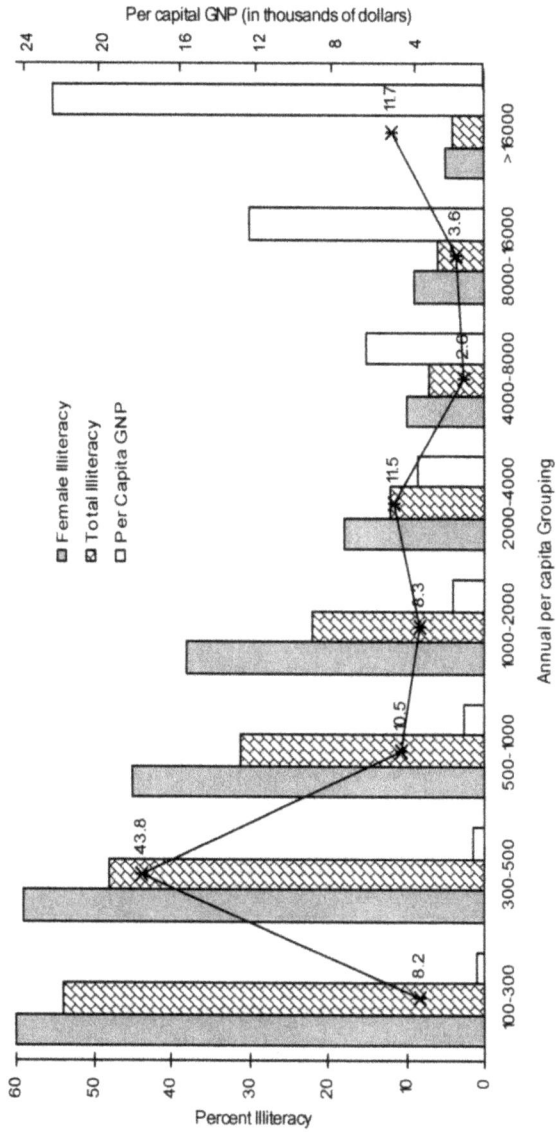

Fig. 3: Literacy and per capital GNP
(the numbers in the diagram indicate the per cent global population under each grouping)

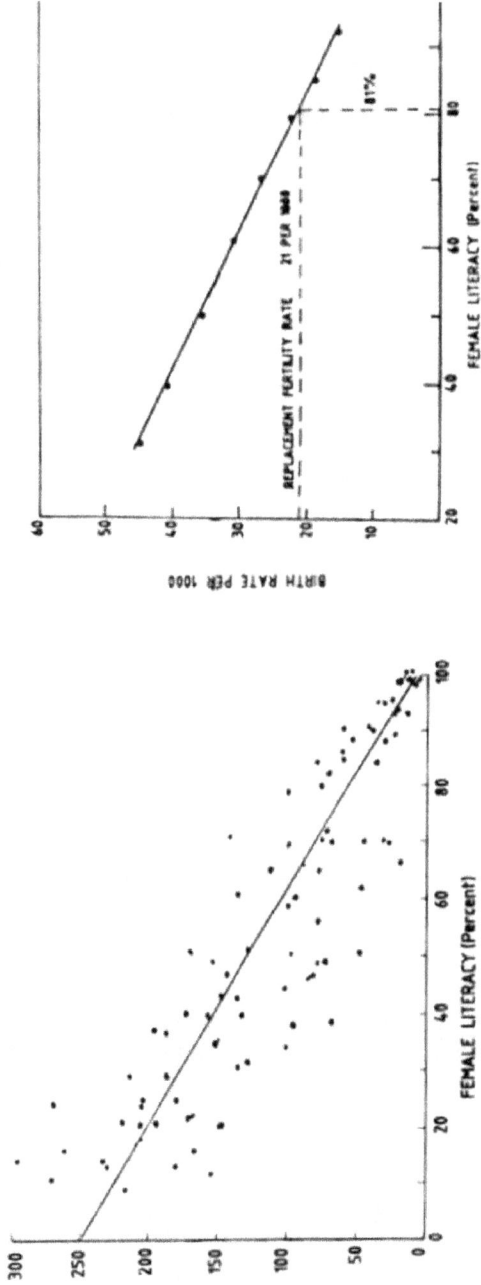

Fig. 4 : Relation between female literacy and fertility
rate and mortality rate

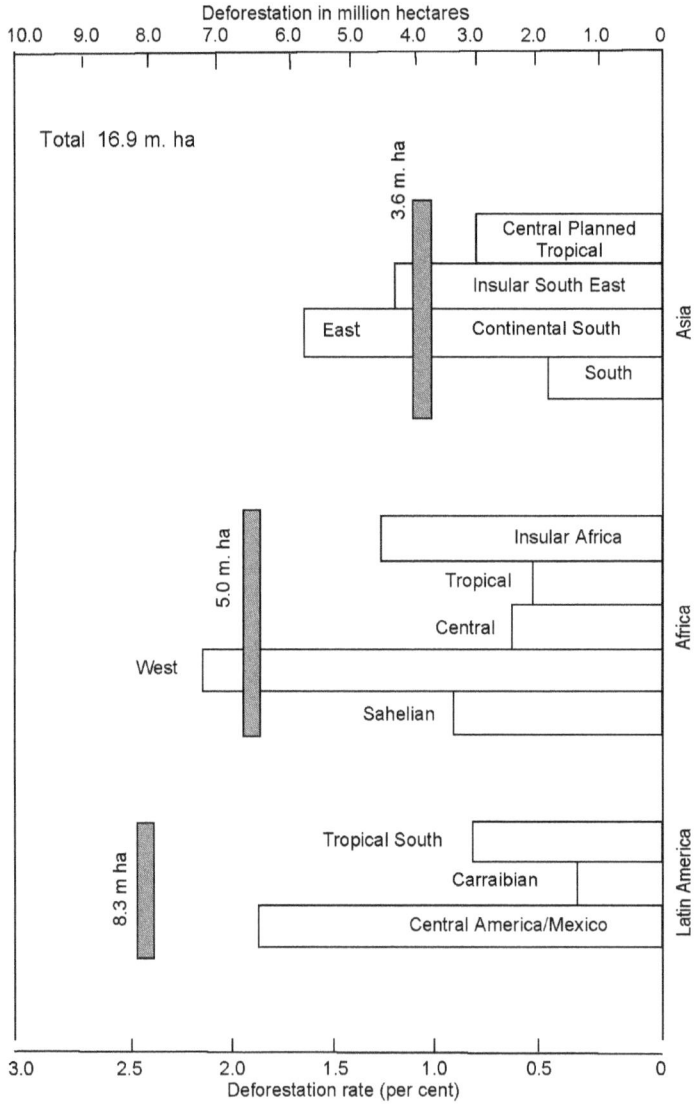

Fig. 5: Annual deforestation in the tropical region (1981–90)

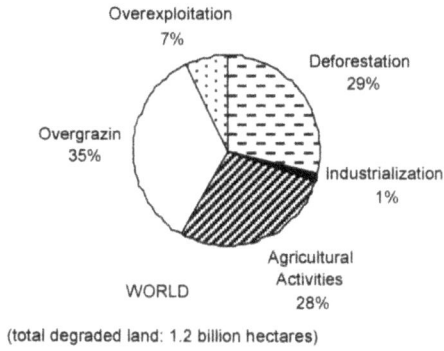

Overexploitation
7%

Deforestation
29%

Overgrazin
35%

Industrialization
1%

Agricultural
Activities
28%

WORLD

(total degraded land: 1.2 billion hectares)

Causes of Land degradation	Per cent of total degraded land						
	Asia	Africa	North America	South America	Central America	Europe	Oceaia
Deforestation	40	14	0	41	22	38	12
Industrialization	1	0	0	0	0	9	0
Agricultural Activities	27	24	66	26	45	29	8
Overgrazing	26	49	30	28	15	23	80
Overexploitation	6	13	4	5	18	0	0

Fig. 6: Causes of Land Degradation in past 45 years

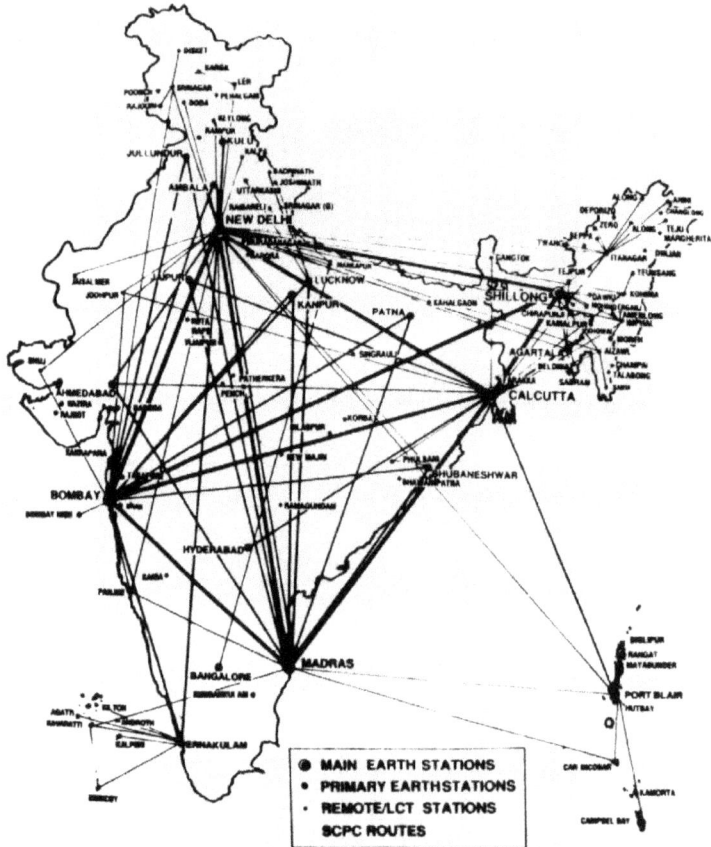

Fig. 7 : Satellite telecommunications in India

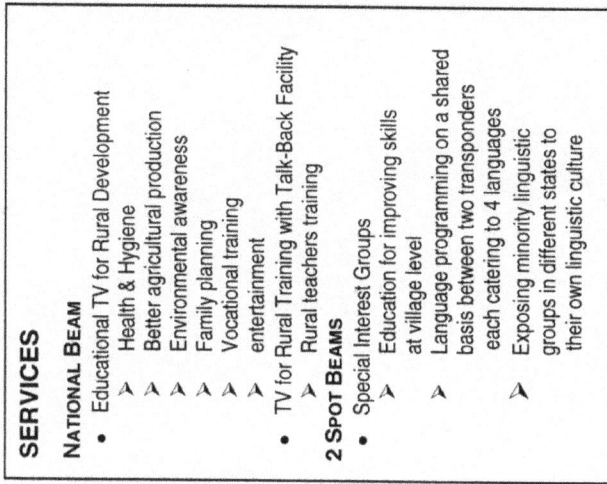

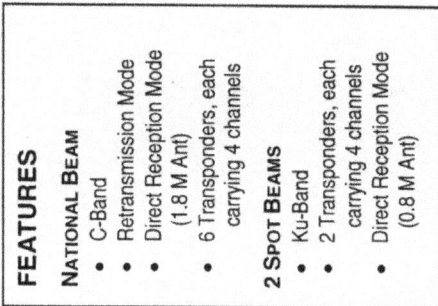

FEATURES

NATIONAL BEAM

- C-Band
- Retransmission Mode
- Direct Reception Mode
  (1.8 M Ant)
- 6 Transponders, each
  carrying 4 channels

2 SPOT BEAMS

- Ku-Band
- 2 Transponders, each
  carrying 4 channels
- Direct Reception Mode
  (0.8 M Ant)

SERVICES

NATIONAL BEAM

- Educational TV for Rural Development
  - Health & Hygiene
  - Better agricultural production
  - Environmental awareness
  - Family planning
  - Vocational training
  - entertainment
- TV for Rural Training with Talk-Back Facility
  - Rural teachers training

2 SPOT BEAMS

- Special Interest Groups
  - Education for improving skills
    at village level
  - Language programming on a shared
    basis between two transponders
    each catering to 4 languages
  - Exposing minority linguistic
    groups in different states to
    their own linguistic culture

Fig. 8 : Gramsat (concept)

43

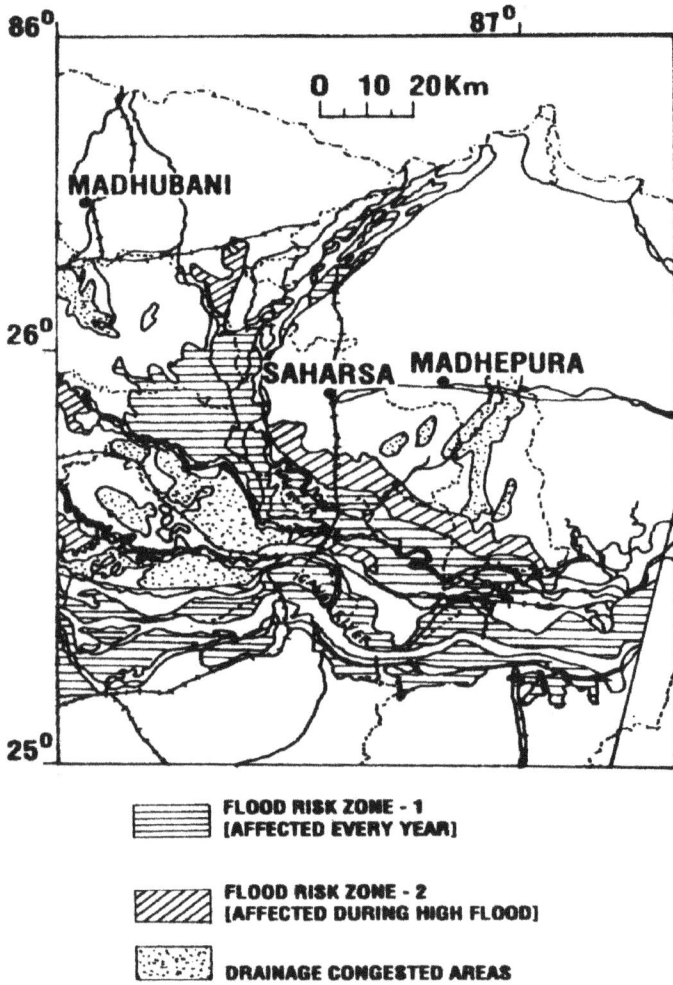

Fig. 9 : Flood risk zone map of part
of Ganga basin

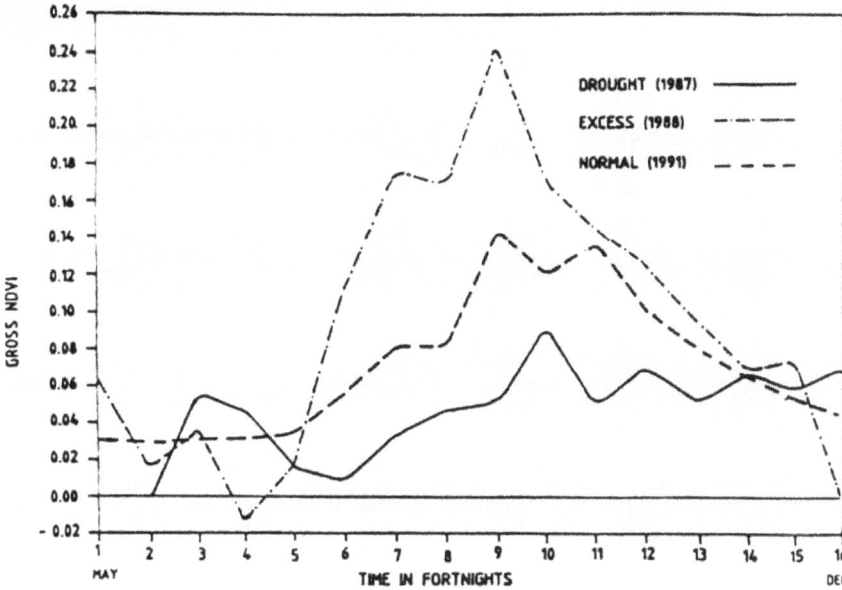

Fig. 10 *NDVI indicating seasonal vegetation conditions (Bhiwani dist., India)*

GENERAL LAND USE

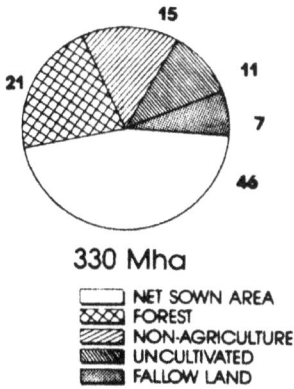

330 Mha

NET SOWN AREA
FOREST
NON-AGRICULTURE
UNCULTIVATED
FALLOW LAND

WASTELAND CATEGORIES

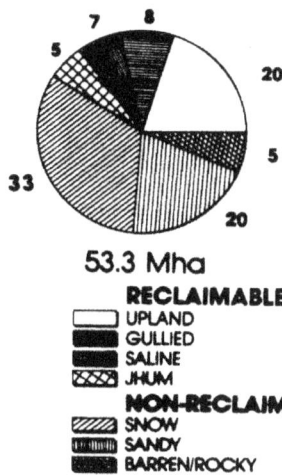

53.3 Mha

RECLAIMABLE
UPLAND
GULLIED
SALINE
JHUM
NON-RECLAIMABLE
SNOW
SANDY
BARREN/ROCKY

Fig. 11 : Typical landuse pattern in a developing country - India

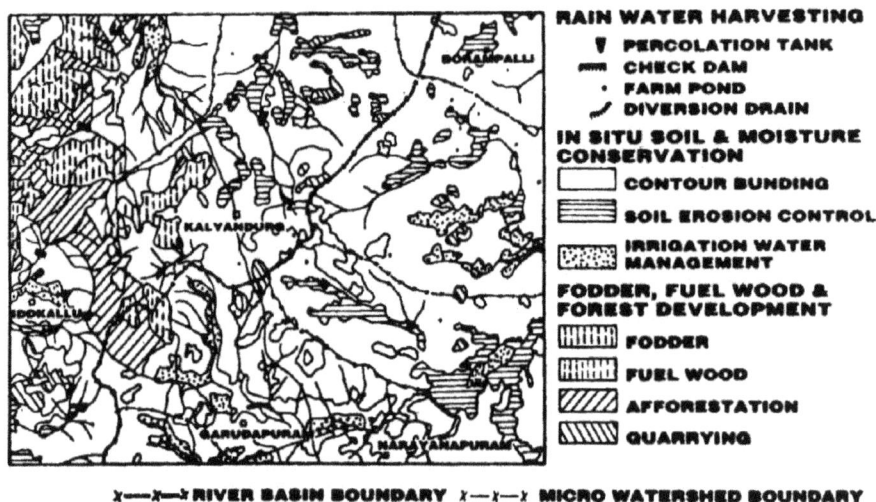

Resources management at microlevel for sustainable development
- Drought prone area

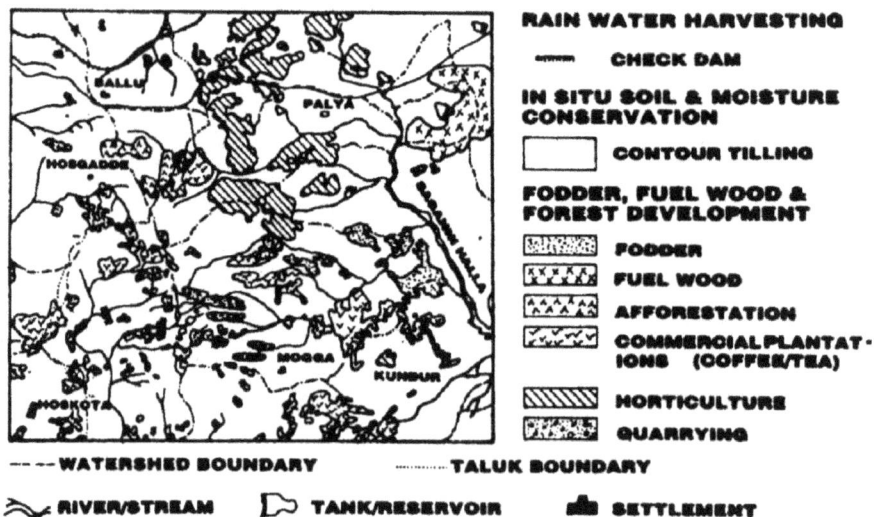

Resources management at microlevel for sustainable development
- Hill area

Fig. 12

References

Brown, L (ed.) (1992), *State of the World,* WW Norton & Co., New York

FIAO (1988), *World Agriculture, Towards 2000,* FAP report, Rome

Gao, F and Rao, UR (eds) (1992), *Space and Education in Developing Countries,* Proceedings of 43rd IAF Congress, Washington DC

Heath, G (ed.) (1994), *Space Safety and Rescue,* Science and Technology Series, Vol. 84, American Astronautical Society, Washington

Koshoo T N (1990), 'Indian Geosphere and Biosphere', in TN Khoshoo and M. Sharma (eds), *Proceedings of National Academy of Sciences,* 178

Liu, D (ed.) (1994), *Satellite Communication for Mass Education,* Proceedings of 45th IAF Congress, Jerusalem

Murai S et al. (1990), 'What population can the earth feed' Report, Mitsubishi Institute, Japan

Pant, N (1994), 'Satellite communication technology and application, 1995 — 2010', *Journal of Spacecraft Technology,* 4(1).

Ramanathan V, *et al.* (1985), 'Trace gas trends and their potential in climate change', *Journal of Geophysical Research,* 90, 5547.

Rao, UR (1987), *Perspectives in Communication,* World Scientific Publishing Company, Singapore, Vol. 2, 1422.

Rao, UR (ed.) (1988), *Space and Humanity,* Proceedings of 39th IAF Congress, Bangalore, India

Rao, UR (1991), 'Remote sensing for sustainable development', Vikram Sarabhai Memorial Lecture, Anna University Madras, India

Rao UR (1993), 'Space Technology for Achieving Socio Economic Revolution', 29th Sri Ram Memorial Lecture, Sri Ram Institute for Industrial Research, New Delhi

Rao, UR (1995a), Space Technology for Sustainable Development, Tata McGraw Hill, New Delhi

Rao, UR (1995b), *Satellite communication in India — Past, Present and Future,* Proceedings of SATCOM ASIA 1995 Conference, Hong Kong

Rao, UR (1995c), 'Space technology for enhancing sustainable carrying capacity', Zaheer Hussain Memorial Lecture, Zaher Hussein Foundation, New Delhi

Rao, UR *et al.* (1987), *Earth Safety and Disaster Response Employing Space Borne Systems,* Proceedings of 38th IAF Congress, Brighton, U.K.

Rao, UR, Chandrasekhar, M G and Jayaraman, V (1995), *Space and Agenda 21 — Caring for the Planet Earth,* Prism Books, Bangalore, India

Swaminathan, M S (1980), *Perspectives in World Agriculture,* CAB.

UN (1992), *Proceedings of UN Conference on Environment and Development*, Rio De Janerio, Brazil.

UN (United Nations) (1994), *World Population Projections*, UN, New York.

World Bank (1993), *The East Asian Miracle,* World Bank Policy Research Report, Oxford University Press, New York.

World Bank (1994), *World Development Report 1994*, Oxford University Press, New York

World Commission on Environment (1987), *Our Common Future*, Report of World Commission on Environment and Development, Oxford University Press, New York.

World Resources 1992–93 (1992), *Report of World Resources Institute*, Oxford University Press, New York

1996 K R Narayanan Oration

Message from the Vice-President

I am happy to see that the Australia South Asia Research Centre inaugurated during my official visit to Australia in 1994 has maintained lively and meaningful contacts with the region and continued the intellectual exploration of its developmental problems. The *K R Narayanan Oration* has become an annual event eagerly looked forward to by the academic community.

I am glad to learn that the third Lecture in the series is being given by the reputed economist Professor Jagdish Bhagwati. Professor Bhagwati is an economist who has made distinctly original contributions to the study and understanding of contemporary Indian and international economic problems. It is of special importance that he is delivering the Lecture in the context of the annual Australian Conference of Economists and as a prelude to the *Australia India-New Horizons* event sponsored by the Government of Australia and scheduled to take place in India later this year. The subject-matter of his lecture: 'India: Retrospect and Prospect' is particularly relevant today when India is entering the Fiftieth Anniversary of its independence.

Compared to the immense needs of the country and the kind of progress made by the *Asian Tigers*, India's achievements during the last 50 years might look unspectacular. But the progress made has been steady and all-round making it possible for the country to move forward rapidly into the future on foundations that are firm and maintaining stability and balance for a vast pluralist society marked by uneven development and baffling social problems.

The most remarkable fact that stands out prominently is that India has developed a democratic system of Government that has faced several social, economic, political and security crises during the last five decades and emerged successful and stronger out of them. In the economic field an achievement of fundamental significance was what has been called the Green Revolution. The magnitude of it can be realised when one recalls the succession of famines that devastated the country before independence and the major famines some of the developing countries had gone through not very long ago. But it has to be recognised that poverty is still with us and that the number of people living below the poverty level is unacceptably high. So is the level of illiteracy in the country. In the world index of human development, India occupies a low position. However, the rise in the average expectation of life from 27 years in 1947 to 60 years today is striking and is the outcome of the slow but steady progress in economic conditions and human development factors. In my state of Kerala which population-wise is equal to two Australia's, the index of human development is more or less the same as that of several advanced developed countries with average expectation of life at 71, literacy level at 100 per cent, infantile mortality rate at 13 per thousand and population growth rate at 1.3 per cent. This is an indication that it might not be impossible for the rest of India also to achieve similar levels of success with proper policies and proper implementation of policies and programmes.

The biggest event happening in India since 1991 has been the massive process of economic reforms with liberalisation and restructuring of the economy and its opening up to the rest of the world. Though in the circumstances of India some caution may have to be observed in regard to speed of liberalisation. It has already led to results that are sizeable and significant. In spite of the daunting nature of the tasks facing Indian development, I should venture to be optimistic about the prospects before India. I would personally look forward to Professor Jagdish Bhagwati's analysis and forecasts in regard to this important issue. I am sure that his Lecture would be a stimulating and rewarding intellectual experience.

K R Narayanan
New Delhi 1996

India: Retrospect and Prospect

Jagdish Bhagwati

At the outset, I must thank you for the great honour that you have extended to me by inviting me to give the K R Narayanan Oration. The honour is twofold.

Vice President Narayanan, whom I have the privilege of knowing well, is a man of great courtesy, charm, acuteness of intellect, and accomplishment. I believe that men and women matter. They defy the tenets of historical determinism, shaping instead of bending to history. They lead themselves, and their nations, to what Prime Minister Jawaharlal Nehru, a great and moving orator, called their 'tryst with destiny'. Dr Narayanan is one of them. But, let me assure the economists assembled here, he is also a man of impeccable taste: he studied economics and even enjoys the dismal science!

And that brings me to the other reason why I am flattered by your invitation today. Australia is in the memories of every Indian of my generation, of course. Many were the days when we ran truant from our school to watch the Indian cricketers locked in combat with the visiting Australians, fascinated in particular by the incredible speed of Lindwall and Miller as they terrified our batsmen: those were the days of exhilarating 5-day Test Matches between Cricket *Teams*, not the fast-track deviants now played between *Squads*! And Don Bradman was to us, as to you, a legend.

But as I grew older, and my tastes turned to Economics, and within that to International Economics, I also realised that Australia had produced many of the best international economists in the world: Murray Kemp, Max Corden, Trevor Swan, Ross Garnaut and Heinz Arndt among them.

For me to come to Australia finally is to come therefore, not just to the country of the irresistible koala, of the exotic kangaroo, of genius in cricket and tennis, of *Breaker Morant* and a wonderful cinema, and of a literature crowned by the Nobel Prize, but also to a great scholarly tradition in the subject closest to my heart. But that is not all. Mr Vice-Chancellor, I must add that your world-renowned university has housed many of the splendid economists that Australia has produced: there could then be no better place for me to be giving this Oration than right here!

Indeed, Mr Vice-Chancellor, I would be remiss if, on an occasion that celebrates the growing friendship between our two countries, I did not also recall the fact that I first met Trevor Swan of your university, a venerated figure among Australian and indeed all economists, in India in 1958, I believe. He had come as part of an advisory team of eminent economists that included Ian Little of Oxford and was led by Paul Rosenstein-Rodan of MIT, a great development economist. Swan had come with enthusiasm, eager to put his expert Australian shoulder to the wheel in India's developmental efforts.

Mr Vice-Chancellor, I must entertain you by recalling the contrasting story of the *reluctant* economic adviser that the Nobel laureate, Princeton economist Arthur Lewis regaled his friends with. Once he found himself invited to a fundraising luncheon by the Princeton University President for the Iranian Ambassador in Washington, a man known only to those who read the Style sections of the newspapers because he used the sudden oil wealth of his nation to entertain flamboyantly the likes of Elizabeth Taylor. So, Lewis was minding his manners and quietly getting through the lunch when he was suddenly startled to hear the President promising the Ambassador: 'We would be happy to send Professor Lewis to Iran to help you with planning your development'. As he walked back morose from the luncheon, Lewis ran into the sociologist Marion Levy, a man of some wit, who asked him what the matter was. When Lewis told him, Levy said: 'Arthur, you should have told the President that Professors can be bought, but not sold.'

As it happens, Trevor Swan's early visit to India provides me with the main theme of the Oration today: the reasons why India's monumental developmental efforts went astray and why, for the very same reasons, the current reforms hold great promise. Swan came to India at a time, in the early 1960s, when India's developmental efforts were attracting attention worldwide. And the attention and interest were equally from economists. To understand this, and also to put the subsequent disenchantment into perspective, let me explain why what we were doing in India through the 1950s was sensible *and* worthy of the huge interest everywhere.

India in the 1950s: On Track, Phase I

At her independence in 1947, India already had a fair degree of industrialisation under her belt. Textiles and steel were among the many industries that had come up exclusively from market forces and with domestic investment, under a colonial government that certainly had not seen itself as a developmental agency and had therefore virtually abstained from 'infant industry' protection or promotion. India also enjoyed the presence of an active entrepreneurial class and a modest but definite integration into the world economy. The country was also endowed with a first-rate civil service and administrative structure, world class leaders and a democratic form of government.

But the poverty was huge, with corresponding standards of living appalling for many, the literacy levels were abysmal even as the higher levels of education were impressive, and the challenge to the new government was clearly immense.

The *key strategy* that defined the resulting developmental effort was the decision to target efforts at accelerating the growth rate. Given the immensity of the poverty, simple redistribution was considered to be both negligible in its immediate impact and of little sustained value. The central anti-poverty strategy had therefore to be the creation of increasing numbers of jobs that would draw ever more of the underemployed and unemployed into gainful employment that would yield them both greater incomes and higher standards of living. Accelerated growth was thus regarded as an instrumental variable, a policy outcome that would in turn reduce poverty, the latter being the true objective of our efforts.

I have often reminded the critics of Indian strategy, who attack it from the perspective of poverty which is juxtaposed against growth, that it is incorrect to think that the Indian planners got it wrong by going for growth rather than attacking poverty: they confuse means with ends. In fact, the phrase 'minimum income' and the aim of providing it to India's poor were very much part of the lexicon and at the heart of our thinking and analysis when I worked in the Indian Planning Commission in the early 1960s.

Equally, the populist notion that pushing growth to kill poverty is a passive and conservative 'trickle-down' strategy is wholly obtuse. In the Indian context, it was an active and radical, what I have called 'pull-up' strategy. Nor were we unmindful that added policy instruments were necessary to ensure that the growth process would indeed extend to all groups. For instance, just as the United States has a 'structural' inner-city problem, we have (among others) a 'tribal' problem: each underprivileged group fails to have equal and ready access to the mainstream economy. Nor were social expenditures relegated to oblivion. The first Five-year Plan itself had addressed this matter, and the Planning Commission had at the time a distinguished social worker, Mrs Durgabai Deshmukh, as a Member who formidably minded her portfolio on the social questions.

But substantial and expanding sums could not be spent on the social questions and on the improvement of the ability of the underprivileged to access the growing mainstream economy *unless* you had growth in the first place. Spending on education and on public health, chief among our concerns, could not be expanded or even sustained unless a growing economy produced the added revenues to finance these and other expenditures.

To those who use the cliche of 'development with a human face', I respond:

> Yes, indeed. But remember that the face cannot exist by itself, except as a mask in a museum, but must be joined to the body; and if the body is emaciated, the face must wither no matter how much we seek to humanise and pretty it up.

So, we return to growth as the centrepiece of the Indian strategy for assaulting poverty and providing minimum incomes to the poor. And we must remember that it was the government's task to accelerate economic growth. I believe that we could say, in a stylised way but with plausibility, that the central conception underlying India's growth-accelerating strategy was the devising of a planning framework that would produce the enhanced investment rates. Thus, the objective was to jolt the economy up into a higher-investment mode that would generate, say, a 5 per cent growth rate as against the conventional lower-investment equilibrium with a 2 to 2.5 per cent growth rate.

The planning framework then rested on two legs. First, it sought to make the escalated growth credible to private investors so that they would proceed to invest on an enhanced basis in a self-fulfilling prophecy. Second, it aimed at generating the added savings to finance the investments so induced.

The Five-year Plan framework was an important aspect of this two-pronged policy. Simply by demonstrating that the government was committed to a higher growth rate, it assured potential investors that demand would grow at higher rates and that the risk of investment would be correspondingly reduced. Besides, at the core of the Plan, there was commitment to substantial governmental spending, mostly on infrastructure, that added yet greater credibility to the high-growth scenario in what was otherwise an 'indicative' Plan in terms of its investment profile. Moreover, the commitment to use fiscal policy to raise public savings to levels necessary to finance the projected growth of investment was also a credibility-enhancing factor for bringing about the enhanced investment.

The bulk of the 1950s can then be called the favourable Phase I of Indian developmental effort; and it broadly coincides, in approach, to much of the East Asian experience where, however, the Five-year Plan framework was not utilised. The governmental intervention, as described, led to an investment boom and hence to an enhanced growth. I may, in fact, recharacterise what happened, in more familiar technical terms, by reference to the Rosenstein–Rodan argument that has now been formalised by Vishny and Shleifer in their fine article in the *Journal of Political Economy* as a case of multiple equilibria.[1] In his classic 1943 *Economic Journal* article, which is arguably the most beautiful piece of creative writing on development, Rosenstein–Rodan was basically arguing that, for developing countries stuck in a Nash equilibrium with low levels of investment, there existed a superior cooperative equilibrium with higher levels of investment and growth.

The Indian planners, in formulating the first Five-year Plan (1951–56), were essentially exploiting this insight. This was an indicative Plan, without the straitjacket of controls and targeted allocations that would presumably reflect the contours of the superior equilibrium. In fact, it is absurd to imagine that anyone, either in India or in East Asia, could have worked out such a Rosenstein–Rodan–Vishny–Schleifer equilibrium even if there had been complete information to do so! What did happen instead was that, as I already suggested, the large component of public spending on infrastructure which was built into these indicative programs made the government's commitment to kicking the system up into some bastardised version of the Rosenstein–Rodan –Vishny–Shleifer equilibrium quite credible to the private sector, triggering the self-fulfilling private sector investment response that lifted the economy into higher investment and growth rates.[2]

What Went Wrong: Derailing after the 1950s, Phase II

What went wrong with India, and was still not entirely manifest when Swan arrived in India, can be characterised by contrasting India with East Asia once we go beyond the 1950s. In fact, by understanding better why East Asia went ahead to build greater success post-1950s helps us to understand why India went ahead to decline instead in her economic performance: hence, I will focus on East Asia's success and its causes for now.

Let me begin by observing that, in my judgment, the critical difference was that India turned to the IS (import substitution) strategy and East Asia to the EP (export promotion) strategy. A central implication, which I have not drawn sharply in my earlier writings (which have focused, not on the inducement to invest, but rather on the social returns from investment) is that India, during this Phase II, handicapped the private inducement to invest, while East Asia wound up enhancing it.

India turned inwards, starting with a balance of payments crisis in 1956-57 which precipitated the imposition of exchange controls which then became endemic to the regime, reflecting the currency overvaluation that implies the effective pursuit of an IS strategy. Again, the explicit pursuit of an IS strategy was also desired, reflecting the economic logic of elasticity pessimism that characterised the thinking of India's planners.

The result was that the inducement to invest in the economy was constrained by the growth of demand from the agricultural sector, reflecting in turn the growth of that sector. But agriculture has grown almost nowhere by more than 4 per cent per annum over a sustained period of over a decade, so that the increment at the margin in India's private investment rate was badly constrained by the fact that it was cut off from the elastic world markets and forced to depend on inevitably sluggish domestic agricultural expansion. Thus, it became customary for Indian economists to talk about 'balanced growth' and about the problem of raising the investment rate which, by the mid-1980s, was still in the range of 19–20 per cent.

By contrast, the East Asian investment rate began its take-off to phenomenal levels because East Asia turned to the EP strategy. The elimination of the 'bias against exports', and indeed a net (if mild) excess of the effective exchange rate for exports over the effective exchange rate for imports (signifying the relative profitability of the foreign over the home market), ensured that the world markets were profitable to aim for, assuring in turn that the inducement to invest was no longer constrained by the growth of the domestic market as in the IS strategy. Private domestic savings were either raised to match the increased private investment by policy deliberately encouraging them or by the sheer prospect of higher returns.

This argumentation is not easy to defend once you face up to what my student Don Davis, now at Harvard, has called the 'tyranny of the Stolper-Samuelson': for, when this theorem holds, wages and rentals on capital are inversely related.[3] When exports are the labour-intensive, the EP strategy may be expected to raise the wage of labour but depress the return to capital, thus depressing, not raising, the inducement to invest. Clearly, therefore, the force of Stolper-Samuelson argument must be broken: as indeed it can be by relaxing one or more of the assumptions underlying that theorem.

Thus, Davis suggests that the forces of comparative advantage may be argued to have been sufficiently strong as to make East Asia specialise in the production of the labour-intensive goods. This

> … decouples factor returns from the factor price frontier for the capital intensive good, leaving wages and rentals dependent only on productivity in the labor intensive good and the price of that good. In moving from autarky to free trade, both factor prices can rise, inducing an accumulation 'miracle'.

Another way out would be to assume productivity differences across countries, as in Ricardian theory. In this case,

> if we assume that the relative productivity gap of East Asia relative to the rest of the world is largest in the capital intensive sectors, and that trade serves to close this gap, then it is again possible for both wages and rentals to rise.'[4]

While therefore it is possible to formalise the argument I have made that the EP strategy increased the inducement to invest, I must also address Dani Rodrik's recent objection that exports were a relatively small part of the economy at the outset so that EP strategy could not have resulted in any significant impact, and therefore the source of the investment must be found in governmental subventions and interventions whereas the growth of trade is simply a *passive* result of the growth induced by these other factors. This argument is unpersuasive because East Asia would have run into precisely the problem of demand constraint that India was afflicted with if an IS strategy had been followed, with the efficacy of these other policies in generating investment seriously impaired. Moreover, the ultra-EP strategy, with its mild bias in favour of the export market and the policy-backed ethos of getting into world markets, meant that export incentives must have played a major role in influencing investment decisions, not just in the exporting industries, but also in the much larger range of non-traded but tradeable industries.[5] In any event, the growth of exports from East Asia was so phenomenal that the share of initial exports in GNP quickly rose to levels that would lay Rodrik's objection to rest, even if it were conceptually correct.

The flip side of the process was, of course, the generation of substantial export earnings that enabled the growing investment to be implemented by *imports of equipment embodying new technical change*.

Now, if the Social Marginal Product (SMP) of this equipment exceeded the cost of its importation, there would be a 'surplus' that would accrue as an income gain to East Asia and would also, as I argue below, boost the growth rate. For this argument to hold, however, the international cost of the newer-vintage equipment must not reflect fully its SMP for East Asia. In a competitive international market for equipment, therefore, I must assume that East Asia was a small player whose higher SMP, did not pull up the world price to reflect the higher SMP i.e., that East Asia could, even without 'piracy' and 'theft' of intellectual property (which was widespread in the region until the new WTO regime), get embodied technology at bargain prices. This seems a reasonable assumption to make, especially when one sees that the world prices of the last-but-one vintage equipment fall drastically due to rapid obsolescence in the presence of quick product innovation: just think of your PCs. (To understand fully the foregoing point, note that an economy in 1970 such as Soviet Russia's which was confined to using its own 1930s-vintage technology in equipment would *not* lose to East Asia which could use a heuristically 20 times more productive 1960s technology if East Asia had to pay a 20 times greater price for it. The surplus arises because East Asia pays, say, only a 5 times greater price in world markets for equipment that is 20 times more productive in East Asia.)

This argument is illustrated in Figure 1 in a simple diagram, with the SMP curve for increasing imports of the vintage capital equipment for East Asia put against the international cost of importing it, the striped area then representing the surplus that accrues to East Asia.

But there may also be another reservation about this argument's effect on the growth rate, as distinct from its effect on income. It is fair to say that, thanks to the focus on the steady state in Solow-type models, it has now become fashionable to assert that the gains from trade, like any allocative efficiency gains, amount to one-time gains, not affecting the growth rate. This is, however, wrongheaded as a general assertion. Thus, consider the simple Harrod–Domar corn-producing-corn growth model with labour a slack variable. If allocative efficiency regarding land use (say, from one inefficient farm to another efficient farm) leads to a greater return to the total amount of ('invested') corn being put into the ground, the marginal capital-output ratio will fall, ceteris paribus, and will lead to a permanently higher growth rate. Similarly, it takes no sweat for a first-rate theorist to construct models where trade in capital goods leads to higher growth rates, without building in externalities etc. and relying exclusively on the fact that they can be imported more cheaply than constructed under autarky.

Thus, TN Srinivasan has extended the Mahalanobis-type putty-clay model to include trade and demonstrated precisely this.[6] Thus, he assumes (in place of just one capital and one consumer good in the autarkic version) that there are two of each class of goods, with the marginal product of capital constant in each sector as in the Harrod–Domar model. The social utility function and the function that transforms the output of the two investment goods into aggregate investment are Cobb–Douglas. There is no intersectoral (i.e., between the consumer goods and the capital goods sectors), as against intrasectoral (i.e., between the two goods in each sector), mobility of capital: this is the clay assumption.

Assuming that all four goods are produced under autarky, that free trade is undertaken at fixed terms of trade, and that the share of investment going to augmenting capacity in each of the two sectors is fixed exogenously, Srinivasan then demonstrates plausibly that free trade in consumer goods (but with autarky continuing in investment goods) will raise welfare relative to autarky but not affect the growth rate of income or utility. On the other hand, freeing trade in investment goods will have a positive effect on transitional as well as on long-run (steady state) growth effect, and also a beneficial welfare effect relative to autarky. The vulgar belief that trade gains cannot affect the growth rate is thus easily disposed of.

However, how does one reconcile the 'surplus' argument with the findings that TFP growth has been a negligible factor in East Asia? So, is my story plausible but not borne out by the facts, as is often the case with our most interesting theories? I think not.

Thus, consider precisely the case where the imported equipment is 20 times more productive in Period 2 than in Period 1, but its price is only 5 times as high. If the valuation of this equipment is at domestic (producer) opportunity cost, as it should be, then it will indeed be priced 20 times higher than the older-vintage equipment of Period 1, so the measure of capital contribution at the level of the industry will rise commensurately and I presume that the estimated TFP growth in the industry will be zero: in that case, my thesis about the surplus is totally compatible with measured TFP emerging as negligible. But, of course, if the equipment is priced at its international cost, then I presume that TFP growth will pick up three-fourths of the gain that accrues from the 'surplus' of SMP over the international cost. My guess then is that, in East Asia, the former was the case. This might have been, not because the accountants were smart and valued Period 2 equipment at domestic opportunity cost, but because I guess that much of the imported equipment may have gone through importing trading firms which collected the three-fourths premium rather than the producing firms.

The role of literacy and education comes in precisely at the stage of the second step in my story above. For, the productivity or SMP of the imported equipment would be greater with a workforce that was literate and would be further enhanced if many had even secondary education. Thus, as shown in Figure 2, the SMP curve could shift to the right with literacy and education, leading to greater surplus for any given international cost of newer-vintage equipment.

Here I may cite Little,[7] using the pretext that a Lecture justifies the informality of argumentation that a Conference paper does not:

> It was largely from the experience of conducting this [1975, South Korean] survey, involving visits to the [28 randomly selected] firms ranging from 1.5 to 3.5 hours, that my own impressions of such matters as the acquisition of technology and skills on the part of the labour force ... were formed. I also visited a number of high exporting medium-size labour-intensive firms in Taiwan in 1976. ... Two points are mainly relevant in the present context. First the technology was simple, non-proprietary and easily acquired ... Secondly, both Korean and Taiwan workers were very quick to learn. Employees would usually reach the expected high level of productivity within a few weeks. This would probably not have been the case if the standards of primary education had not been high.

Of course, as these economies grew rapidly, the demand for secondary and higher education in turn would rise and a virtuous circle would follow: primary education would enhance the growth that the EP strategy brought whereas the enhanced growth would demand and lead to a more educated workforce. I see therefore primary education and literacy as playing an enhancing, rather than an initiating, role in the EP-strategy-led East Asian drama.

Thus, my story of East Asia's success, and by contrast that of India's failure, combines in its own way three major elements, in that order: (i) the enhanced inducement to invest due to the EP strategy; (ii) the benefit from the surplus of domestic SMP over international cost of imported newer-vintage capital equipment; and (iii) the raising of this SMP by the presence of a literate workforce. But if the main plot is this, the story has doubtless many sub-plots. I will touch on just one of them, especially as the analysis dates back to the early

1970s and to the NBER project which I had the pleasure of codirecting with Professor Anne Krueger, yet another of Australia's gifts to Economics.

In my synthesis volume[8] for the NBER Project findings, I had noted that among the advantages of the EP strategy, which the Project had found beneficial, one had to count the fact that trade barriers-jumping DFI in the IS countries was likely to be limited for these countries by the size of the domestic market by which it was motivated — there are shades here of the inducement-to-invest argument I have made today, but only in the faintest strokes. Secondly, such DFI as was attracted in the IS countries was also likely to be less productive because it would be going into economic regimes characterised by significant trade distortions that could even generate negative value added at socially-relevant world prices — a possibility that was discussed by me (based on an extension to the DFI issue of the contribution by Harry Johnson to the theory of immiserising growth in tariff-distorted economies)[9] and then nailed down in well-known articles into a certainty under certain conditions by Hirofumi Uzawa[10] and by Richard Brecher and Carlos Diaz Alejandro[11] independently. I should mention that both these (thoroughly plausible in terms of their economic rationale) hypotheses have been examined, with some success, in cross-country regressions by another former student of mine, V N Balasubramanyam at Lancaster University and his co-authors.[12] So, this element may also be added to the explanation of East Asia's superior performance relative to that of IS-strategy-plagued countries such as India.[13]

Indeed, the inefficiency of the limited investment that did occur is the other side of India's miseries in the post-1950s Phase II. As India turned inward, the absence of competition and its salutary effects on efficiency were also lost. This loss was further compounded as the original, promotional apparatus established in the Ministry of Industry (the DGTD) turned swiftly into a restrictive agency instead. The government turned from indicative planning to a mechanism for masterminding, with the aid of a stifling licensing system, the production, investment and import decisions in the economy to a degree unimaginable to anyone outside the regime. I am reminded that, eventually when, in the early 1990s just prior to the beginning of the reforms in earnest in 1991 under what we might call Phase III, *The Economist* ran a long piece on India, describing and denouncing its policies, a visiting Russian economist, Maxim Boycko, who then went on to play a major part in the Russian privatisation program of Anatoly Chubais, told me: 'that article could well have been describing the Soviet Union'. We had clearly reproduced beautifully the disadvantages of communism without any of its benefits!

In addition, the early policy adopted in the 1950s itself, under which a growing share of the country's investments would occur in the public sector, spawned inefficient public sector enterprises whose losses would make a significant contribution to a macro crisis in the 1980s and which, in addition, crippled the efficiency of the private sector as well since the public sector enterprises supplied, or rather failed to adequately and efficiently supply, infrastructure inputs such as electricity and transportation over which they were granted monopoly of production.

So, if I were to summarise briefly the period of three decades between the end of the 1950s and of the 1980s, I would reach the following sobering conclusion:

We had started out in the 1950s with:

- high growth rates
- openness to trade and investment
- a promotional state
- social expenditure awareness
- macro stability
- optimism; and hence
- admiration of the world.

But we ended the 1980s with:

- low growth rates[14]
- closure to trade and investment
- a license-obsessed, restrictive state
- inability to sustain social expenditures
- macro instability, indeed crisis
- pessimism; and therefore
- marginalisation of India in world affairs.

Why Did the Reforms Happen? The Sources of Phase III

The full story of why the reforms finally began to happen in 1991, under the minority government of Prime Minister Rao, awaits research: we are still too close to it. But I have some candidates that have a bearing on my speculation as to the prospects of India not reversing the existing reforms and of her continuing to undertake further reforms.

First, 1991 saw India perilously close to declaring bankruptcy as the reserves shrank rapidly towards nothing. The macroeconomic crisis, developing steadily as the internal budget deficit got out of hand and reliance on external borrowing became unprecedented, was finally at hand. As many have observed for South America, a macroeconomic crisis, where you rush for the lifeline that the Bretton Woods institutions provides, clears your head as well as the prospect of a hanging. The notion that India, during what I have called Phase II here, had now come to a turning point where it was more readily manifest than ever that her economic policies could not be allowed to continue unchanged. And so the changes, attempted sporadically in the past, would finally begin in earnest.

But then add also the fact that no Bretton Woods support would have been forthcoming without a dose of conditionality pointing in the same direction. The spread of reforms worldwide, before India was getting to them, meant that the IMF–World Bank conditionality could no longer be dismissed as ideological; it had been legitimated as sensible prescription which only reflected what we had all learned in three decades of experience.

But I suspect that it also reflected a sense in the leadership of the Prime Minister and his chosen Finance Minister who would spearhead the reforms that they had here a chance to make history, putting the economy finally on to a path that was bound to work and bring them glory. An India which had played a major role in world affairs in the 1950s was now a marginal player on that very stage, a reflection of her having shot herself in the foot. The historical parallel was with Gorbachev contemplating the decline of the Soviet Union and seeking to seize the moment with *perestroika*: the English Sovietologist has recorded how Gorbachev and Scheverdnadze had discussed that things simply could not go on as they had in the Soviet Union, and that they had to seize the moment.

India's elite, including the bureaucracy, also came to realise that there was a growing dissonance between India's traditional claim to respect and attention and her shrinking ability to command them as her economic policies and failure became more widely known and a subject of derision. I suspect that the worst psychological state to be in is to have a superiority complex and an inferior status!

The Reforms to Date and Prospects

The reforms that have been initiated are many; and they continue to arrive in many little moves, almost continually. But much of importance remains to be done. Should we condemn the reformers for hastening only slowly?

Remember that, to some extent, changing India's uniquely damaging policy framework, nourished over three decades, is a task akin to cleaning up after a typhoon: the task is enormous and cannot be done all at once. It is also hard to double guess politicians beyond a point when, while they move in the right direction, they claim that they must be allowed to traverse the political minefields in a democracy as they, and not we technocrats, see fit as far as speed and strategy are concerned. The last time when technocratic full-speed-ahead advice to a reforming government backfired badly was when shock therapy was prescribed for Russia, with a backlash that gave Russia much political turmoil and little economic progress while returning Jeffrey Sachs unceremoniously to begin a life again at Harvard. I am reminded of his famous line: 'you cannot cross a chasm in two leaps', to which Padma Desai (I should confess my bias since she is my wife) replied: 'you cannot cross it in one leap either unless you are Indiana Jones; so you drop a bridge instead'.

Yet governments can indeed be too slow for their own, and their societies', good. My judgment is that the initial speed and scope of reforms in India were just about right. India took very definite and substantial steps towards freeing the economy: the industrial licensing system has been virtually dismantled, current account convertibility is virtually in place, and the astringent attitude to direct foreign investment (DFI) which had led to an incredibly low annual inflow of equity capital of just about US $100 million annually by 1990, has been reversed both in rhetoric and in policy actions.

This early harvest is not yet sumptuous, for these reforms are still to be deepened further. The current account convertibility still goes hand in hand with wholly muddled thinking that permits nearly all consumer goods to be still subjected to strict import controls on the silly ground that we 'do not need such imports'! The DFI policy, while better, is still far from what is necessary to attract substantial inflows: the Enron affair, and now the withdrawal on grounds of inordinate delays in clearance by Amoco from a $ 1 billion coal based methane gas project again in energy-starved India, just reported in the *Asian Wall Street Journal* (September 20–21, 1996), suggest that much needs to be done, and fairly quickly, if India is to move effectively into its outward orientation mode nearly a quarter century after the East Asian NIE countries did and about a decade after the other Asean NECs have done. I am an optimist on this front since I believe that these dramatic instances will, given India's open democratic system, lead to enough pressure from below to weed out the remaining inefficiencies.

The greater difficulties lie, however, in the speed at which important residual reforms can be carried out, now that the Rao government has been replaced by a weak coalition government. The two areas where reforms are necessary and critical, if the outward orientation is to produce growth rates of 9–10 per cent rather than of 6 per cent, are the public sector which cries out to be privatised now and the ability of firms to extract greater efficiency from its labour force, including through changed laws that permit the laying off of workers as necessary, though with appropriate safeguards. In neither area can one expect this coalition government, which has two Communist cabinet members with trade union backgrounds, to bite the bullet. True, the communists in Bengal have shown flexibility in going out to get DFI and talked the talk of 'capitalist roaders'. But what you do when the rules are set by the center which you have no part of, and you must compete for resources in the market place at the state level, is entirely different from what you would do if you are at the center making the rules.

On the other hand, the new Prime Minister is pragmatic and his personal experience of the Global Age is from the Silicon Valley in Bangalore in his own state of Karnataka: and that gives him an optimistic view of the benefits to India from integrating rapidly into the world economy. And the new Finance Minister is as committed to reforms as the old one; in fact, the two had joined hands in the Rao government as the leading reformers of their time.

So, you can be an optimist or a pessimist as to whether we in India will change from second to third gear in our reforms or whether we will coast along in second gear. Only time will tell.

FIGURE 1

FIGURE 2

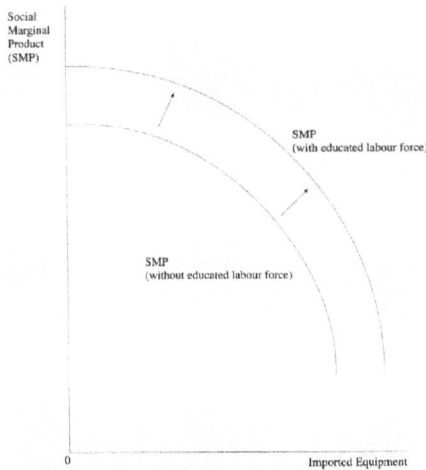

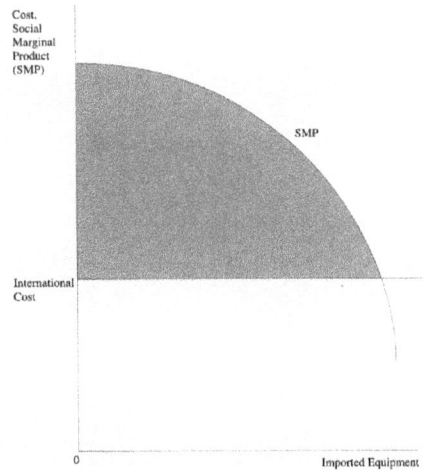

Endnotes

[1] Shleifer, Andrei and Robert W Vishny (1988) 'The Efficiency of Investment in the Presence of Aggregate Demand Spillovers', *Journal of Political Economy*, 96(6) December, pp. 1221–31.

[2] Dani Rodrik seems to share broadly this view of how private investment rose but seems to err in two ways. He seems to suggest, presumably in sympathy with the Amsden–Wade thinking, that the bureaucrats could figure out the sectoral contours of the superior equilibrium, a presumption that I find ludicrous especially having seen the best bureaucrats in India confess to their inability to choose industrial favorites on any rational grounds. Moreover, he extends the argument well beyond the 1950s whereas, as I argue later in the text, this makes little sense. See Dani Rodrik, 'Getting Interventions Right: How over the home markets South Korea and Taiwan grew Rich'*Economic Policy,* April 1995.

[3] I am drawing here on the preliminary draft of Don Davis's paper, 'Miracles of Accumulation: Models of Trade and Growth in East Asia' (mimeo), Department of Economics, Harvard University, January 1996.

[4] Don Davis, *ibid.,* page 2. Davis proceeds to formalize these ideas in a dynamic framework, more appropriate to the accumulation problem at hand.

[5] Rodrik (op.cit) also seems to think it pertinent that the export incentive, in the shape of the real exchange rate, did not continue improving. However, it is not necessary for it to be improving continuously for the export incentives to operate. Thus, an excess of the effective exchange rate for

exportables over that for importables (as distinct from continuous increase in this difference) will suffice to provide a continuing incentive for the export Martin Wolf has also critiqued Rodrik's anti-EP-strategy argumentation, as also the Krugman argumentation, in two excellent recent columns in the *Financial Times*, 'The Tyranny of Numbers' and 'A Lesson for the Chinese'.

[6] See his Comment on 'Two Strategies for Economic Development: Using Ideas and Producing Ideas', by Romer, *Proceedings of the World Bank Annual Conference on Development Economics 1992*, World Bank, Washington DC, 1993. Srinivasan also makes the valid point that the Mahalanobis–Feldman putty-clay models are among the earlier examples of 'endogenous' growth theory since the growth rate is determined by the discretionary policy choice of the share of investment goods being allocated to the capital goods sector. The neglect of the considerable literature on such models by the originators of the current endogenous growth theorists is to be attributed to the fact that these theorists have come to their models from the Solow model and have no acquaintance with the growth models that came up in the context of developmental problems in the 1960s. Of course, most of us are rediscovering great ideas all the time!

[7] Little, Ian (1994) 'Picking Winners: The East Asian Experience', *Social Market Foundation Occasional Paper*, London.

[8] Bhagwati, Jagdish N (1978) *Anatomy of Consequences of Exchange Control Regimes*, NBER, Cambridge Mass: Ballinger.

[9] See Jagdish Bhagwati, 'The Theory of Immiserising Growth: Further Applications', in Michael Connolly and Alexander Swoboda (eds), *International Trade and Money*, Toronto University Press: Toronto, 1973.

[10] Uzawa, Hirofumi, 'Shihon Jiyuka to Kokumin Keizai (Liberalisation of Foreign Investments and the National Economy)', *Economisuto*. Vol. 23, December 1969, pp. 105–122.

[11] Brecher, Richard and Alejandro, Carlos Diaz, 'Tariffs, Foreign Capital and Immiserising Growth', *Journal of International Economics*, 1977.

[12] See, in particular, V N Balasubramanyam and M A Salisu, 'EP, IS and Direct Foreign Investment in LDCs', in A Koekkoek and L B M Mennes (eds), *International Trade and Global Development: Essays in Honour of Jagdish Bhagwati*, Routledge: London, 1991, for the former hypothesis; and V N Balasubramanyam, M A Salisu and David Sapsford, 'Foreign Direct Investment and Growth in EP and IS countries',*Economic Journal*, January 1996, for an indirect test of the latter hypothesis (explaining growth as the dependent variable).

[13] Of course, as Magnus Blomstrom has reminded me, I should also note that there is considerable evidence at the microlevel of beneficial spillover effects from DFI, including from several studies he has undertaken in developing countries. However, reconciling this evidence with the contention that there is little evidence of TFP in the Lau–Young type studies remains an unresolved issue.

[14] The 1980s had higher than the 'Hindu growth rate' of 3.0 to 3.5 per cent during the preceding two decades but, as has been discussed by many, it was based on excessive internal spending and both internal and external borrowing, and hence was clearly unsustainable. It in fact led directly to the huge external crisis that forced the reforms of *Phase III*.

1999 K R Narayanan Oration

Message from the President

I am glad that the annual lecture to commemorate the inauguration of the Australia South Asia Research Centre in April 1994 at The Australian National University has been taking place every year without interruption. These lectures delivered by distinguished economists have contributed meaningfully to the understanding of vital aspects of the South Asian economy in this period of change and reforms. I am glad to learn that this year the oration is given by Mr P Chidambaram, a former Finance Minister of India who played a leading role in the liberalisation process of the Indian economy. Mr Chidambaram with his profound knowledge of economics and wide ranging experience in Government and public life of India would, I am confident, make the Lecture an illuminating exercise in the understanding of the complex process of economic transformation that is taking place in India in all its multiple dimensions.

It is refreshing that Mr Chidambaram will give special emphasis in his Oration upon the third tier of Government in India, that is, at the grass-roots level. What invests the Indian experiment with depth and significance is that the reform process is not a superficial phenomenon affecting the upper crust of society, but involves the participation of millions of men and women at the village level. The Panchayati Raj institutions in India have made democratic decentralisation a reality. Three million elected representatives of the people at the grass-roots level, one million of whom are women, are today participants in both decision-making and implementation of developmental programmes at the grass-roots level. The 474 District *Panchayats*, 5906 intermediate level *Panchayats* and over 227,000 village *Panchayats* now constitute powerful self-propelled engines to promote the developments goals of the country. The success of this exercise of unprecedented scale in devolution of power has varied in different parts of the country depending on the extent of devolution of finances and responsibilities along with necessary training and capacity building. There is no doubt however, of the potential for these evolving institutions to become vibrant vehicles of self-governance, transforming the quality of life in India's villages with democratic participation and paying heed to the demand for social justice by the generality of the people.

I am confident that Mr Chidambaram will more than do justice in his oration to this very import subject which has far reaching consequences for India's polity and development, and which would be of interest to all democratic countries.

K R Narayanan
New Delhi 1999

Stronger Branches, Deeper Roots: The Democratisation of India's Economic Reforms

P Chidambaram

It is a privilege to be invited to The Australian National University. ANU has had a long association with India. Sir John Crawford, one of your former Chancellors, played a key role in the 1960s in making the green revolution possible in India, and we are grateful for that. Few institutions around the world have a centre dedicated to research on South Asia. This University has set an example by establishing the Australia South Asia Research Centre (ASARC). I have no doubt that the seed that was sown in 1994 will grow into a huge tree, providing opportunity to hundreds of scholars to study the unfolding South Asian drama.

There could have been no better occasion for me to visit here — which is also my first visit to your beautiful country — than to deliver the K R Narayanan Oration. It is my privilege to have known Mr Narayanan personally for many years. Mr Narayanan is a distinguished son of India and has impeccable intellectual and moral credentials. He has served his country with commitment and far-sightedness. His rise to the high office of President is a modern-day version of 'log cabin to the President's House', and throughout his life he had no assets other than hard work, integrity and humility. I hope I can measure up to the great honour attached to a lecture that bears his name.

The Development Challenge

India is a large and diverse country and its development has many dimensions. A population of nearly a billion people is just one aspect that sets it apart from most developing countries. True, China makes a good comparison. But China does not have the religious, ethnic, social or cultural variations and diversities that mark India. No other nation has such a large underclass — of backward castes and classes — that seeks empowerment. We cannot also forget that, unlike in many other developing countries, democracy has flourished in India for over five decades now and has struck deep roots. Its federal polity and the division of political power make the nature of State intervention in the economy somewhat different from other systems. Therefore, while comparisons with East Asia and China could certainly help in analysing India's economic trajectory and the success or failure of its policy responses, such an approach suffers from obvious limitations. India's development problem has to be probed on its own and solutions found that are specific to its needs. The theme that I have chosen for my lecture today rests on this premise. My endeavour would be to look at both the political and economic aspects of the development challenge in India.

Soon after India launched its reforms in 1991, its economy responded strongly to the bold initiatives taken by the government. The foreign exchange crisis of 1991 had brought down the GDP growth rate to a mere 0.8 per cent in 1991–92. The rebound thereafter was strong and, during the five years ending 1996–97, GDP growth rate averaged 6.9 per cent, the highest ever for a five-year period. This was accompanied by a turnaround in macro-economic balances. The current account deficit improved from a high of 3.5 per cent in 1991 to 1.2 per cent in 1996–97 and the debt-service ratio declined from 32.4 per cent to 23 per cent. External debt as a percentage of GDP fell to 25 per cent in 1996–97 from a high of 37 per cent a few years earlier. Fiscal deficit of the Centre declined from 8.6 per cent in 1990–91 to 5.1 per cent in 1996–97. Foreign exchange reserves improved dramatically, rising from a mere billion dollars to over 27 billion dollars now. And this has happened despite substantial liberalisation of the trade regime and reduction in tariffs.

While the improvement in the macro economy has been remarkable, no less remarkable have been the changes that have taken place at the grass roots. Let me give you a flavour of the impact of economic reforms on the rural population of India who constitute the bulk of our poor, illiterate and deprived. Between the National Sample Survey 46th round (July 1990 — June 1991) and the 53rd round (January 1997 — December 1997), the total number of employed in rural India increased from 268 million to 294 million, a gain of 26 million in the space of six years. While no accurate estimates are yet available for changes in rural per capita income, an indication can be had from the changes in real wages of unskilled agricultural labour. After a sharp decline in 1991–92, the first year of reform, real wages increased at an average annual rate of 3.6 per cent in the next six years. Gross capital formation in agriculture, another useful indicator, shows a 50 per cent rise at constant prices in the six years between 1991–92 and 1996–97. What is more remarkable is that there is a clear shift in favour of private investment in agriculture, and the share of private investment has increased from 75 per cent to 83 per cent. These changes are also reflected in the social indicators for rural India. Infant mortality rate for rural areas has declined from 86 per thousand live births to less than 80 per thousand (the national average is 71). Literacy in rural areas has improved from 44.7 per cent to 56 per cent (the national average is 62 per cent). The birth rate for the whole country has declined from 29.5 per thousand to 27.2 and the death rate from 9.8 per thousand to 8.9. These tentative trends are consistent with the view that rapid economic growth has brought about an improvement in the living standards of the people in general.

During the last two years, however, while macro-economic balances have not deteriorated, growth rate of GDP has tended to slow down to about five per cent. The IMF's forecast for the current year (1999–2000) is that the GDP growth would once again be only 5.1 per cent. The sector responsible for the slowdown is manufacturing, where growth has slipped from a peak of 15 per cent in 1995–96 to less than four per cent in 1998–99. What has also raised concern is that during the nineties, as a whole, trend growth rate in agriculture has been lower than it was in the eighties.

Recent researches have confirmed that economic growth has contributed much more to reduction of poverty in India than subsidies or the government's anti-poverty interventions targeted at the poor. The rate of decline in the poverty ratio in the late 1980s and early 1990s has been double the rate achieved in the 1970s. This happened because the average growth rate of GDP improved from 3.5 per cent in the 1970s to 5.3 per cent in the 1980s and even higher to seven per cent during 1994–95, 1995–96 and 1996–97. Clearly, India needs to sustain GDP growth rates of seven per cent plus to eliminate poverty over the next fifteen to twenty years. What is also required is some sort of balanced growth across sectors because of the pivotal role of agricultural growth in poverty alleviation.

Three Constraints

Among the constraints to sustainability of high growth and poverty reduction in India, three are most apparent.

First, India's infrastructure is in urgent need of repair and expansion. Huge amounts need to be invested in ports, power generation and distribution, telecommunication, railways, roads and bridges, irrigation systems and water resources, infrastructure in urban and rural settlements, and afforestation and rehabilitation of degraded land.

Second, the quality of India's human resources is abysmally poor. India has the highest number of illiterate people among all countries. A third of India's children between the ages of six and ten do not get to school. Of the children that do, a good number drop out well before they acquire the skills needed to earn a decent wage. India has also the world's largest share of children who remain malnourished. A large proportion of the Indian population does not have access to basic health-care or basics like drinking water, shelter and toilets. Communicable diseases and prenatal and maternal mortaity cause about 470 deaths per 100,000 persons in India — a rate four times that of China. In sum, a third of all Indians are poor, malnourished, illiterate and in bad health, and a robust growth rate of population only adds more to the bottom third of the Indian people. In a country like India, reduction in population growth becomes a crucial variable. Experience of some Indian States clearly suggests that a fall in population growth rate has strong linkages with social indicators like health and literacy, particularly of women.

Third, the government needs to redefine itself both in terms of what it should do and what it must spend on. While deregulation has already reduced the role of government in industry, infrastructure and services, and has expanded the space for the private sector, much more needs to be done. The process of privatisation remains tardy. But deregulation and privatisation alone will not help. This is because high fiscal deficits continue to threaten the sustainability of the growth process. Huge borrowings by the government hamper resource mobilisation by the private sector and keep interest rates high. It follows that redefinition of government is closely linked with fiscal reform, especially reduction of the deficit and re-orientation of expenditure.

Trends in Indian Polity

It is necessary to look at these constraints within the setting provided by the emerging trends in the Indian polity and society. The most visible feature of the polity is the emergence of regional political and social forces and their urge for autonomy and empowerment. Over the last decade or so these urges have found a vehicle in regional political parties and they have played a key role in coalition governments at the Centre. The coalition governments have responded to the growing clout of regional parties by devolving more powers of decision-making from the Centre to the States. This trend cannot now be reversed as its roots go deep. Indeed, State governments are also under pressure to further decentralise power and resources to local bodies. Indian society is witnessing a process of great churning. The old order is dead. Sections at the lowest rung of society, the *dalits* [1] and the backward castes, minorities and women are now seeking social equality and their rightful place in the power structure. Alongside, there has been a surge in the activities of thousands of non-governmental organisations seeking to find decentralised solutions to developmental, cultural and social problems faced by the people. This social change, as well as the people's urge to participate in the development agenda and seek localised solutions to their problems, is bringing to the fore the role of local bodies, called Gram (i.e., village) panchayats, Nagarpalikas and Zila parishads.

The initial phase of reforms under the Congress government (1991–96) was driven by compulsion, external pressure and a few committed individuals. By a quirk of fate, many parties that had long opposed structural reforms came to power in 1996 under the banner of the United Front government. The United Front government surprised its critics by not only reaffirming the reform process but vigorously pursuing reforms in new areas. For instance, it was the United Front government which reformed direct taxes, began dismantling the administered price mechanism for petroleum products, and won the approval of the Inter-State Council (a body comprising the Chief Ministers of all the States) to accept 29 recommendations on Centre-State financial relations.

That Government also introduced a slew of draft legislations ranging from Company Law to Income-Tax to Foreign Exchange to Insurance. The BJP-led Government which assumed office in March 1998 came in with a reputation of being a right-wing coalition, rooted, however, not in reform but in atavism. After farcical posturing with outdated ideas like Swadeshi (self-reliance, or, more accurately, autarchy) and outrageous suggestions like withdrawal from WTO, the government settled down to the business of governance and categorically reaffirmed both the content and direction of the economic reforms that had started in 1991. The positive fall out of this was a new policy on Information Technology and a major overhaul of excise duties. Thus, the 1990s has witnessed the forging of an unspoken consensus among all the parties which cover the entire political spectrum of India. The Congress and the BJP have emerged as the two poles. Regional parties which dominated the United Front have shown a tendency to gather around one or the other pole. Many observers discern a definite trend towards a two-party system. While there is some basis for this conclusion, I do not think political life in India would ever be so simple. As the two major parties move towards the centre, they are in danger of losing their USP, although, I must confess, in the case of the BJP it would be better off if it loses its Unwanted Selling Points more rapidly! I also believe that there is political space for the Communist parties; there is space for a Green party as well. The two-party system would eventually dominate India's system with a peculiar Indian variation: the Congress and the BJP will be the two dominant parties at the Centre, but at the State level it is possible that the two party system may be dominated by two regional parties excluding either or both the Congress and the BJP.

Even if single-party governments replace coalitions at the Centre, they will have to accommodate regional and sub-regional aspirations and even nurture them. They will also have to provide representation to backward castes, the _dalits_ , the minorities and women. Indeed, both the leading national political parties, the Congress and BJP, are now supporting demands by sub-regional forces for formation of new States. Both are wooing the _dalits_ , backward castes and minorities and debating legislation to reserve seats for women in elected bodies. There is a realisation across the political spectrum that if the country were to be governed effectively, its diversity would have to be respected and nourished. The constraints to India's growth which I noted earlier would have to be addressed within this changing political matrix.

Indeed, this framework is no different from the one visualised by the architects of India's Constitution five decades ago. They clearly defined the division of responsibilities between the Centre and the States and enumerated them in the Union list, the States' list and the Concurrent list. These lists entrust the State governments with substantial responsibilities for development. Thus, States play a determining role in development of agriculture, water resources, land relations, environment and forests, rural roads and state highways, minor ports, electricity and rural and urban services. They are also responsible for human development through investments in key areas as health and education. To enable them to fulfill their responsibilities, the Constitution also empowers them with rights to raise taxes, get a share in funds available with the Centre, and levy user charges on various economic and social services provided to the people. The Constitution also provides for rights and responsibilities of local bodies like panchayats and municipal bodies. The Indian Constitution envisages that the States are as much, if not more, responsible for development as the Centre.

One may ask that if the framework was already provided for in the Constitution, then what went wrong? The framework worked, but only for a few years after independence. Thereafter, India suffered a phase when the Centre encroached upon the powers and autonomy of the States. The States in turn usurped the powers of local bodies. This was a logical fall-out of the centralised model of planned development India chose in the mid-fifties, which ensured that all economic decisions were directed by the Centre. The result was that the Centre sought to assume a larger responsibility for development than assigned to it in the Constitution. It floated centrally-sponsored schemes and procrastinated on sharing all the tax revenues with State governments. States were required to seek clearances from the Centre for setting up projects for infrastructure and human development. Before the economic reforms of 1991, the States had little autonomy in attracting private domestic or foreign capital because investment, financial, industrial, sectoral and locational policies were controlled by the Centre. Local initiatives, especially initiatives that would have been possible through local bodies, perished under the Centre-directed and Centre-controlled economic model of development. In turn, States neglected their local bodies: in many States local bodies ceased to exist as elections to such bodies were not held for 10–20 years.

The coincidence of economic reforms and the emergence of regional political forces in the nineties have acted as a catalyst to trigger devolution of power to the States. The United Front government (1996–98) offered to abolish or transfer to the States centrally-sponsored schemes. It also liberalised policies to allow States to attract more private capital. The United Front government also accepted the recommendation of the Finance Commission that 29 per cent of all central tax revenues should be shared with the States. The change in the correlation of forces in favour of States is evident from the fact that the BJP-led coalition government that followed has continued with decentralising power to the States.

Is Empowerment of States Enough?

But empowerment of States is just one side of the coin. To deliver on the development front, the States will have to perform and not just rest content with acquiring more powers. The overall record thus far has been uninspiring. Most States' finances are in a mess and they often have to resort to overdrafts to pay salaries to their employees. The latest figures show that the States' combined fiscal deficit had increased to a high of 3.6 per cent of GDP. In 1985–86, this figure was 2.7 per cent.

Disturbingly, the States' fiscal deficit is rising not because they are spending more on development. The bulk of the States' expenditure is devoted to salaries and pensions, interest payments, and covering losses of public enterprises or losses incurred by electricity and irrigation boards. The interest burden on States has risen from 1.4 per cent of GDP in 1985–86 to 2.3 per cent now. Not surprisingly, their development effort is faltering: capital expenditure on social and economic services has fallen from 3.1 per cent of GDP in 1985–86 to around two per cent now. The States' expenditure on key social services like health and education is falling as a proportion of their total expenditure. Likewise, their commitment to developing critical infrastructure has weakened. They are unable to find resources even for maintenance of existing roads, public transportation systems and irrigation facilities. They cannot meet the growing energy needs of industry and agriculture because the state electricity boards have accumulated losses of over Rs. 150 billion. The urban and rural settlements are in a state of decay. And even as their wasteful expenditures are going beyond control, their taxation systems have lost the ability to deliver the revenue growth needed to plug the widening resources gap.

It will be evident that the three constraints to growth and development I outlined earlier are in full play at the level of the States. Since the States are responsible for a substantial part of the development effort, it is plain that reforms at the Centre alone cannot resolve the issue. The answer clearly lies in reforms at the State level: reforming States hold the key to India's economic future.

Fortunately, some States have seen the writing on the wall and launched welcome initiatives. Orissa, Haryana, Andhra Pradesh and Uttar Pradesh have launched comprehensive power sector reforms to dissolve their electricity boards and establish separate companies for generation and distribution of power, and have drawn up plans for privatisation of both generation and distribution. They have set up regulatory agencies to eliminate government's interference in the power sector, and to set tariffs for various categories of consumers. Hopefully, the huge subsidies being doled out will now be phased out and the power sector in these States would become financially sustainable. The power reforms experiment in these four States has motivated other States like Karnataka to launch similar reforms. Incidentally, these five States are ruled by five different political parties.

Similar initiatives have been launched in other areas of infrastructure. Karnataka and Andhra Pradesh have created infrastructure funds to boost investments in large infrastructure projects. Andhra Pradesh and Gujarat are upgrading their State highways and are revamping their road departments to improve the quality of road construction and maintenance. Many States are seeking private investors to rebuild high-density corridors into toll-based highways or expressways. Almost all States along India's large coastline are inducing private investors to build new ports on a BOT basis.

Some States have also launched new programmes in the social sector. States like Rajasthan, Uttar Pradesh and Madhya Pradesh have embarked on improving their primary school systems to universalise primary education. Andhra Pradesh and Karnataka are reforming their health systems to improve the quality and reach of health services. Some States have launched ambitious programmes for reproductive health and women and child development. Kerala and Tamil Nadu have already reached the replacement level of fertility of 2.1.

Fiscal Reform: The Critical Variable

While all these are steps in the right direction they still fall far short of the truly enormous requirements of the large Indian population. Even as many States are deregulating to woo private investors, it is obvious that private capital cannot satisfy all the requirements. There are critical areas in social sector and infrastructure where only the government can provide the necessary money as well as drive. Many of the programmes, especially in the social sector, are not backed by fiscal reform and realignment of public expenditure. In the absence of fiscal reform, the critical minimum effort in infrastructure and human development is sadly missing. Fiscal reform at the state level is the one crucial element for redirecting State governments' energies towards the social sector and infrastructure.

Furthermore, these programmes would not be sustainable unless they are conceived, designed and owned by the people and communities themselves. Most Indian States have large populations: a good number have more than 60 million people and one is large enough to qualify as the sixth largest country in the world! Within each State there are substantial regional variations in social structures and ethnicity, resource endowments, land relations, agro-climatic conditions, cropping patterns and the like. Quite often programmes and projects conceived in State capitals fail to account for such variations, and communities are not taken into confidence. Also, centralised implementation of projects prevents transparency and vested interests tend to gain at the expense of the people. A good example is the plethora of anti-poverty programmes and subsidies targeted at the poor. Their achievements in terms of poverty reduction have been found to be questionable and far from commensurate with the huge amount of funds poured into them. If the States have to ensure that reforms deliver at the grass roots they have no option but to decentralise in favour of local elected bodies at the village and municipal levels.

Panchayats: The Third Tier

Over two-thirds of the one billion Indian population lives in over 500,000 small villages and the remainder in a few thousand urban and semi-urban settlements. As I said earlier, the setting for development may change from one set of villages to another. To ensure that these varying needs are addressed and programmes are implemented in a decentralised manner, the Congress government under Rajiv Gandhi (1985–1989) sought to strengthen the role of the 'third tier' in India's administrative structure comprising elected local bodies. Subsequently in 1992, the Indian Parliament enacted two critical changes in the Indian Constitution, called the 73rd and 74th amendments, that created a multi-level structure of 'Panchayati Raj' institutions at the district, intermediate and village levels. The aim was to put in place elected local bodies as institutions of self-government and enhance their role in development.

This Constitutional and legal initiative opened a new window of opportunity for State governments to deal with the constraints that thwart India's development. However, not many States have grabbed the opportunity and the establishments in State capitals continue to resist decentralisation of power and resources. Fortunately, some States are utilising the constitutional changes to empower their local bodies. A noteworthy example in this context is the manner in which Madhya Pradesh, a large Indian state, is implementing a programme to universalise primary education through a programme called the Education Guarantee Scheme (EGS). It has redefined the Indian State by including in it the village panchayat and the local community and excluding the civil service apparatus that allocates money and manages a large educational bureaucracy. Any community that has 25 children but does not have access to a primary school can demand a school. The demandeurs should select a locally available teacher and present a claim to the gram panchayat, which passes it on to the authorities at the district level. The district administration shall respond within 90 days of the demand. While the government lays down the curriculum and pays for textbooks, mid-day meals for children, and the salary and training of the teacher appointed by the village panchayat, the latter, along with the community, has to provide land for the school. This demand-driven system has been phenomenally successful: in 1998, over 40 primary schools have come up each day of the year. More has happened for primary education in Madhya Pradesh over the last two years than in the five decades prior to the launch of the EGS. The success of EGS belies the argument that tradition-bound communities are not alive to the value of education for their children. It also shows that they are willing to take charge of primary education for their children, and can do a better job than the bureaucracy.

Another bold initiative is underway in the state of Andhra Pradesh. In June 1997, the State legislature passed the 'Andhra Pradesh Farmers Management of Irrigation Systems Act'. The Act provides for creation of Water Users Associations all over the State which in turn elect their Managing Committees. The State government has empowered the WUAs and their committees to manage the irrigation systems at the level of the village i.e., beyond the main feeder canal. They maintain records of water use, collect dues from member farmers, ensure proper distribution of water, and are also allowed to spend on repair and maintenance of the network. Over 10,000 such associations have been formed. Preliminary assessments show better maintenance of the irrigation system, increase in the area of cultivated land and improved collection of revenues. This needs to be set against the abysmal performance of irrigation departments in most States, which are bankrupt, and unable to maintain the existing channels, let alone create new ones.

The government of Andhra Pradesh has launched another new development initiative called 'Janmabhoomi'. The programme is based on identification and prioritisation of needs by the communities themselves through the institution of the village panchayat. People share the cost of community works to which government also contributes, they execute the works through self-help groups, review and audit the expenditure and own the assets thus created. The projects executed through the programme include roads, drains, buildings for schools and colleges, drinking water, health clinics, irrigation facilities etc. Over the last two years a number of such projects have been completed and commissioned. Even allowing for some waste and leakages, assets worth billions of rupees have been added to the community, and there is a growing sense of community ownership and responsibility.

Many more such community-based programmes are under implementation in the States. The common feature that marks all such success stories is participation by people's institutions like elected local bodies, self-help groups or co-operatives. True, in all these success stories there are other features like meticulous planning, social leadership, external technological and managerial inputs and availability of resources. However, there is little doubt that people's participation, and the resulting beneficiary orientation of such schemes, has been the critical input.

Another feature of successful development programmes has been their holistic approach. It has been realised that the development of the poor cannot be achieved through any one single activity. Development has to be a multi-dimensional process that addresses problems of illiteracy, ill health and infrastructure. The range of activities being addressed in the Janmabhoomi programme in Andhra Pradesh illustrates this point. Janmabhoomi also confirms the fundamental fact that only programmes identified by the community deliver the maximum results. Development occurs when it is an interactive and democratic process, because then alone it addresses the numerous dimensions of backwardness.

As I said earlier, the potential for sustainable development revealed by the 73rd and 74th amendments is still not being tapped by most State governments, although some have begun to move in that direction. In most States, the power elite continues to resist decentralisation, and implementtation of 'Panchayati Raj' has turned out be an exercise in bureaucratic expansion. The concept itself continues to be plagued by numerous problems. There are legal ambiguities that allow States to keep local bodies weak and ineffective, and some more constitutional changes may be necessary to plug the loopholes. Another problem is the lack of resources available to local bodies, as State governments and State Finance Commissions have yet to work out the terms of sharing of taxable resources. Local bodies have also not yet been fully empowered to levy and collect taxes, user charges and other revenues. Only in a few cases have municipalities been allowed to issue bonds. Another hurdle is the limited expertise at the village level considering the high levels of illiteracy among village communities and their relative isolation. And not to be overlooked is that the villages and communities have their own elite and inequitable power structures, patron-client relations, and caste equations, which resist and arrest any social or economic change. There are numerous such problems that I need not spell out here. Scholars at this Centre interested in pursuing the subject can easily dip into the vast body of literature available.

The Tree: With Branches and Roots

Friends, a discussion on economic reforms in India tends to look at what the Indian government in New Delhi is doing. Investors and even scholars often base their judgement on the pace and quality of reforms by assessing the actions of the Central government. There cannot be any doubt that the overall policy environment has to be created by the Centre. For instance, some of the constraints to growth in India lie in the policies concerning the financial sector, international trade, privatisation of public sector enterprises, legal systems, taxation, and fiscal issues like subsidies. The Central government has to continue reforms in all these areas to improve the environment for growth and development. None can underestimate the catalytic role played by the policy framework created by the Centre.

But the role of the Central government in the Indian reform process ought not to be exaggerated either. For example, fiscal reforms, easily the most important macro-economic issue, cannot be assessed only in terms of measures outlined in the central budget. Fiscal deficits in the States are as substantial and as relevant. My endeavour today has been to draw your attention to the large and crucial space occupied by two other layers in the institutional framework for reform in India: the State governments and the third tier comprising local bodies or other elected community-based organisations. India cannot sustain high rates of growth and make its people prosper without activating these two layers as well. Indeed, all three have to move in tandem, with each one reinforcing and invigorating the other. If the policy framework at the Centre is the main trunk of the Indian tree of development, the States are like its branches and local bodies and people-based organisations are its roots. The tree can grow bigger and its trunk more sturdy only if the branches are stronger and wider and the roots go deeper into the earth. I can see democracy driving this process in India.

We have put behind us the years when moderate growth rates ensured small islands of prosperity in a sea of poverty. Today, every section of the Indian people aspires for a better life. For the very poor, better life will mean, in their lifetime, perhaps no more than better water, better housing, better schools, and better medical care. The road to that better life is in better governance, and the very poor have awakened to the fact that self-governance is indeed better governance. The 73rd and 74th Amendments to the Indian Constitution ensured the democratisation of India's polity. Out of 227,000 village panchayats, fully one-third are headed by women. The _dalits_ control up to 22.5 per cent of the elected offices. The minorities and the backward castes have also discovered 'empowerment'. Driven by aspiration and fortified by empowerment, the people of India will reap the benefits of an open and competitive economy. More and more people will share the benefits of growth and development.

The democratisation of India's economy is underway. And therein lies the reason for our hopes and our dreams.

Endnotes

[1] The former untouchables who suffer the worst discrimination

2001 K R Narayanan Oration

Message from the President

I am glad that since the establishment of the K R Narayanan Oration in 1994 to commemorate the inauguration of The Australia South Asia Research Centre of The Australian National University, remarkable personalities from the academic, intellectual and public spheres have delivered orations on a variety of issues of contemporary significance. Beginning with Dr Raja Chelliah who delivered the first Oration in 1994, other outstanding personalities such as Jagdish Bhagwati and Mr P Chidambaram through their masterly orations have enriched our understanding of different subjects. It is particularly noteworthy that all these prominent figures have played major roles in fashioning India's agenda for development both at the academic and practical levels.

I am glad that this year's Oration is being delivered by another renowned economist Dr C Rangarajan, who is presently serving as the Governor of Andra Pradesh. I am happy that the topic of Dr Rangarajan's lecture is 'Monetary Policy in a Developing Economy — The Indian Experience'.

Hailed as one of the chief architects of India's monetary policy for several years, Dr Rangarajan during his long and distinguished career, particularly during his association with the Reserve Bank of India as Deputy Governor and subsequently as Governor, devised a monetary policy which would facilitate growth and ensure price stability. Most of the measures such as simplification and deregulation of interest rate structure, policy formulations for improving lendable resources of the Reserve Bank of India, upgradations of the information technologies and introduction of competition in the financial system, have contributed to lay down the foundation of a monetary policy to further strengthen India's new economic environment.

While doing so Dr Rangarajan has proved that in developing countries growth of the economy and price stability can be appropriately blended. New economic policies must not only ensure prosperity and growth, these must also serve other defined goals for the society as a whole. As a moving force behind the liberalisation of our economy and as an active player and economic strategist for building up of a dynamic economy, Dr Rangarajan's contributions have become significant. I am sure that his Oration will be an insightful exercise in understanding the economic transformation of India in all its ramifications. I am sure the range of ideas, the depth of understanding and the wide experience of Dr Rangarajan will be of importance for all developing countries grappling with the emerging realities of liberalisation and financial reforms.

K R Narayanan
New Delhi 2001

Monetary Policy in a Developing Economy — The Indian Experience

C Rangarajan

It is a great honour to be asked to deliver the K R Narayanan Oration of this year. It is an honour in more ways than one. First, the invitation has come from the prestigious South Asia Research Centre of The Australian National University which has done commendable work in studying the political and economic developments in South Asia and particularly India. The growing integration of the world economy has made the work of the Centre extremely valuable and relevant. Second, the Oration is named after one of the most distinguished sons of India, who today occupies the exalted position of the President of India. Narayanan's contributions to India's public life are immense. With quiet diplomacy and skillful and strategic interventions, he has steered the country during difficult times, particularly in the last few years. Through his scholarship and statesmanship, he has endeared himself to one and all. It is truly a great privilege to deliver the lecture bearing his name.

Developments in Monetary Policy

I have chosen to speak to you today on the Indian experience with respect to monetary policy as an instrument of economic management. Developments in monetary policy closely mirror the changes in overall economic policy. The decade of 1990s has seen far reaching changes in India's economic policy. The content and approach to economic policy underwent a sea change. The country has become a more open economy. The roles of state and market are getting redefined. There is a common thread running through the various measures introduced since 1991 and that is to improve the productivity and efficiency of the system. This is sought to be achieved by imparting a greater element of competition in the system. It is in this context that monetary policy in India acquired a new role. Financial sector reforms which were an integral part of the economic reforms programme created a new institutional environment in which monetary policy had to operate.

In industrially advanced countries, after decades of eclipse, monetary policy re-emerged as a potent instrument of economic policy, in the fight against inflation in the 1980s. Issues relating to the conduct of monetary policy came to the forefront of policy debates in the 1980s. The relative importance of growth and price stability as the objective of monetary policy as well as the appropriate intermediate target of monetary policy became the focus of attention. Over the years, a consensus has emerged among the industrially advanced countries that the dominant objective of monetary policy should be price stability. Differences, however, exist among central banks even in these countries as regards the appropriate intermediate target. While some central banks consider monetary aggregates and, therefore, monetary targeting as operationally meaningful, some others focus on the interest rate. There is also the more recent practice to ignore intermediate targets and focus on the final goal such as inflation targeting.

A similar trend regarding monetary policy is discernible in developing economies as well. Much of the early literature on development economics focused on real factors such as savings, investment and technology as mainsprings of growth. Very little attention was paid to the financial system as a contributory factor to economic growth even though attention was paid to develop financial institutions which provide short term and long term credit. In fact, many writers felt that inflation was endemic in the process of economic growth and it was accordingly treated more as a consequence of structural imbalance than as a monetary phenomenon. However, with the accumulated evidence, it became clear that any process of economic growth in which monetary expansion was disregarded led to inflationary pressures with a consequent impact on economic growth. Accordingly, the importance of price stability and, therefore, the need to use monetary policy for that purpose also assumed importance in developing economies. Nonetheless, the debate on the extent to which price stability should be deemed to be the overriding objective of monetary policy in such economies continues.

The Reserve Bank of India was set up in 1935. Like all central banks in developing countries, the Reserve Bank has been playing a developmental and a regulatory role. In its developmental role, the Reserve Bank focused attention on deepening and widening the financial system. It played a major part in building up appropriate financial institutions to promote savings and investment. In the realm of agricultural credit, term finance to industries and credit to export, the apex institutions that are now operating were essentially spun off from the Reserve Bank. Strengthening and establishing new institutions to meet the country's requirements is a continuing process. The promotional role had taken the Reserve Bank into the area of credit allocation as well. Pre-emption of credit for certain sectors and that too at concessional rates of interest became part of the overall policy. Commercial banks over time had been required to provide a certain percentage of their total credit to certain sectors which were regarded as 'priority sector'.

An active role by the Reserve Bank of India in terms of regulating the growth in money and credit became evident only after 1950s. During the 1950s the average annual increase in the wholesale price was only 1.8 per cent. However, during the 1960s, the average annual increase was 6.2 per cent and in the 1970s, it was around 10.3 per cent. In the early years of planning, there was considerable discussion on the role of deficit financing in fostering economic growth. The First Plan said: 'Judicious credit creation somewhat in anticipation of the increase in production and availability of genuine savings has also a part to play'. Thus, deficit financing, which in the Indian context meant Reserve Bank credit to the Government, was assigned a place in the financing of the plan, though its quantum was to be limited to the extent it was non-inflationary. Monetary growth, particularly in the 1950s, was extremely moderate. However, as each successive plan came under a resource crunch, there was an increasing dependence on market borrowing and deficit financing. These became pronounced in the 1970s and thereafter. The single most important factor influencing the conduct of monetary policy after 1970 had been the phenomenal increase in reserve money contributed primarily by the Reserve Bank credit to the Government.

To summarise, the system as it existed at the end of 1970s was characterised by the following features. The Reserve Bank of India as the central monetary authority prescribed all the interest rates on deposits and lending. The commercial banks were required to allocate a certain percentage of credit to what were designated as 'priority sector'. Credit to parties above a stipulated amount required prior authorisation from the central bank. After the nationalisation of major commercial banks in 1969, nearly 85 per cent of the total bank assets came under public sector. Apart from small private banks, foreign banks were allowed to operate with limited branches.

The increase in the scale of borrowing by the Government resulted in (a) the steady rise in statutory liquidity ratio requiring banks to invest higher and higher proportion of their deposits in Government securities which carried less than 'market rates' and (b) the Reserve Bank of India becoming a residual subscriber to securities and Treasury Bills leading to monetisation of the deficit. The Reserve Bank had, therefore, to address itself to the difficult task of neutralising to the extent possible the expansionary impact of deficits. The increasing liquidity of the banking sector resulting from rising levels of reserve money had to be continually mopped up. The instrument of open market operations was not available for this task since the interest rates on Government securities were well below 'market rates'. The task of absorbing excess liquidity in the system had to be undertaken mainly through increasing the cash reserve ratio. In fact, in mid 1991, the cash reserve requirement was 25 per cent on incremental deposits. In addition, the statutory liquidity ratio was 38.5 per cent. Thus, nearly 63.5 per cent of incremental deposits was pre-empted in one form or another.

In 1983, the Reserve Bank of India appointed a Committee under the Chairmanship of the distinguished economist Prof. Sukhamoy Chakravarty to review the working of the Indian Monetary System. I was a member of the Committee. The Committee's Report covered a wide range. One of its major recommendations was to regulate money supply consistent with the expected growth rate in real income and a tolerable level of inflation. Recognising the fact that Government borrowing from the Reserve Bank had been a major factor contributing to the increase in reserve money and therefore, money supply, the Committee wanted an agreement between the Central Government and the Reserve Bank on the level of monetary expansion and the extent of monetisation of the fiscal deficit. Without such a coordination, the Committee felt that Reserve Bank's efforts to contain monetary expansion within the limits set by expected increase in output could become impossible. While this recommendation of the Committee was accepted in principle, it could take a concrete shape only in the Nineties.

In the wake of the economic crisis in 1991 triggered by a difficult balance of payments situation, the Government introduced far reaching changes in India's economic policy. Monetary policy was used effectively to overcome the balance of payments crisis and promptly restore stability. An extremely tight monetary policy was put in place to reap the full benefits of the devaluation of the rupee that was announced. However, it did not stop with that. Financial sector reforms became an integral part of the new reform programme. Reform of the banking sector and capital market was intended to help and accelerate the growth of the real sector. Banking sector reforms covered a wide gamut. The most important of the reforms was the prescription of prudential norms including capital-adequacy ratio. In addition, certain key changes were made with respect to monetary policy environment which gave to commercial banks greater autonomy in relation to the management of their liabilities and assets. First and foremost, the administered structure of interest rates was dismantled step by step. Banks in India today enjoy the complete freedom to prescribe the deposit rates and interest rates on loans except in the case of very small loans and export credit. Second, the Government began borrowing at market rates of interest. The auction system was introduced both in relation to Treasury Bills and dated securities. Third, with the economic reforms emphasising a reduction in fiscal deficit, pre-emptions in the form of cash reserve ratio and statutory liquidity ratio were steadily brought down. Fourth, while the allocation of credit for the priority sector credit continued, the extent of cross subsidisation in terms of interest rates was considerably brought down because of the reform of the interest rate structure.

Monetary policy in the 1990s in India had to deal with several issues, some of which traditional but some totally new in the context of the increasingly open economy in which the country had to operate. In the first few years, monetary policy had to contend with the consequences of devaluation and the need to quickly restore price stability to obtain the full benefits of devaluation. While the fiscal deficit was being brought down, the question of monetisation of the deficit continued to remain an issue and a solution had to be found. This eventually led to a new agreement between Government and RBI on financing deficit. The system of ad-hoc Treasury Bills under which Government of India could replenish its cash balances by issuing Treasury Bills in favour of the Reserve Bank and which had the effect of monetising deficit was phased out. It was replaced by a system of Ways and Means advances which had a fixed ceiling. The Reserve Bank of India continued to subscribe to the dated securities at its discretion. During 1993 and 1994, for the first time monetary policy had to deal with the monetary impact of capital inflows with the foreign exchange reserves increasing sharply from $9.2 billion in March 1992 to $25.1 billion in March 1995. In 1995–96, the change in perception with reference to exchange rate after a prolonged period of nominal exchange rate stability vis-a-vis the US dollar brought into play the use of monetary policy to stabilise the rupee — an entirely new experience for the central bank. Similar situations arose later on also at the time of the East Asian crisis. Monetary policy had begun to operate within a changed institutional framework brought about by the financial sector reforms. It is this change in the institutional framework that gave a new dimension to monetary policy. New transmission channels opened up. Indirect monetary controls gradually assumed importance. With the progressive dismantling of the administered interest rate structure and the evolution of a regime of market determined interest rate on Government securities, open market operations including 'repo' and 'reverse repo' operations emerged for the first time as an instrument of monetary control. Bank Rate acquired a new role in the changed context. The Nineties paved the way for the emergence of monetary policy as an independent instrument of economic policy.

Monetary policy in the 1990s had also to be conducted in the context of the financial sector reforms. The need to reduce non-performing assets and to conform to the new prudential norms put the banking industry under great strain. While introducing banking sector reforms, care had to be taken to ensure that there was no compromise with the basic objectives of monetary policy.

In the post reform period, the Indian economy has done well. Since 1992–93 the average annual growth rate of the economy in real terms has been 6.3 per cent. The average inflation rate, as measured by the wholesale price index in the 1990s has been 7.2 per cent. However, the significant fact to note is that the average inflation rate since 1996–97 has been less than five per cent. Broad money grew at an average annual rate of 17 per cent per annum. The exchange rate of the rupee in terms of US dollar has declined by 24 per cent since July, 1997. This decline is smaller than what other countries in this region have experienced. The current account deficit has averaged since 1992–93 at one per cent of the GDP. The foreign exchange reserves in the country have risen from about $5 billion to $43 billion as of a recent date. These broad macro economic indicators show a substantial improvement in the Indian economy, even though several concerns such as slow reduction in poverty ratio and slow growth rate in agriculture persist.

Issues of Concern

Let me now focus on some of the issues which came to be debated extensively during 1990s. These issues are not specific to India or developing economies. They have been debated in the context of the developed countries also. Nevertheless, these issues which I want to highlight have a special significance for developing countries like India.

Objective

The first question that needs to be addressed relates to the objective or objectives of monetary policy. A recurring question is whether monetary policy should be concerned with all the goals of economic policy. The issue of 'objective' has become important because of the need to provide a clear guidance to monetary policy makers. Indeed, this aspect has assumed added significance in the context of the increasing stress on the autonomy of Central Banks. Autonomy goes with accountability and accountability in turn requires a clear enunciation of the goals.

Since the inception of development planning, the broad objectives of India's economic policy have been to achieve a faster rate of growth, ensure reasonable degree of price stability and promote distributive justice. Working of monetary policy in India over the past several decades would reveal that monetary policy has emphasised these broad objectives of our economic policy. In one of my earlier articles, I had said:

> In a broad sense the objectives of monetary policy can be no different from the over all objectives of economic policy. The broad objectives of monetary policy in India have been: (1) to maintain a reasonable degree of price stability and (2) to help accelerate the rate of economic growth. The emphasis as between the two objectives has changed from year to year, depending upon the conditions prevailing in that year and in the previous year.

The question of a dominant objective arises essentially because of the multiplicity of objectives and the inherent conflict among such objectives. Jan Tinbergen had argued decades ago that there should be as many instruments as there are objectives, if all objectives are to be fulfilled. Faced with multiple objectives that are equally relevant and desirable, there is always the problem of assigning to each instrument the most appropriate objective. This 'assignment rule' favours monetary policy as the most appropriate instrument to achieve the objective of price stability. It is this line of reasoning which has led to the single objective approach.

The crucial question that is being debated in India as elsewhere is whether the pursuit of the objective of price stability by monetary authorities undermines the ability of the economy to attain and sustain high growth. A considerable part of the relevant research effort has been devoted to the trade-off between economic growth and price stability. Empirical evidence on the relationship between growth and inflation in a cross country framework is somewhat inconclusive because such studies include countries with an inflation rate as low as one to two per cent to those with inflation rates going beyond 200 to 300 per cent. These studies, however, clearly establish that growth rates become increasingly negative at higher rates of inflation.

The case of price stability as the objective of monetary policy rests on the assumption that volatility in prices creates uncertainty in decision-making. Rising prices adversely affect savings while they make speculative investments more attractive. The most important contribution of the financial system to an economy is its ability to augment savings and allocate resources more efficiently. A regime of rising prices vitiates the atmosphere for promotion of savings and allocation of investment. Apart from all these, there is a social dimension particularly in developing countries. Inflation adversely affects those who have no hedges against it and that includes all the poorer sections of the community. The fiscal consolidation also becomes easier in an environment of reasonable degree of price stability. In a period of rising prices, the gap between revenues and expenditures widens. Expenditures tend to grow at a faster rate than revenues because many components of expenditures such as employees' compensation are closely linked to variations in prices.

The question that recurs very often in the minds of the policy makers is whether in the short run, there is a trade-off between inflation and growth which can be exploited. In the industrial countries, a solution is sought through the adoption of Taylor's rule which prescribes that the signal interest rate be fixed taking into account the deviations of inflation rate from the target and actual output from its potential. In this rule, the coefficient of inflation deviation term is fixed at a level higher than unity. While the rule is intuitively appealing, there are serious problems in determining the value of the coefficients. In this context, the critical question to raise is: At what level of inflation, do adverse consequences begin to set in? It is this inflation threshold which will provide some guidance to the policy makers. Below and around this threshold level of inflation, there is greater maneuverability for the policy makers to take into account other considerations. Interestingly, the Chakravarty Committee regarded the acceptable rise in prices as 4 per cent. This, according to the Committee, will reflect changes in relative prices necessary to attract resources to growth sectors. I have myself indicated that in the Indian context, inflation rate in the range of 5 to 6 per cent may be acceptable. There is some amount of judgment involved in this, as econometric models are not in a position to capture all the costs of inflation. This approach provides some guidance as to when policy has to become tight or to be loosened. It is also necessary for the policy makers to note that this order of inflation is higher than what the industrial countries are aiming at. This will have some implications for the exchange rate of the currency. While the open economy helps to overcome domestic supply shocks, it also imposes the burden to keep the inflation rate in alignment with other countries.

Intermediate Target

The second issue relates to the intermediate target. In India since the mid Eighties the target chosen has been broad money. The Chakaravarty Committee recommended a system of flexible monetary targeting. It is true that central banks in several countries in the industrial world have abandoned intermediate targets and have focussed on the final target such as inflation control. While this has the advantage of specifying the ultimate objective in clear and precise terms, it must be admitted that there is some uncertainty regarding the route through which this will be achieved. One of the reasons for the abandonment of intermediate targets in these countries has been the breakdown of the relationship between monetary aggregates and the inflation rate. The demand function for money has been found to be unstable. However, in India, studies show that the money demand function is a stable function of select variables and it can be used to reasonably predict inflation. Several statistical functions of the demand for money estimated by using the equilibrium and disequilibrium analysis provide overwhelming evidence on the long run stability of the money demand function. Perhaps some of the factors that have contributed to the instability of the demand function for money in the industrially advanced countries such as financial innovations and large movements of funds across the border are yet to have the same impact in India. In the demand function for money in India, income emerges as the most dominant variable. Such a function enables the authorities to estimate the appropriate growth in money supply, given the expected increase in real output and the acceptable level in price increase. With the freeing of the interest rate structure, interest rate may also emerge as an appropriate intermediate variable in the coming years. In fact, with the inflation rate coming down and remaining in a narrow range, it will be possible to focus on interest rate along with overall monetary aggregates. However, as of now, money supply seems to be an appropriate target. Such a target is relatively well understood by the public and provides unambiguously the stance of monetary policy.

The literature on monetary economics talks of four distinct monetary transmission channels. They are (1) Quantum Channel, especially relating to money supply and credit, (2) Interest Rate Channel, (3) The Exchange Rate Channel and (4) The Asset Prices Channel. While the emphasis in India so far has been on the quantum channel, with the development of financial markets and closer integration of such markets, the interest rate channel will assume importance. It must be noted that at the equilibrium both quantity and price are determined. Changes in interest rates cannot be ordained. The appropriate quantitative changes in money will have to be brought about even though the signal for change may be given by the price variable like interest rate.

Level of Interest Rate

Another question of importance that has arisen relates to the appropriate level of interest rate. The nominal interest rate comprises of three elements: (1) the real rate of interest; (2) inflation expectations; and (3) a discount factor for uncertainties. The effectiveness of monetary policy to bring down the nominal interest rate will depend on the impact that this policy will have on inflation expectations and on the perception of uncertainty in the economy. A monetary policy that is geared to maintain reasonable price stability, if it is successful, can help to bring down the interest rate in sympathy with the downward drift in inflation. Inflationary expectations can be broken, if the monetary authority enjoys high credibility. However, this leaves the real rate of interest to be determined. The real interest rate is not an observed variable. The real interest rate is influenced by several long-term factors such as saving and investment balance in the economy and the rate of return on capital. Theory tells us that on an economy-wide basis, this rate should not exceed the real rate of growth. In fast growing economies the real rate of interest will be higher. In South Korea during the years of very rapid economic growth the real rate of interest was around six to seven per cent in several years. The real rate of interest is thus related to the rate of growth of the economy. In the early 1990s in India, the real rate of interest was low because the inflation rate was in the range of 8 to 10 per cent. However, with the break in the inflation rate beginning 1996–97, the real rate of interest has gone up. As mentioned earlier, the inflation rate on an average has remained at less than five per cent since 1996–97. However, it must be kept in mind that the real rate of interest will have to be relatively higher in developing economies which seek to maintain a high savings rate and which aim at growing at more than six to seven per cent per annum. This is typically the situation in India. A situation of high real rate of interest accompanied by high growth rate must be distinguished from other situations when real rates of interest may remain high. In this context, it is worth noting that the high level of nominal interest rate in developing economies may also be due to high intermediation costs. Improved efficiency can reduce the spread between the deposit rate and lending rate and bring the lending rate in closer alignment with fundamental factors.

Exchange Rate Management

The role of monetary authority in exchange rate management came into focus in the 1990s. Since 1975, the exchange rate of the rupee was determined with reference to the daily exchange rate movements of a selected number of currencies of the countries which were India's major trading partners. The Reserve Bank of India was required to maintain the exchange rate within a band on either side of a base 'basket' value. This allowed the achievement of a medium-term real effective exchange rate (REER) objective through changes in the NEER. Such a regime could be maintained only with the support of extensive exchange controls and import controls. The reform measures introduced in 1991 included significant changes in the foreign trade regime and exchange rate management. The devaluation of the rupee in mid 1991 was followed by a system of dual exchange rate system in March 1992. A year later, the dual system was abolished and the country moved towards a unified market determined exchange rate system. The monetary authority does not intervene in the market process of rate determination as long as orderly conditions prevail in the exchange market and the exchange rate reflects macro economic fundamentals.

The approach to exchange rate by the monetary authorities in the developed world generally has been to let the market determine the rate. However, there have been several exceptions. There have been occasions when central banks in these countries have intervened, some times in a concerted way, when exchange markets became volatile. The Indian experience with market determined exchange rate system is that there have been several occasions when the RBI had to intervene strongly to prevent volatility. This happened in 1995 and 1996 and later in 1997 and 1998 at the time of the East Asian crisis. The impact of the East Asian crisis on the Indian market was minimal. This was partly due to the reason that while India subscribed to current account convertibility under Clause VIII of the IMF agreement, the capital account liberalisation was undertaken cautiously. Besides, India's current account deficit during this period was low. In fact, in 1991, a High Level Committee on Balance of Payments had made specific recommendations regarding the level of current account deficit, the size and composition of capital flows, the management of external debt including short-term debt and the quantum of foreign exchange reserves. Implementation of these recommendations stood India in good stead at the time of the East Asian crisis.

In narrow under developed markets like in India, there is a tendency for the herd instinct which amplifies the fluctuations. This can cause volatile and destabilising movements in the exchange rate which may go beyond any correction, required by the fundamentals. Even in developed markets there is a tendency for the market to 'overshoot', when a critical mass in terms of the perception of overvaluation in the exchange rate is reached. With narrow markets, the danger is greater. On such occasions, the monetary authority has to step in to ensure orderly market conditions. The monetary authority must, however, recognise that integration of markets is inevitable and therefore action must be spread across the markets to achieve results.

In developing economies like India, trade flows both visible and invisible, dominate the balance of payments. That is why for the exchange rate regime in India, continuous monitoring of the real exchange rate with an appropriate base becomes important. It provides valuable information to the authorities on the behaviour of the current account to which it is intrinsically linked. A monetary policy geared to domestic price stability in this situation helps to avoid disruptive adjustments in the exchange rate. In that sense monetary policy and exchange rate management become intertwined.

Financial Stability

Increasingly macroeconomic stability as an objective of central banking is closely linked to financial stability. It is easy to see how the two are inter linked. Financial stability broadly implies the stability of the important institutions and markets forming part of the financial system. Financial stability requires that the key institutions in the financial system are stable, in that, there is a high degree of confidence about meeting contractual obligations without interruption or outside assistance. While the complementarity between the objectives of macro stability and financial stability is easily recognised, the one question that needs to be addressed is whether there can be a conflict between the two objectives. It is not inconceivable to have situations in which the price stability objective might call for a restrictive policy, while the financial market conditions may demand a somewhat liberal policy to provide relief. The Reserve Bank of India was extremely conscious of this dilemma. Banking sector reforms were in full swing in the 1990s which necessarily put the banking system under strain. While facilitating the smooth transition, RBI took care that there was no dilution of the basic objectives of monetary policy. However, viewed as part of overall economic stability, financial stability need not run at cross-purpose with other dimensions of macro economic stability. Normally, price stability should provide an environment favourable to financial stability. If on occasions dealing directly with financial stability becomes necessary, it must be done as in the case of intervention in the foreign exchange markets. Actions to maintain financial stability in those circumstances may be in the long run interest of economic stability.

Autonomy of Central Banks

Autonomy of central banks has become an article of faith in the industrial countries. It has been written into the constitution setting up the European Central Bank. The literature on this subject is growing. There is a general consensus to give instrument independence to central banks among countries that have decided that the single objective of monetary policy is inflation control. Autonomy implies discretion to central banks to decide on the timing and nature of monetary policy intervention. It also calls for transparency in relation to both objectives and strategies. The increased use of explicit targets by central banks is part of the broader move to build credibility through transparency. It is quite true that in India, monetary policy has been very much conditioned by the stance of fiscal policy. The system of the scheme of *ad hoc* Treasury Bills facilitated monetisation of the fiscal deficit without limit and without prior approval.

The 1990s saw the phasing out of the system and the introduction of the scheme of Ways and Means Advance. This was a major step towards the achievement of greater discretion. The Fiscal Responsibility Bill that is now before the Indian Parliament takes this to its logical conclusion. When enacted this would be a great step forward not only in fiscal but monetary management. Two associated comments may be made in this context.

First, an autonomous central bank does not mean lack of coordination with the Government. Nor does it imply lack of harmony. In fact, harmony in the sense in which it is used in classical symphonic music will be achieved. In a symphony, different artistes play different notes simultaneously but in effect create a blend that produces the best of music. However, the stances of monetary policy and fiscal policy cannot run at cross-purposes. For example, a lax fiscal policy accompanied by a tight monetary policy can lead to a sharp increase in interest rate. On the other hand, an accommodative monetary policy in a period of lax fiscal policy can lead to explosive increase in prices. While monetary and fiscal coordination is desirable, it is important at the same time that the monetary authority which has its own specific agenda must have the institutional autonomy and should not be burdened with functions which may come in conflict with its own special objective. It is in this context that the Reserve Bank of India and Government of India are examining the issue whether the management of public debt can be delinked from RBI.

Second, the emergence of an autonomous central bank does not mean that the 'state of bliss' has arrived. It only enables the central bank to pursue a consistent monetary policy over a long time. Then the onus of responsibility for the conduct of monetary policy will rest on the shoulders of the Reserve Bank, where it should logically rest. In an open economy, the task of the central bank will be rendered more difficult if it does not have the autonomy and discretion to make changes quickly in response to external shocks.

There was a time when it was said that central banking was neither a science nor an art but a craft. This is at best a half-truth. Central banking has never been a case of applying well known remedies to well known problems. 'Rules versus discretion' has been a subject of long-standing debate in monetary policy. Rigid rules such as those implicit in gold standard will give to central banks no room for maneuverability. On the other hand, total discretion with respect to objectives and instruments will make monetary policy indeterminate. That is why the new phrase 'constrained discretion'. This will require the central banks to be transparent and explicit with respect to objectives and strategies, while leaving the freedom to them to choose the timing and nature of their actions. This is the type of autonomy towards which every central bank should move.

2002 K R Narayanan Oration

Message from the President

I am delighted to know that the 'K R Narayanan Oration' instituted at the Australia South Asia Research Centre (ASARC) of The Australian National University during the visit to this center by my predecessor-in-office during 1994 has now become a regular feature of the Centre's calendar and that eminent personalities from various fields of life have delivered these orations on topics of immediate relevance to India.

I am happy to note that ASARC is continuing with its high tradition of inviting those personalities who have made outstanding contributions in their sphere of work, which is relevant to India. It is in this light that I see the name of Professor Meghnad Desai of the London School of Economics who is delivering this year's oration on 'Democracy and Development: India 1947–2002'. Professor Desai needs no introduction. We are all aware of the intellectual prowess and the policy analytical framework, which he has brought to bear upon contemporary development economics and the related social sciences. Having seen the birth and the early days of independent India first hand, I am sure there can be no better person to walk the august audience through the first fifty years of our Independence and the working of our democracy and its institutions.

This will be an excellent opportunity for our friends in ASARC and in Australia at large to get to know about India's experience of working a democracy after over two hundred years of subjugation under alien rule. We have identified five areas where India has a core competence for an integrated action for transforming India into a developed nation: 1) Agriculture and Food Processing — we have set a target of 360 million tons of food and agricultural production. Other areas of agriculture and agro food processing would bring prosperity to rural people and speed up economic growth; 2) Reliable and quality electric power for all parts of the country; 3) Education and Healthcare — we have seen, based on experience that education and healthcare are inter related; 4) Information and Communication Technology — this is one of our core competences. We believe this area can be used to promote education in remote areas and also to create national wealth; and 5) Strategic sectors — this area, fortunately, witnessed growth in nuclear technology, space technology and defence technology.

These five areas are closely inter-related and lead to national, food and economic security. A strong partnership among and between R&D academics, industry, business and the community as a whole with Government Departments and agencies will be essential to accomplish this vision. The key to success is in various forms of connectivity such as physical, electronic, knowledge, and economic. I am sure Professor Desai's oration will also give the audience sufficient intellectual queries and knowledge. I wish the event all success

A.P.J. Abdul Kalam
New Delhi 2002

Democracy and Development: India 1947–2002

Meghnad Desai

It gives me a particular pleasure to be giving the Narayanan Oration at The Australian National University. President Narayanan is a perfect example of how despite numerous obstacles merit will shine through. His life exemplifies the progress India has made, warts and all, over the entire 20th century but especially since Independence. Names of Harold Laski and Jawaharlal Nehru play a major part in his early story. On a personal note, he has also showed me immense kindness but perhaps more because I teach at his alma mater than for anything personal to me.

It is also a great pleasure to come back to the ANU where I twice spent a term teaching in 1980 and 1984 and where I claim many friends. Australia has taken a great interest in South Asia as the centers here and in other Australian universities testify.

India Since 1991

It is eleven years since India had the economic shock of its life and had to rethink its economic policy and rearrange its economic institutions. It was nearly ten years ago that I had the opportunity to welcome the drastic change and wish that it would be more rather than less drastic, not a popular position among my economist friends in India at that time (Desai 1993). This is thus a good opportunity to see how far India has got in its response to the shock of near bankruptcy in early 1991.

But a lot more has also happened to India in its political life since 1991. Indeed it is hard to say whether it is the political or the economic map that has changed more in the last ten or more years. In various articles written over these years I have also tried to chart the political dynamics of the 1990s (see various references in the Bibliography). While there was always implicitly a political background to my economic comments and an economic background to my political comments, I would like to take this opportunity of the Narayanan Oration to try a synthesis.

The separate strands which need to be synthesized are as follows:

- In its first phase lasting just over three decades (1947–1980), India's economic policy was driven by a model of national self-sufficiency. It was built around, indeed pioneered, an Import Substitution Industrialisation (ISI) strategy. It also chose (and this is separate strictly from ISI) a capital intensive programme hoping that matters of employment creation, consumer goods supply especially foodgrains would take care of themselves. Political developments in the mid and late 1950s forced a situation in which the Planning authorities had to reverse the neglect of agriculture. The Green Revolution which occurred by accident in the 1960s corrected the earlier urban biases of the Second and Third Five Year Plans but the poor performance of the manufacturing sector — in terms of inefficiency, excess capacity and low quality — persisted in both the private and public organized sectors. The growth rate was low relative both to early aspirations (Bombay Plan for instance) and to the rates achieved by other countries. This was the so-called Hindu Rate of Growth. 3.5 per cent per annum and 1.3 per cent per capita.

- Over this period 1947–1980, India's political life exhibited a lot of stability and a solid, indeed unique achievement among post colonial polities in creating and sustaining a vibrant political democracy. Single Party Dominance nurtured this democratic life except during the infamous Emergency which was brief and was reversed by that very democratic process it tried to subvert. The dominant vision of nationalism was built around secularism, non alignment and socialism. There was however beginning to be an assertion of the various regional, caste and religious — by and large 'ubaltern' forces — in the federal polity. Indeed the Janata Government of 1977–1979 reflected this.

- During the 1980s, there was a decade of restoration of Single Party Dominance but a relaxation of the imperative of economic self-sufficiency. There was borrowing from abroad — from the IMF, from foreign commercial banks and then from NRIs. But the economic institutions of permit-license Raj did not change and there was no relaxation of domestic economic policy in parallel with foreign borrowing. Growth rate went up to 5.5 per cent, 3.5 per cent per capita.

- The decade of the 1980s stored up much trouble for political life later on. Secularism was compromised into a parallel populism with accommodation of the orthodoxies of the two major religions as Rajiv Gandhi's decisions on Shah Bano case and the shilanyas at Ayodhya showed. The subaltern elements continued to grow powerful at regional levels.

- The 1990s ruptured the old model in two ways. Economic dirigisme — often mislabeled socialism — became untenable as India could not repay its commercial borrowings without drastic reform. At the same time the end of Congress dominance unleashed forces — implementation of the recommendations of the Mandal Commission with all it meant about valorization of caste distinctions, rise of the Hindutva parivar, dalit militancy — which ended for the decade and more any hope of a single party government. In a strange combination, the arrival of globalisation saw India modernise and liberalise on the economic front but become less secular and more ethnically divided than before politically. Modernity in India thus took a different path from what its champions in the early days after Independence had charted for it. It is not a secular socialist democratic India but a liberal, increasingly Hindu nationalist democratic India that is shaping its own future.

- On the economic front the reform forced upon India by the trauma of 1991 has proved irreversible and effective. Despite much hesitation, the reform process has persisted and raised the growth rate nearer to 6.5 per cent for GDP and 4.5 per cent per capita. The liberalization process has been slow relative to countries of Eastern Europe but it has been consensual. Even as politicians compete in populist rhetoric about protecting the jobs and the poor, it is clear that no possible combination of parties exists which upon gaining power would or even could reverse the liberalization process.

- There is one solid continuity despite the change in party dominance and in economic philosophy over the last fifty-five years. This is the nationalist programme of a militarily strong India. Even as India preached peace and non-alignment in 1950s it built up its military production capacity especially its atomic and nuclear research. Whether Congress or BJP, whether Nehru, Indira and Rajiv Gandhi or Vajpayee, the determination to make India militarily strong has been common. There is no peace party in India. Indeed, it can be seen now that the ISI strategy and the insistence on self-sufficiency arose from a defence policy that meant India to be a powerful regional power. The election of President Narayanan's successor has crowned that policy with official recognition.

It is this cluster of trends that I wish to explore. The decline of secularism and socialism, the rise of liberalism and religiosity, the persistence of nationalism as a force even as its nature has changed. Democracy has been the universal solvent in this process. In order to appreciate the importance of Indian democracy, it is necessary to go back to the early history of Independent India.

The Revolution of 1946–1949: The Constituent Assembly in Action

The decision to adopt universal adult franchise with a Westminster style parliamentary system was a revolutionary decision of the Constituent Assembly. It was not inevitable nor was it a conservative decision. Given the experience of almost every other post colonial country with constitutional change, it is a miracle that the Constituent Assembly (the Assembly hereafter), elected as it was on a restricted franchise got it so right. But this choice revolutionary as it is, profoundly constricted and shaped the subsequent trends.

The Assembly rejected the Gandhian option — a decentralized village republic with local autonomy and indirect democracy with an obviously weak Centre.

A strong Centre was basic to Indian nationalism as its one great fear was, indeed is, of India breaking up into many nations. In the wake of Partition, a weak Centre was not going to be chosen whatever the Father of the Nation may say. The Assembly also firmly ruled out any role for the feudal order — the hundreds of native princes, for whom a role was envisaged in the 1935 Government of India Act. Unlike Malaysia, India did not give these kings even a ceremonial role. In copying the Westminster system, it replaced the Crown by an elected President with similar powers. It also rejected a single party polity which must have been tempting as it was for many African and Asian countries under the spurious rationalisation that multi party democracy was a Western luxury that a poor country could ill afford. The Communist alternative was also rejected. Private property, including foreign property, was not disturbed but could be subject to state takeover with compensation. Land was not confiscated or nationalized but land reform was made feasible.

The democracy that was chosen was radical in other ways as well. There was to be no recognition of any ethnic, religious or caste basis of citizenship. There were to be no separate electorates, no religious qualification for holding office, nor a literacy test. Women were given the vote on the same terms as men when even in the developed countries e.g., France, women's suffrage had only recently (i.e., 1945) been granted. But by the same token there were no guarantees of minority rights qua minority; no consociational arrangement in a formal sense whereby a minority had veto rights over drastic abridgements of its rights by the Majority vote Minorities, like majorities were treated qua Westminster as collections of individuals rather than ethnic blocks and therefore were to be looked after as part of the democratic process by legislative or by executive actions. Thus despite its being elected from a small and restricted franchise which could have made it conservative, the Assembly chose an individualist atomistic model of democracy for India rather than one grounded in caste, religion and language identities. Secularism was the implicit guarantee that a religious minority had nothing to fear from majority rule. Religion was not to be a subject which could be legislated about.[1]

It will be my contention that this bold revolutionary choice was crucial in shaping subsequent choices and indeed in making some of these subsequent choices less bold than they could have been. In making the Constitution, ethnicity-blind and religion-blind, the Founding Fathers were rejecting the trauma which had led to the Partition and hoping to avoid further fragmentation. But they were also denying reality, not only of the country at large but even of their own personal identities. Indians were individuals of course like anyone else but they also lived in a vital sense their ethnic, religious regional, linguistic identities. These identities were not to be left behind when they entered the political arena. Nor were these identities an invention of the colonial masters or a badge of poverty or under-development ready to disappear at the first whiff of economic progress as Nehru in his more passionate moments thought.

Indian democracy was shaped by these ignored identities as they asserted themselves in the daily course of electoral politics. At the elite level, their own orthodox upbringing, their upper caste loyalties if they were Hindus, their relatively prosperous state meant that the choices taken were their choices. But they were also the progeny of Macaulay and had absorbed western ideas of progress and equality, of liberty and the greatest good of the greatest number. They may have lived much as their fathers did at home but they thought and spoke the Englishman's language.

Social Conservatism and Economic Radicalism

Two crucial choices were made early in the years after Independence. One was to be socially conservative and not use the State apparatus to abolish the caste system with its inegalitarian logic of hierarchy and status. Primary education and adult literacy were state subjects and thus left to stagnate in those conservative states in the Hindi heartland where literacy, especially female and dalit literacy, were seen to be threats to the social order. Although untouchability was made illegal in the Constitution, the attendant evils of caste were left undisturbed. Muslim society was even more delicately handled. As far as Hindu society was concerned an attempt was made mainly at Nehru's behest to codify and systematise Hindu Family Law, though he met with resistance in his desire to modernise it from the then President Dr Rajendra Prasad. But Muslim Law was out of bounds even for Nehru. Thus political independence and the revolutionary decision to adopt democracy did not result in any state-led political programme of social reform. Indian society was allowed to reform itself in a *laissez faire* way.

In the economic sphere, on the other hand, radicalism was the order of the day. India had, by 1947, one of the oldest modern industries in the Third World (though it was not so called till later). It had the largest group of native modern capitalist entrepreneurs, the largest jute industry, a cotton textile industry which was globally competitive and was the seventh largest industrial country in terms of volume of industrial output. But the perception of the nationalist movement was that India had been deindustrialised by British rule and that industrialisation was the first priority. Free trade and foreign capital imports were to be shunned. India would become a self-sufficient industrialised country by relying on planning led by the State.

This was not particularly surprising both in terms of the thinking of the Congress as moulded by Nehru and the climate of the times. Free market ideology was on the retreat and many thought that capitalism too was on its way out. India had been much taken by the Soviet example and indeed even by the

German example of planning in a mixed economy. What was not necessary, however, to this strategy was to neglect if not punish the Industries already established, especially the cotton textile industry and shifting resources to machine building. There was rampant export pessimism, unjustified as subsequent investigations showed (see articles in Ahluwalia and Little (1997) by Bhagwati, Desai and Sen). The strategy failed to take advantage of India's early start in modern industry and reinvented many of the things which were there but were tarred with foreign brush.

Thus India created a dependent entrepreneurial class in place of one that had survived foreign rule, depressed modern consumer goods industries and fostered small scale ones which were capital wasting and inefficient, built at an enormous expense a basic goods sector with a long lead time before it could bring better consumer goods to the people and failed to generate industrial employment. The public sector, mainly in services, became the biggest provider of employment in the modern sector. Jointly the private and public organised industrial sector became a stagnant and highly privileged pool of a limited number of employees. Together the public services and the organized industrial sector employed 15 per cent of the labour force. This was called socialism (Desai 1993).

The strategy was wasteful of scarce capital and quite perverse in its determined neglect of the rules of efficient allocation. It is one thing not to get prices right but quite another to deliberately get them wrong. Restrictions on interest rates, multiple exchange rates, subsidies to inefficient industries, taxation on movement of agricultural commodities which constituted a tax on agriculture, perks to labour in the organized sector and de facto taxation of the informal sector by a lack of subsidies etc. All this was done by an elite fully economically educated but determined to flout the rules of western economics.

The results were predictable — slow growth of output and employment and persistence of poverty and inequality through the first phase of thirty years. With slow growth of jobs in the private sector, government jobs at all levels became much sought after and the democratic electoral system was harnessed to provide patronage. The first task of government became provision of jobs through the public fisc and then the sale of permits and licenses.

Triangulation Indian Style

Thus we get a unique triangular interaction. Economic radicalism leads to slow growth biased towards elite jobs. Social conservatism strengthens caste, regional and religious loyalties. Political democracy allows the mobilization of these loyalties in an electoral competition to capture governments at state and then at central levels. This capture then translates into jobs for the newly included. Yet the economic surplus does not expand by this route. So the system crashes in the 1970s under the weight of its own demands. A way out had to be found. It was the economic radicalism which began to be abandoned because that was the only way surplus could be enhanced. This is the way the model unfolded itself.

The interaction of social conservatism and economic radicalism in the context of political democracy produced a most interesting mutation. To get the fruits of patronage, non elite groups had to get organized and they did this through their caste and regional identities. Linguistic states had to be created during the 1950s in response to popular pressure from the local capitalists as well as local middle classes who wanted public jobs and public contracts. Next came in the 1960s the pressure from the rural areas to divert resources to agriculture. This happily bore fruits in the form of the Green Revolution with input subsidies as well as price guarantees for outputs. But even then the discontent due to slow growth continued. This broke into a flood of protest from tribal dalit and lower caste groups in the 1970s, and were brought together under the Lokayan banner. This was what unhinged Indira Gandhi and led to the Emergency. Groups previously downtrodden were finding their voices and using the unreformed social structures of caste and religion to make their claims on the surplus. But the surplus was not expanding due to the elitist policies being followed.[2]

The Escape from Triangulation

The Janata government was the transition between the first and the second phase. By itself ineffective, it mirrored the subaltern groups which had come to stake their claim to power. But Janata had no organizing vision to unite these groups as the elite vision of Nehruvian nationalism had. What Mrs Gandhi learned from her defeat was that the new India could not be run on old elite lines. She reinvented the Nehruvian vision keeping the rhetoric of socialism and secularism but changing the content.

The two major changes were that in the economic sphere she abandoned self-sufficiency as a goal but retained dirigisme (socialism). Foreign loans were taken but the economy not restructured. On the political side she used both Hindu and Muslim imagery to garner Hindu vote banks, and of course Muslim ones too. The foreign loans and some liberalization on import account led to higher growth. The Green Revolution was also now routinely yielding good harvests so food imports were no longer an item on the balance of trade. Of course not all the regional and linguistic loyalties could be bought off. The demand for Khalistan was a demand too far and Indira Gandhi gave her life in her determination to combat that.

What was happening on the ideological front was less obvious but no less important for that. Indian nationalism had suffered a body blow with the Partition. The India that Nehru had 'discovered' during his final prison term was not the India that he came to be the leader of. He gave a new vision to the nation — of a non-aligned, secular modern, even socialist India. But the war with China shattered the non-alignment. Pragmatic consideration forced Indira Gandhi to replace secularism by parallel and simultaneous flattery of Hindu and Muslim religiosity. Socialism hung by a slim thread of dirigisme but one reinforced by foreign loans. Elsewhere Asian countries were marching ahead economically; China had abandoned Maoism in favour of Deng's pragmatism. Even Pakistan was no inferior to India in terms of income levels or industrial performance.

What was going to be India's vision of nationhood if the modernist Nehruvian vision with its secularism, socialism and non-alignment was no longer adequate? There were two rival models on offer. One was the religious Hindutva model which had been shunned aside in favour of the Congress one early in the independence movement which now began to be revived by the Jan Sangh/BJP. The other model — less articulated — was the one which came to the forth in the first Round Table Conference in 1929. This was the India of regions, languages, religious and ethnic identities. This was how the British saw India but the Congress rejected this vision in favour of a 'unity in diversity' vision. But this vision somewhat subaltern was what would have ruled India had the Cabinet Mission's plan been accepted. India would have remained united, unpartitioned but would have been a confederation. With provincial autonomy for big states like Panjab and Bengal and Sind, local nationalisms would have flourished.[3]

In the years since 1947, it was this vision which strengthened itself as linguistic and caste parties became electorally successful. It is these forces which have become the challenge to the Hindutva vision. Under the leadership of Mulayam Singh Yadav or Laloo Prasad Yadav or Karunanindhi/Jayalalitha or Chandrababu Naidu this confederate vision is also secular and can align either with the Left or the Centre Right (Congress). As the Congress hegemony fell apart at the end of the 1980s, this vision became a pillar of Indian politics.

The decisive change did not come with Rajiv Gandhi but after his defeat. He confirmed the abandonment of social reform by capitulating on the rights of Muslim women in the Shah Bano case and yielded to Hindu pressure on shilanyas for the potential Ramajanmabhumi temple on the site of the Babri mosque. It was electoral cynicism but it did not pay. But what a decade of growth at 5.5 per cent did was to create opportunities in the private sector which the old elite could exploit. It began to disengage from public sector jobs. There were better perks in the private sector. This created room for meeting the next explosion in subaltern demands which V P Singh tried to accommodate by undertaking to implement the Mandal recommendations.

The Crisis of 1991 and the New Dispensation

The uplift in the economic growth rate during the 1980s had been bought with foreign borrowings but without restructuring the economy. The economy's autarchic orientation continued and this meant that insufficient export income was generated to pay back the foreign debt. Had the borrowings been invested in exportables and India been given an open economy orientation, then repayment would have been easier. Had the capital come as equity rather than debt, the repayment would have not been a problem. But borrowings were made in debt form to retain political control over resources and this proved to be fatal. The economy crashed as it became unable to service its debt.

The political system crashed at the same time in as much as neither V P Singh nor Chandrashekhar could sustain a majority. The Budget for 1991 had to be postponed and central bankers had to scurry around raising money to pay back debt. The election of 1991 did not settle the issue though Congress (without Rajiv Gandhi) came back to power without a majority. A break away from the old model was now urgent in the economic sphere. Of the three sides of the triangle — social, political and economic, it was the economic which was the easiest to change quickly. But the change rapid as it was soon became mired into a reluctant transformation. The two other dimensions constrained the speed and thoroughness of the abandonment of the old dirigiste model in favour of economic liberalism.

Through the 1990s and into the 21st century, coalition governments persisted. In its first forty-two years after independence, India had six Prime Ministers of whom three had ruled for thirty eight years. In the next thirteen years there have been six more prime Ministers. Political continuity in the sense of one-party dominance has now gone. Economic self-sufficiency as an ideal has also been abandoned. The contending visions of nationhood have resulted in a marked rise in political and communal violence. There are caste wars in Bihar, Hindu Muslim violence in 1992/1993 and again in Gujarat in 2002 with smaller episodes in between. There is violence against dalits and Christians from those who prefer a Hindu India.

At the same time India has remained a democracy in a most resilient fashion. For someone who grew up when the world was worried about After Nehru who?, the question today seems absurd. Coalition governments have carried on Westminster politics in a most Indian fashion. Politics is more consensual, less elitist but at the same time more corrupt and self-serving. Democracy is too deeply entrenched now to imagine any other form of governance in India. Which by the same token makes it very difficult to imagine any drastic change in the second pillar of social conservatism. Thus castes are valorized as are regional and religious divisions. They are cards to play in the electoral game. Political power is the solvent which brings gains of patronage to communities which have little chance in the liberal market order for economic gain. Of course by resorting to political patronage, these 'backward' castes and scheduled castes dig themselves deeper into the mire of dependency. This strengthens the appeal of conservatism. The fact that some caste leaders spout secular or socialist slogans does not make them modern in any sense.

Thus the burden of keeping the show on the road, of plastering the differences together falls on the economic dimension. Economic reform over the last ten years has been slow, hesitant but consensual. The strategy of implementing reform through the democratic process has meant that unlike in Eastern Europe there has been no shock therapy, no convulsion. The reformers of today were the dirigistes of yesterday. There is continuity. Thus the growth rate has gone up only modestly (relative to East Asian countries) to between six and six and a half percentage points. There has been a slow trickle of FDI and India's export performance remains modest. The rate of privatization has been slow for a long time though it has perked up in the last year or so. Infrastructure development is urgent as is the need for restructuring of public sector infrastructure provision if FDI is to be attracted. Budget deficits of the Centre and the states together are too large and represent a waste of savings.

But then the deficits are the price of the twin pillars of social conservatism and political democracy. Coalition politics and the patronage politics of social factions combine to make government expenditure a variable outside political control. Despite the misgivings of IFIs and credit rating agencies, Indian finance ministers carry on with the deficits as they are, knowing full well that any effective curbing of government spending would end any coalition. The same is the case with corruption and the crime/politics nexus. The quality of public life has gone lower as India's democracy has become more inclusive. The costs of this democracy now constitute a non negligible burden on India's growth rate. If even half of the deficit now running at 10 per cent of GDP is avoidable, we are speaking of around 2 per cent per annum in GDP growth rate.

The Prospect

In one sense India is super stable and very resilient against drastic reform, social or economic. The strength of India's democracy vouches for its super stability. The revolutionary choice of the Constituent Assembly in 1946/1949 has had counterrevolutionary consequences, much as it happened in 19th century France following the French Revolution. The country is immune to radical change. If there is a danger anywhere it comes from the overarching ideology of nationalism. Let me spell this out.

There are as I said above three competing visions of Indian nationhood (Desai 2000). The Nehru vision of secularism, socialism and non-alignment is now moribund if not dead. The BJP Hindutva vision is in ascendance. It is non-secular, non socialist though uncomfortable with foreign capital. The third alternative is the confederate nationalist one which is deeply embedded in caste, language and religion. It is secularist and dirigiste if not socialist. (The Left parties — CPI, CPM — are a small presence in Lok Sabha and perhaps disproportionately large in India's political and intellectual life. They can be clubbed together with either the Congress or with the third cluster of confederationist parties.)

At present, Congress is secularist but against economic liberalization. This is partly because it is in opposition and partly because the older vested interests in the socialist model are housed in the Congress. The rhetoric is all about the poor and anti Western multinationals. The BJP and its parivar is split on economics. The RSS is anti foreign capital and anti reform. But the parliamentary wing of the BJP is led by people who have made their peace with economic reform. This is again because they are in office and not in opposition. But the old Jan Sangh was always derided as a party of shopkeepers and merchants. It has anti-dirigiste instincts. Of course being in electoral competition, the financing of patronage makes every party love the public sector. The third cluster is anti-capitalist in most of its rhetoric.

The dilemma facing India is that it can have a secular but anti reform coalition or a non secular but economically liberal coalition. The latter variant is in power now but it may lose the next election to a combination of Congress and a number of smaller parties. Only a Grand Coalition of the type German politics has seen, one between Congress and BJP may overcome this dilemma. I have been long an advocate of such a coalition which everyone considers quite utopian.

Such a coalition would become a reality only for one reason. If India is to be a militarily powerful force in Asia comparable to China then it does need to accelerate its economic growth. While the obsession with Pakistan lasts, China is not clearly perceived as a challenge. But sooner or later Indian nationalists of whatever cluster will realize that China is the only serious competitor for India — a rival not an enemy. To catch up with China could yet become a nationalist ambition. To achieve that India will have to set aside its fear of economic change and its parochial concerns with religious divisions.

References

Ahluwalia, Isher and Ian Little (1998), *India's Economic Reforms and Development: Essays for Manmohan Singh* (Oxford: OUP).

Ayres, Alyssa and Philip Oldenburg (2002), *India Briefing: Quickening the Pace of Change* (Armonk, NY: M E Sharpe).

Desai, Meghnad (1993), Capitalism, Socialism and the Indian Economy (EXIM Bank Lecture: Mumbai, EXIM Bank).

—— (1995), 'Economic Reform: Stalled by Politics?', in Oldenburg.

—— (1996), *India's Triple Bypass: Economic Liberalism, the BJP and the 1996 Elections'*, *Asian Studies Review*, 19(3), April.

—— (1998), 'Development Perspectives: Was There an Alternative to Mahalanobis?', in Ahluwalia and Little.

—— (2000), 'Communalism, Secularism and the Dilemma of Indian Nationhood', in Leifer.

—— (2002), 'Death, Development and Democracy in India 2002' (Delhi: *Encyclopaedia Britannica Hindu*).

Jaffrelot, Christophe (2002), 'The Subordinate Caste Revolution', in Ayres and Oldenburg.

Leifer, Michael (2000), *Asian Nationalism* (London: Routledge).

Lijphart, A (1996), 'The Puzzle of Indian Democracy: A Consociational Interpretation', *The American Political Science Review*, 90(2): 258–68, June.

Oldenburg, Philip (1995), *India Briefing 1995* (Armonk, NY: M E Sharpe).

Endnotes

[1] Lijphart (1996) has argued that India's polity is de facto consociational. I have my doubts.

[2] See for a most thoughtful account of the lower orders' entry into politics Christopher Jaffrelot (2002)

[3] See for a fuller discussion Desai (2000).

Political-Economy and Governance Issues in the Indian Economic Reform Process

Pranab K. Bardhan

I am grateful to ASARC for the invitation to deliver the 2003 Narayanan Oration and am happy to be here at The Australian National University. I do not know ex-President Narayanan personally but we have a good common friend (K N Raj) from whom I had often heard glowing accounts about Dr Narayanan. Exactly 20 years back I gave the Radhakrishnan Lecture[1] at Oxford University, and I now have great pleasure in getting this opportunity to honour another distinguished south Indian ex-President.

My subject today is political economy and governance issues in Indian economic reform. Political economy is concerned with distribution of economic and political power, and inequality in this distribution poses important questions in a democracy. In 1949, as the Indian Constitution was getting ready and the debates in the Constituent Assembly were being wound up, B.R Ambedkar, a founding father of the Indian Constitution, said in a speech in that Assembly:

> On the 26th of January, we are going to enter a life of contradictions. In politics we will have equality and in social and economic life, we will have inequality ... How long shall we continue to live this life of contradictions?

More than 50 years later in India we still live this life of contradictions, although there have been many changes, some of which would even have taken Ambedkar by surprise.

I will start with some historical and social factors which provide the context for Indian democracy and have shaped its complex unfolding in the last five decades, and then relate these to the various disjunctures between economics and politics that have developed in the on-going economic reform process in the last decade or so.

The historical origins of democracy in India are sharply different from those in much of the west, and these differences are reflected in the current functioning of democracy in India, making it difficult to match the Indian case to the canonical cases in the usual theories of democracy. At least five of these differences are:

1. While in Europe democratic rights were won over continuous battles against aristocratic privileges and arbitrary powers of absolute monarchs, in India these battles were fought by a coalition of groups in an otherwise fractured society against the colonial masters. Even though part of the freedom struggle was associated with on-going social movements to win land rights for peasants against the landed oligarchy, the dominant theme was to fight colonialism. And in this fight, particularly under the leadership of Gandhi, disparate groups were forged together to fight a common external enemy, and this required strenuous methods of consensus-building and conflict management (rather than resolution) through co-opting dissent and selective buyouts. Long before Independence the Congress Party operated on consensual rather than majoritarian principles. The various methods of group bargaining and subsidies and 'reservations' for different social end economic categories that are common practice in India today can be traced to this earlier history.

2. Unlike in western Europe democracy came to India before any substantial industrial transformation of a predominantly rural economy, and before literacy was widespread. This seriously influenced the modes of political organization and mobilization, the nature of political discourse, and the excessive economic demands on the state. Democratic (and redistributive) aspirations of newly mobilized groups outstripped the surplus-generating capacity of the economy, demand overloads sometimes even short-circuiting the surplus generation process itself,

3. In western history the power of the state was gradually hemmed in by civil society dense with interest-based associations. In India groups are based more on ethnic and other identities (caste, religion, language, etc.), although the exigencies of electoral politics have somewhat reshaped the boundaries of (and ways of aggregating) these identity groups. This has meant a much larger emphasis on group rights than on individual rights.[2] A perceived slight of a particular group (in, say, the speech or behaviour of a political leader from another group) usually causes much more of a public uproar than crass violations of individual civil rights even when many people across different groups are to suffer from the latter. The issues that catch public imagination are the group demands for preferential treatment (like reservation of public-sector jobs) and protection against ill-treatment. This is not surprising in a country where the self-assertion of hitherto subordinate groups in a hierarchical society takes primarily the form of a quest for group dignity and protected group-niches in public jobs.

4. In western history expansion of democracy gradually limited the power of the state. In India, on the other hand, democratic expansion has often meant an increase in the power of the state. The subordinate groups often appeal to the state for protection and relief. With the decline of hierarchical author-

ity in the villages and with the moral and political environment of age-old deference to community norms changing, the state has moved into the institutional vacuum thus left in the social space. For example, shortly after Independence popular demands of land reform legislation (for the abolition of revenue intermediaries, for rent control and security of tenure), however tardy and shallow it may have been in implementation, brought in the state to the remotest corners of village society. With the advantage of numbers in electoral politics as hitherto backward groups get to capture state power, they are not too keen to weaken it or to give up the loaves and fishes of office and the elaborate network of patronage and subsidies that comes with it.[3] This serves as a major political block to the (largely elite-driven) attempts at economic liberalization of recent years, as we will discuss later.

5. For a large federal democracy India, by constitutional design, differs from the classical case of US federalism in some essential features. Not merely is the federal government in India more powerful vis-a-vis the states in many respects (including the power to dismiss state governments in extreme cases and to reconstitute new states out of an existing state in response to movements for regional autonomy), but it has also more obligation, through mandated fiscal transfers (via the Finance Commission and the Planning Commission), to help out poor regions. In classical federalism the emphasis is on restraining the federal government through checks and balances, in India it is more on regional redistribution and political integration. Stepan (1999) has made a useful distinction between 'coming-together federalism' like the US, where previously sovereign polities gave up a part of their sovereignty for efficiency gains from resource pooling and a common market, and 'holding-together federalism' as in multinational democracies like India or Belgium or Spain, where compensating transfers keep the contending nationalities together and where economic integration of regional markets is a distant goal, yet incompletely unachieved even in more than 50 years of federalism.

Given these social and historical differences in the evolution of democracy in India its impact on inequality and poverty has been rather complex. In the history of western democracies extension of franchise has been associated with welfare measures for the poor. In the more recent data for a large number of countries cross-country regressions have found a positive association between democracy and some human development indicators[4] (relevant largely for the poor) or incomes of the lowest quintile of income distribution.[5] What has been the performance over time of the Indian democracy in terms of economic inequality and poverty? If we examine inequality in terms of the Gini coefficient there has not been much change overall. According to household consumer expenditure data collected by the National Sample Survey, during 1983 to 2000 for example, rural inequality in consumption decreased a bit whereas urban inequality increased somewhat. Poverty has fallen significantly, though. In 1983 46 per cent of the population was below the Planning Commission poverty line whereas in 1999–2000 this figure was about 29 per cent. Despite this fall, India remains the largest single-country contributor to the pool of the world's extremely poor, illiterate people. Anti-poverty programs constitute a substantial part of the budgets of federal and state governments, but it is widely noted that a large part of them do not reach the real poor. The poverty figures are based on NSS consumption data and not data on income. Some fragmentary data on income suggest that the Gini coefficient for income distribution remains quite high, around 0.41 (and the Gini coefficient for asset distribution substantially higher). Some people contend that in the last decade or so the top 1 per cent of the population has become much richer, and their income or consumption is not captured in the usual survey data.

On the other hand, democracy has clearly brought about a kind of social revolution in India. It has spread out to the remote reaches of this far-flung country in ever-widening circles of political awareness and self-assertion of hitherto subordinate groups. These groups actually have increased faith in the efficacy of the political system and they vigorously participate in larger numbers in the electoral process. In the National Election Study[6] carried out by the Centre for the Study of Developing Societies, the percentage of respondents who answered positively to the question, 'do you think your vote has effect on how things are run in this country?', went up between 1971 and 1996 from 48.4 per cent to 58.7 per cent for the total population, from 45.7 per cent to 57.6 per cent for 'backward caste' groups (designated as OBC in India), from 42.2 per cent to 60.3 per cent for the lowest castes (designated as scheduled castes), and 49.9 per cent to 60.3 per cent for Muslims (only later data can show if this figure has now changed for Muslims in view of the recent happenings in parts of the country).

Yet, this faith in the efficacy of the political system is very inadequately translated into concrete results on economic progress for the median member of the poor disadvantaged groups. Let us explore this particular disjuncture between economics and politics in India a bit further. The politicians are seldom penalised by the Indian electorate for endemic poverty; poverty is widely regarded among common people as a complex phenomenon with multiple causes, and they ascribe only limited responsibility to the government in this matter. In any case the measures of government performance are rather noisy, particularly in a world of illiteracy and low levels of civic organization and formal communication on public issues. As we have indicated before, a perceived slight in the speech of a political leader felt by a particular ethnic group will usually cause much more of an uproar than if the same leader's policy neglect keeps thousands of children severely malnourished in the same ethnic group.[7] The same issue of group dignity comes up in the case of reservation of public sector jobs for backward groups which, as we have said before, fervently catches the public imagination of such groups, even though, objectively the overwhelming majority of the people in these groups have little chance of ever landing those jobs, as they and their children drop out of school in large numbers by the fifth grade. Even when these public job quotas mainly help the tiny elite in backward groups, as a symbol and a possible, though distant, object of aspiration for their children, they ostensibly serve a valuable function in attempts at group upliftment.

Particularly in north India there seems to be a preoccupation with symbolic victories among the emerging lower-caste political groups; as Hasan (2000) points out, with reference to BSP, a politically successful party of the oppressed in UP, these groups seem less concerned about changing the economic-structural constraints under which most people in their community live and toil. Perhaps this is just a matter of time. These social and political changes have come to north India rather late; in south India, where such changes have taken place several decades back, it may not be a coincidence that there has been a lot more effective performance in the matter of public expenditures on pro-poor projects like health, education, housing and drinking water. This reflects the fact that in south India there has been a long history of social movement against exclusion of lower castes from the public sphere, against their educational deprivation, etc. in a way more sustained and broad-based than in north India. One may also note that the upper caste opposition to social transformation is somewhat stronger in north India, as demographically upper castes constitute in general a somewhat larger percentage of the population than has been the case in most parts of south India. So new political victories of lower castes in north India get celebrated in the form of defiant symbols of social redemption and recognition aimed at solidifying their as yet tentative victories, rather than in committed attempts at changing the economic structure of deprivation.

From this major disjuncture between politics and economics in India let me now move on to the various kinds of disjuncture that have appeared in the Indian scene between the policy of economic reform and the on-going political and administrative processes. Economists often ignore these, and are surprised when things do not proceed in the way they want. In the last two decades, particularly since the early nineties, India has launched a widely-heralded process of economic reform with a view to unleashing the entrepreneurial forces from the shackles of the nightmarish controls and regulations that have hobbled the economy for years. Yet many commentators have noted our ways of lumbering, proceeding two steps forward, one step backward. We need to have a better understanding of why reform is so halting and hesitant, why there is no substantial and durable political constituency for reform (outside the small confines of India's metropolitan elite), why even the few supporters of reform underplay it at election time. In the rest of this lecture I shall point to ten different kinds of disjuncture that may be linked to this phenomenon.

1. Any process of sustained economic reform and investment requires a framework of long-term policy to which the government can credibly commit itself. But the political process in India seems to be moving in the opposite direction. While becoming more democratic and inclusive in terms of incorporating newer and hitherto subordinate groups, it is eroding away most of the structures of institutional insulation of long-run economic management decisions against the wheeling and dealing of day-to-day politics. There are very few assurances that commitments made by a government (or a leader) will be kept by successive ones, or even by itself under pressure. A political party that introduces some reforms is quick to oppose them when it is no longer in power.

2. With the extensive deregulation of the last two decades it was expected that corruption that is associated with the system of permits and licenses will decrease. There are no hard estimates, but by most anecdotal accounts corruption has, if anything, gone up in recent years. Although there may have been some decline in smuggling, black market in foreign exchange, or real estate. Some of the newer social groups coming to power are quite nonchalant in suggesting that all these years upper classes and castes have looted the system, now it is their turn. This has implications for the milking of the remaining obstructive regulations, particularly at the level of state governments (for example in matters of water and electricity connections to factories or enterprises, and in land acquisition and registration). As elections become more and more expensive the demands on business from the politician-regulator are unlikely to relent.

3. Much more than economic reform the major economic issue that captures public imagination, as we have noted before, is that of job reservation for an increasing number of 'backward' groups, which is accepted by all political parties. In the last decade of market reform more and more of the public sector job market has been carved up into protected niches. Cynics may even argue that the retreat of the state, implied by economic reform, is now more acceptable to the upper classes and castes, as the latter are losing their control over state power in the face of the emerging hordes of hitherto subordinate groups, and they are opting for greener pastures in the private sector and abroad. As these hitherto subordinate groups capture state power they are not likely to easily give up the lucrative benefits of office and the elaborate network of patronage distribution that goes with it. This is more acutely the case at the state government level where these groups are more secure in power.

4. There have been few substantive reforms in the agricultural sector, and the non-agricultural informal sector has been hurt by the credit crunch. Yet these two sectors constitute 93 per cent of the total labor force. No wonder they are not enthused by the reforms carried out so far. In fact even organised farm lobbies (with few exceptions) have not been very active in demanding reforms of agricultural controls like those on storage and distribution and on domestic and foreign trade. They may be worried that the dismantling of the existing structure of food, fertilizer, water and electricity subsidies in exchange of receiving, say, international agricultural prices may be too complex and politically risky a deal. In any case the high administered procurement prices for grains have now eroded India's earlier (largely unexploited) competitive advantage in world grain markets.

5. Political power is shifting more to regional governments and regional parties, which makes national coordination on macro policy more difficult. For example, fiscal consolidation in general and a substantial reduction in the budget subsidies in particular are difficult when the national government depends on the support of powerful regional parties that assiduously nurse their parochial interest lobbies with a liberal use of subsidies (implicit or explicit). As the logic of economic reform and increased competition leads to increased regional inequality, it is not clear how the Indian federal system will resolve the tension between the demands of the better-off states for more competition and those of other states (which a politically weaker Centre can ill afford to ignore politically) for redistributive transfers. Can, for example, a coalition government at the Centre, dependent for its survival on the large number of MPs from weak states (like Bihar or UP), ignore their redistributive demands to compensate them for losing out in the inter-state competition for private investment? It is also the case that a large number of entry taxes on goods imposed by governments even in otherwise leading states in economic reform (for example, Maharashtra, Tamil Nadu) are making the goal of reformers to unify an integrated all-India market that much more distant.

6. While the political power of regional governments is increasing, at the same time their fiscal dependence on the Centre is also increasing. (Between the middle 1950s to middle 1990s, the fraction of states' current expenditures financed by their own revenue sources declined from around 70 per cent to around 55 per cent). A significant part of the central transfers is discretionary (examples are the numerous central sector and centrally sponsored schemes); these and discretionary subsidized loans are often used by the Centre more for political influence in selected areas than for the cause of fiscal or financial reform or of poverty removal.

7. Reform would have been more popular if it was oriented to aspects of human development (education, health, child nutrition, drinking water, women's

welfare and autonomy, etc.). Reformers usually are preoccupied with problems of the foreign trade regime, fiscal deficits, and the constraints on industrial investments in the factory sector, and they believe that once these are handled right, trickle-down will take care of the issues that concern the masses. In particular, the reformers have paid little attention to the crucial problems of governance in matters of achieving human development, which will be inexorably there even if trade, fiscal and industrial policy reforms were successful. Ravallion and Datt (2002) show from an analysis of household survey data across 15 states over 1960 to 1994 that non-farm growth is less effective in reducing poverty in states with poorer initial conditions in terms of rural development, human resources and land distribution. For example, nearly two-thirds of the difference between the elasticity of headcount poverty index to non-farm output for Bihar and Kerala is attributable to the latter's substantially higher initial literacy rate. If the administrative mechanism of delivery of public services in the area of human development remains seriously deficient, as it is today in most states, chances of constructing a minimum social safety net are low, and without such a safety net any large-scale program of economic reform will remain politically unsustainable, not surprisingly in a country where the lives of the overwhelming majority of the people are characterized by a brutal lack of economic security.

Of course, decentralization of governance which the 73rd and the 74th constitutional amendments in the early 1990s ushered in most of the country (around the same time as serious economic reforms were also launched) has raised hopes for better delivery of public services, sensitive to local needs. In some sense this is quite a landmark in administrative reforms. But so far the progress in this respect has been disappointing in most states, both in terms of actual devolution of authority and funds, and the outcome variables of services actually delivered. Let me just quote from one general evaluation, by Pal (2001): 'With some exceptions in Kerala, Madhya Pradesh, Tripura and West Bengal, nothing worthwhile has been devolved to the panchayats. The bureaucracy at all tiers of panchayats is holding the balance.' Note also that in Kerala and West Bengal decentralization with regular panchayat elections started long before the constitutional amendments. In many states not just the bureaucracy (which often has overlapping functions with the panchayats) has been reluctant to let go, the local MLAs, in order to protect their patronage turf, have hijacked the local electoral and administrative process (even in otherwise better-run states like Tamil Nadu). In Andhra Pradesh, a state supposedly at the forefront of economic reform, the Chief Minister is reportedly using information technology to further centralise (and personalise) the administrative process. Even in the relatively successful case of West Bengal the major role of panchayats has been in identifying beneficiaries of government programmes and the management and implementation of local infrastructure projects like roads and irrigation, funded by tied grants from the Central or state government. There is no serious involvement of the panchayat in the management or control of basic public services like primary education, public health and sanitation or in raising local resources. Of course, prior land reforms in Kerala and West Bengal have made the panchayats somewhat less prone to capture by the village landed oligarchy as compared to parts of north India.

8. Another potential link between economic reform and decentralization largely un-utilized in India relates to small-scale, particularly rural, industrialization. (In fact, rural non-farm employment grew at a much slower rate in the nineties than in the eighties). The Chinese success in the phenomenal growth in rural industries is often ascribed to decentralization, by which the Central and provincial governments gave 'positive' incentives to the local government-run village and township enterprises (by allowing them residual claimancy to the money they make) and 'negative' incentives to keep them on their toes (in the form of refusing to bail them out if they lose money in the intense competition with other such enterprises). In India decentralization is usually visualised only in terms of delivery of welfare services, not in terms of fostering local business development, and yet if this link could be established, economic reform would have been much more popular, as local informal-sector industries touch the lives of many more people than the corporate sector. A program of economic reform that involves curbing the petty tyranny and corruption of the small industry inspectors (who currently act as serious barriers to potential entry), encouraging micro-finance and marketing channels, and providing the 'positive' and 'negative' incentives of Chinese-style decentralization, has the potential of opening the floodgates of small-scale entrepreneurship in India. Examples of successful cooperative business development with the leadership of the local government, though rare in India, are not entirely absent. Take the case of the Manjeri municipality in the relatively backward district of Malappuram in north Kerala, with not much of a pre-existing industrial culture. In this area the municipal authorities, in collaboration with some NGOs and bankers, have succeeded in converting it into a booming hosiery manufacturing centre, after developing the necessary skills at the local level and the finance. This and other award-winning panchayats in Kerala dispel the common presupposition that civic bodies in the villages and small towns of India do not have the capability to take the leadership in developing and facilitating skill-based small-scale and medium-scale industries.

9. It is anomalous to expect reform to be carried out by an administrative setup that for many years has functioned as an inert, arbitrary, heavy-

handed, often corrupt, uncoordinated, monolith. Economic reform is about competition and incentives, and a governmental machinery that does not itself allow them in its own internal organization is an unconvincing proponent or carrier of that message. Yet very few economists discuss the incentive and organizational issues of administrative reform as an integral part of the economic reform package. We have an administrative structure dominated by bureaucrats chosen on the basis of a generalist examination (rank in that early entry examination largely determines the career path of an officer no matter how well or ill suited s/he is in the various jobs s/he is scuttled around, each for a brief sojourn), and promotions are largely seniority-based not merit or performance-based. There are no well-enforced norms and rules of work discipline, very few punishments for ineptitude or malfeasance, and there are strong disincentives to take bold, risky decisions. Whether one likes it or not, the government will remain quite important in our economy for many years to come, and it is difficult to discuss the implementation of economic reform without the necessary changes in public administration including incentive reforms, accompanied by changes in information systems, organizational structure, budgeting and accounting systems, task assignments, and staffing policies. In these matters there is a lot to learn from the (successes and failures of) innovative administrative reform experiments that have been carried out in many developing countries in the last decade or so.

10. Finally, in large parts of the country the judiciary (particular at the lower end) is almost completely clogged by the enormous backlog of cases and the legal system is largely paralysed by delay and corruption. Even more important, the institutional independence of the police and criminal justice system is regularly undermined by politicians of whichever is the ruling party. As result, the rule of law, which is as much the foundation stone of a regime of market reforms as of political democracy, is often sadly missing. (The N.N. Vohra Committee Report of a few years back, now shelved, clearly spelled out the nexus between politicians, bureaucrats, the mafia, and even some members of the judiciary.) This politicisation of police and the administrative system is also the institutional background of the state-abetted carnage in Gujarat last year. This shameful chapter of recent Indian history took place in a state which is supposed to be a leader in economic reforms, indicating an alarming disjuncture between politics and economics in India today.

But much more than hostility of certain religious groups is involved here; what is basically at stake is a political failure of the Indian state. In large parts of India sectarian interests are fishing in the troubled waters mainly caused by a failed state, when the state cannot deliver the essential services (health, education, a minimum safety net and the rule of law). When public schools, for example, do not deliver education to the poor, they sometimes are compelled to send their children to the schools run by Hindu fanatics or madrasas run by Muslim fanatics. Market reformers, instead of trying to organize the retreat of the state, should devote a large part of their energies to the cause of reform of the state machinery, to administrative and judicial reform to make the state more accountable to the common people, and to prevent the hijacking of the police and the criminal justice system by the politician-criminal nexus.

In this lecture I have started with a delineation of the different social and historical context of Indian democracy, compared to the West, how it adds complexity to its relation with problems of inequality and poverty. In this discussion I have underlined the various kinds of disjunctures that have appeared, and unless these are addressed not much reform or reduction of poverty and inequality will be sustainable, in spite of the many strides of undoubted social and economic progress the country has taken over the last five decades.

References

P. Bardhan (1984), *The Political Economy of Development in India,* Oxford University Press, with an expanded edition in 1998, New Delhi.

Z. Hasan (2000), 'Representation and Redistribution: The New Lower Caste Politics of North India', in F.R. Frankel *et al.* (eds), *Transforming India: Social and Political Dynamics of Democracy,* Oxford University Press, New Delhi.

M. Lundberg and L. Squire (1999), 'Growth and Inequality: Extracting the Lessons for Policymakers', Working Paper, World Bank, Washington D.C.

A. Mani and S.W. Mukand (2000), 'Democracy and the Politics of Visibility', Working Paper, Vanderbilt University.

M. Pal (2001), 'Documenting the Panchayat Raj', *Economic and Political Weekly,* 8 September.

A. Przeworski, M. Alvarez, J.A. Cheibub, and F. Limongi (2000), *Democracy and Development: Political Institutions and Material Well-being in the World, 1950–1990,* Cambridge University Press, Cambridge.

M. Ravallion and G, Datt (2002), 'Why Has Economic Growth been More Pro-poor in some States of India than Others?', *Journal of Development Economics,* August.

Y. Yadav (2000), 'Understanding the Second Democratic Upsurge: Trends of Bahujan Participation in Electoral Politics in the 1990s', in F. Frankel, *et al.* (2000), *Transforming India: Social and Political Dynamics of Democracy,* Oxford University Press, New Delhi.

Endnotes

[1] See Bardhan (1984, 1998).

[2] One of the early leaders who carried in him the tension between individual and group rights was Ambedkar himself, a formidable constitutional lawyer concerned with individual liberty, but who was also a major spokesman of an oppressed caste group.

[3] In some sense this is familiar in the history of American municipal politics in big cities when one after another hitherto disadvantaged ethnic group captured the city administration and distributed patronage.

[4] See A. Przeworski, M. Alvarez, J.A. Cheibub, and F. Limongi (2000).

[5] See M. Lundberg and L. Squire (1999).

[6] See Yadav (2000).

[7] For a formal analysis of the role of visibility in influencing government resource allocation across multiple public goods in an electoral framework, see Mani and Mukand (2000).

2004 K R Narayanan Oration

Message from the President

I am delighted that The Australian National University is holding the 2004 Narayanan Oration on the theme 'India — On the Growth Turnpike' on April 27, 2004.

Today the GDP growth rate is about 8 per cent; it has to grow to 10 per cent and then be sustained for a decade. This is possible only by enriching 70 per cent of our population which lives in six hundred thousand villages. To realise this transformation, the nation is poised for the execution of PURA (Providing Urban Amenities in Rural Areas) programme. This programme aims at bridging the rural urban divide and achieving balanced socio-economic development. PURA consists of four connectivities: physical, electronic, knowledge, all three of which lead to economic connectivity. This will enhance the prosperity of the village clusters. Economic connectivity will generate markets and production establishments for serving them. PURA has all the ingredients to be a business enterprise with global dimensions.

My greetings and felicitation to all those associated with the University. I wish the Oration all success.

A.P.J. Abdul Kalam
New Delhi 2004

India: On the Growth Turnpike

Vijay L. Kelkar[1]

I

It is a great honour and privilege for me to be invited to deliver the 2004 Narayanan Lecture at The Australian National University. ANU is one of the premier universities of the world, and to speak at this great university itself is an honour. Further, to be associated with Dr Narayanan, one of our great Presidents, amplifies the honour manifold.

Dr K R Narayanan, a noble son of India, exemplifies all that is good in India. He was President in the year when I was involved in budget-making as the Finance Secretary. As you know, in India, it is the President, who as the head of state, sends the budget to Parliament for its consideration. Hence, it is customary for the Finance Minister and the Finance Secretary to brief the President on the Budget before he gives his assent to its transmission to Parliament.

As it was my first time, I was nervous, but I was told that this would be a short and pleasant affair. The President was very warm and gracious but he asked some penetrating questions, particularly about what this budget would mean to a common citizen, and how it would accelerate growth. I was very impressed by his grasp of complex economic issues. He emphasized the need for policies that foster accelerated growth and address problems of equity. Today, in my lecture, I will endeavour to discuss some aspects of these great questions.

II

My lecture is titled *India: On the growth turnpike*. The term 'turnpike' — which is typically North American — refers to an expressway, and today, I propose to present logic and evidence which suggests that economic growth in India will considerably accelerate further in the coming decade.

Macroeconomic Trends and the Setting

A lot has been said and written about India's exciting growth story, which can be dated to the beginning of the 1980s. Let me start with the most interesting and important facts about India's growth experience.

From the early 1980s onwards, India got strong GDP growth, averaging 5.7 per cent over the last 24 years. This year, in 2003–04, GDP growth is expected to be 8.2 per cent, and GDP is expected to reach $625 billion. India's high GDP growth is sharply visible when GDP comparisons are done on a purchasing power parity basis. As of 2001, India came in at 4th place, with output of $3 trillion. It is likely that by 2004, India will reach 3rd place, displacing Japan. That will give us a global ranking of US, China, and India in that order.

Looking back, it seems to me that we had two broad phases in our growth experience: Before 1980, and after. Before 1980, GDP growth had a mean of 3.5 per cent with a standard deviation of 3.5 per cent. In the 24 years after 1980, the mean rose to 5.7 per cent, and the standard deviation dropped to 1.9 per cent.

Many people have noticed India's high sustained growth over the last 24 years. But the low volatility of GDP growth is equally striking. For a comparison, over 1960–99, the median value for industrial countries was 2.18. For developing countries, it was 4.28. So we have had two big changes around 1980 as a breakpoint: mean GDP growth went up, and GDP growth volatility went down.

I find it useful to look at the acceleration of growth in India using the tool of 'rolling window' growth rates, where at each point, we compute the average growth over the last decade. A decade is a broad enough window, which allows us to smooth out the fluctuations caused by an unusual monsoon or two. So every year, we look back at the last 10 years, and compute the mean and standard deviation of GDP growth over that decade.

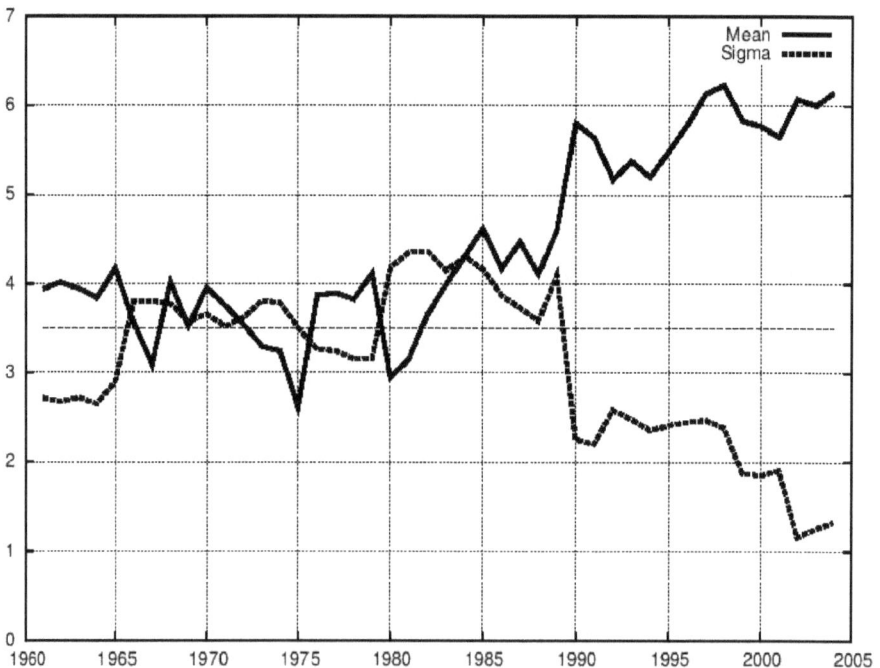

This graph gives us new insights into familiar facts about the acceleration in India's GDP growth.[2] We departed from the 'Hindu rate of growth' of 3.5 per cent in 1982, and reached levels like 6 per cent from 1996 onwards. In this lecture, I am going to argue that we will go further up to substantially higher growth rates in the years to come.

We have also obtained a sharp reduction in GDP growth volatility. Along with this, inflation and interest rates have also come down sharply. We seem to have thus created an extremely benign macroeconomic environment, with low inflation, low interest rates and high GDP growth.

	GDP growth (%)		Years to double
Period	Aggregate	Per-capita	p.c. GDP
1972–1982	3.5	1.2	57
1982–1992	5.2	3.0	23
1992–2002	6.0	3.9	18

Let me talk about this in a different way — as growth of per capita GDP. While GDP growth has accelerated, population growth rates have gone down slightly. These have combined to give an even sharper acceleration of GDP growth per capita. In the 1970s, this was 1.2 per cent and it went up to 3.9 per cent in the 1990s.

I want to emphasise that 1.2 per cent and 3.9 per cent both sound like small numbers, but there is a huge difference between the two in terms of their human impact. At 1.2 per cent a year, per capita GDP takes 57 years to double. A man sees one doubling in his adult life. At 3.9 per cent a year, per capita GDP takes 18 years to double. A man who lives to 72 sees three doublings as compared with the standard of living that he saw at age 18. This is an enormous difference!

Why did India Exhibit Resilience to Shocks?

A remarkable feature of India's growth experience has been its resilience to shocks. In many countries, short periods of high growth appear to be punctuated by years of poor growth.[3] Largely speaking, this has not been the case in India over the last 25 years. This is reflected in the figure above, which shows a sustained increase in average GDP growth rates, coupled with a sharp *decline* in GDP growth volatility from the decade 1980–1990 onwards.

This resilience of growth in recent decades is an important change when compared with preceding decades. In 1973 and 1979, growth in India was adversely affected by oil shocks. In the later period, this vulnerability appears to have been greatly reduced.

This aspect is important in understanding India's growth experience. It is important to address the questions: *Why has India's growth been so consistent?*

Why has growth accelerated from decade to decade, without encountering the difficulties which are observed in many other developing countries? Why has India exhibited such resilience to shocks?

One could maintain a hypothesis that the Indian economy was exposed to smaller external shocks in the period after 1980; that this drop in volatility is an artefact of a benign external environment. However, this is just not true. In these years, the economy has faced many shocks, including international financial crises, security tensions, international sanctions, etc. From roughly 1995 onwards, the world has emphatically not been a quieter place. Hence, the drop in GDP growth volatility seems to reflect a genuine improvement in macro stability and not a lack of shocks.

Another possible hypothesis is rooted in currency flexibility. A broad consensus that appears to be emerging in the literature suggests that greater flexibility in exchange rates is conducive to enhanced macro-stability. A recent paper[4] by Edwards and Yeyati finds that terms of trade shocks are exacerbated in countries with more rigid exchange rate systems. In their empirical work, under flexible exchange rates, the effects of terms-of-trade shocks on growth are approximately one half of those under pegged regimes. They also find that under inflexible exchange rate regimes, output growth is more sensitive to negative than to positive shocks.

If the economic reforms in recent decades had moved towards greater currency flexibility, then this could have been pointed to as a key source of improved resilience. However, a series of recent papers[5] have demonstrated that in India's case, currency flexibility has been broadly unchanged since 1979. Hence, a *change* in the currency regime does not constitute a feasible explanation for this decline in GDP growth volatility.

One element of an explanation appears to be the improvement in price flexibility that took place in many *other* areas of the Indian economy. While price flexibility on two important markets — currency and food grains — did not go up, price flexibility rose sharply in the 1990s in myriad other areas such as interest rates, steel, cement, etc. In these areas, price volatility had been stifled in the traditional command-and-control paradigm of economic policy, and prices were freed up in the 1990s. This is expected to have improved the ability of the economy to adjust to shocks through changes in prices. A second explanation that we offer relates to the maturing processes of democracy, which I will come to later.

Globalisation

One of the most important phenomena about the Indian economy in the 1990s was the growth of international trade. We see striking changes in the one-decade period following 1991–92. India has engaged in unilateral removals of barriers to trade, and this process has been assisted by our WTO obligations.[6]

Through these, gross trade flows almost tripled over this period from $56.7 billion in 1991–92 to $155.5 billion in 2001–02. Expressed as a fraction of GDP, the trade-GDP ratio went up from 21.3 per cent to 33.1 per cent over this ten-year period. This was a fairly rapid pace of change for a structural parameter like the trade/GDP ratio.

A key feature of India's experience with trade has been the rapid growth of services exports. Over this decade, merchandise exports grew by 145 per cent but services exports grew by 275 per cent.

This high growth of services exports has been based on two distinct components. In the earlier period, invisibles revenues were primarily obtained through remittances from Indians working outside India. In recent years, improvements in telecommunications have implied that many services, which were previously non-tradable, could now be produced in India as part of global production chains. Export-oriented services production in India ranges from high volume production of low-end services like accounting, all the way to services that require highly specialised and high-wage staff, like research and development. For example, research laboratories located in India by major US companies have filed for over 1,000 patents with the US Patent and Trademark Office.

The high degree of public awareness about India's success in these IT-enabled services exports has led to a widespread perception that India is faring extremely well in services exports but has failed in obtaining growth in manufacturing exports. This perception is inconsistent with the high growth which is *also* seen with merchandise exports. Particularly in the last five years, growth rates of manufacturing and services exports have been rather alike.

India's success on exports growth has made a big difference to the overall outlook on the external sector. We began the decade of the 1990s with a BOP crisis. Today, India is widely seen as having an extremely strong position on the external sector. This was achieved through several elements: currency depreciation, export buoyancy, and policies of avoiding foreign currency debt. Our foreign currency reserves are now roughly as big as our external debt, so there can be little question of a BOP crisis shaping up.

Political Economy of Growth

One of the most interesting features about India's growth is the way it has been achieved under a democratic framework. There is a view that democracy impedes economic growth and India would eliminate poverty faster if we are willing to sacrifice freedom and democracy.

I quite disagree with this perspective. I believe that democracy is a 'growth fundamental', that we have come where we have come *because* of democracy, and not despite it. I found one insightful way of thinking about this in a 1988 paper[7] by Dani Rodrik, which offered an interesting framework for understanding resilience of output growth, when faced with external shocks.

$$\Delta \text{ growth } =$$
$$- \text{ external shocks } \times \frac{\text{latent social conflict}}{\text{Institutions of conflict management}}$$

This 'equation' seeks to explain the impact on GDP growth of a given external shock. This is linked to three explanations:

1. The size of the external shock matters — bigger external shocks should obviously give a bigger impact on growth,
2. The extent of 'latent social conflict'. Rodrik defines this in terms of ethnic and religious heterogeneity.
3. Rodrik focuses on 'institutions of conflict management' as the tool through which countries are better able to absorb external shocks.

Going by his definition, India has substantial 'latent social conflict', given the ethnic and religious diversity present in the country. Yet, we know that the output loss associated with shocks in India was small. How did this happen?

By Rodrik's argument, this suggests the high quality of the institutions of conflict management in the country. This is achieved through political institutions, and the functioning of democracy. As is well known, India is the world's largest democracy. Freedom of speech, regular elections, and an independent judiciary have characterised India's 57-year post-independence experience.

While India started out with very strong majorities for a single party (the Congress) in Parliament, over the decades, the political system has learnt how to obtain consensus through coalition governments. For example, in recent years, bipartisan support was essential for every piece of legislation. Milestones in economic legislation, such as the Electricity Act, the Foreclosure law, or the Fiscal Responsibility and Budget Management Act, would not have been possible without bipartisan support.

In many countries, the introduction of market-oriented reforms has been highly unpopular with the larger populace. This appears to have not been a constraint in India. One litmus test of this problem is found in the labour market. One revealing statistic about this is the number of strikes and the man days lost through strikes in 1992 and 2002. Major changes in economic policy have been actually accompanied by a sharp *diminution* in the incidence of unrest on the part of organised labour.

How was such a consensus in favour of market-oriented reforms forged? In the early period, market-oriented reforms may have appeared relatively novel and required consensus building to support embarking on relatively unknown territory. These innovations in policy were better accepted in India, as compared with the experience of many other countries, since they were crafted through the processes of a participatory democracy. In recent years, the consensus in favour of market-oriented reforms has been cemented by the results which better economic policy has delivered. One of the reasons for this has been the better sequencing of reforms which enabled 'early harvest' of the benefits.

The most important area of progress is that of poverty reduction. A shocking fact, embedded in Indian history, is the stagnation of the headcount of the poor at 320 million for the two-decade period from 1973 to 1993. From 1993 to 1999, in a short six-year period alone, the headcount of the poor dropped by 60 million. Taking into account various factors, it can be said that 100 million people have been brought out of poverty by the growth process of the last decade. This is an astonishing achievement, and it has had a positive impact on the political acceptance of economic reforms.[8]

As mentioned before, per capita GDP now shows three doublings in an adult life, as compared with one doubling in an adult life that used to be observed earlier. These changes have been accompanied by a reduction in the volatility of GDP growth, which has helped alleviate fears about the vagaries of the free market. All these changes have been manifestly visible in the political system and public discourse, and have helped cement the consensus in favour of economic reforms.

While democratic institutions are very valuable things to have, this is not to say that it is easy for a country to learn how to operate democratic institutions. Many countries have lost high GDP growth rates for a decade or more, in learning to make the transition from dictatorship to democracy. By now, India appears to have absorbed the costs of learning to operate vibrant democratic institutions.

Recent Themes in Reforms

A lot has been written about the economic reforms process in India. I would like to once again be brief and selective, and talk about a few big things that are going on.

I think the general principles that are driving the reforms process may be summarised as follows. We are trying to focus on *incentives*, and give the right people the right incentives to do the right things. We are trying to reduce frictions and transactions costs, so as to enable more transactions and more trading. We are trying to harness network externalities and obtain increasing returns to scale. Finally, we are trying to emphasise the 'meso-economic reforms', to put a focus on that in-between space between the macro and the micro, which consists of major institutions and 'rules of the game'.

Deepening Globalisation

Let me start with *globalisation*. As emphasised above, our trade/GDP ratio went up sharply from 22 per cent of GDP to 33 per cent of GDP over a 10-year period. India has digested the lessons of the 1960s and 1970s, about the enormous distortions and harmful political economy that is induced by protectionism. So we have made much progress in doing unilateral trade liberalisation, and in exploiting the WTO process. We have eliminated quantitative restrictions, and brought down the peak customs rate on manufactured goods from over 150 per cent to a present level of 20 per cent.

What is particularly striking is that this year, with elections impending, we were able to sharply cut tariffs, and this was criticised by some observers as a 'populist' thing to do! This highlights the sea change that has taken place in India's attitude towards trade integration with the world economy. India, which was once described as a 'hesitant globaliser', has become a 'willing globaliser'!

The elimination of QRs, and the drop in the peak rate from 150 per cent to 20 per cent, was obviously costly for many firms and individuals. There are real costs that have to be paid in terms of obsolete business plans, and factors of production had to shift into areas where India has a comparative advantage. In my view, this is a subtle reason behind the upsurge of bad loans in the banking industry in the mid-1990s.

However, the difficult part of our adjustment to eliminating tariffs and QRs now seems to be behind us, and we are well on our way to single digit tariffs. It is striking to observe that while the multilateral discussions about trade reforms are still talking in terms of multi-decade horizons for adjustment, India has been able to move much faster, and unilaterally make progress on trade reforms.

Going from the current account to the capital account, there is now a broad consensus that capital controls are ineffective when there is a large and free current account. There are simply too many opportunities for moving capital across the globe by over invoicing, under invoicing, transfer pricing by multinational corporations, and trade in gold. Hence, India has steadily made progress on freeing up the capital account, particularly in the last five years. For foreign institutional investors, we are 100 per cent convertible. Indian firms can take up to 100 per cent of their net worth out of the country. Domestic citizens can take up to $25,000 out of the country, which is a lot when compared with the per capita income. The opening up of the capital account has enormous implications for the conduct of Indian macro policy. The impossible trinity is now with us, so that a restrictive currency policy comes at the price of monetary price autonomy. Hence, this is a new and exciting phase for Indian macroeconomics.

As an aside, I want to highlight some non-economic factors which have been at the foundation of India's success in rapid integration into the world economy. These consist of: our strong IT and telecom sectors, our use of English, and our vibrant democracy. Our strengths in IT and telecom have helped us to exploit the Internet, which is an important highway of globalisation today. Our use of English has meant lower transaction costs in interacting with the global economy. Our democracy has helped us avoid the difficulties and hindrances that come into the picture when repressive regimes try to block ideas from flowing in through the Internet. For example, we in India have multiple competing private sector Internet service providers, with high speed lines that reach into the outside world, with no large government effort at censorship or selective blocking of content.

Infrastructure Sector: Unfolding Mesoeconomic Reforms

Let me turn to infrastructure. In the early 1990s, infrastructure was high on our minds. The public goods of transportation and communications were clearly a bottleneck to efficiency, and to internal and international trade. In the presence of those constraints, our ability to harness gains from trade was limited, owing to the high transactions costs of engaging in trade. Our inefficiencies in transport and communications ultimately filtered into the exchange rate, where the rupee had to devalue enough to obtain rough parity on the current account.

India chose to go down the path of moving towards competitive markets in infrastructure, with private sector production, under a framework of sound regulation. I believe that this was the right path to go down. But as we all know, this is a difficult path to take. There are truly subtle difficulties in finding the right policy mix, the right 'rules of the game' which provide sound incentives to private firms to produce adequate quantities of these goods, while at the same time avoiding monopolistic profit rates. I look at the difficulties in California on electricity, and in the US on broadband telecom, and I sympathise with the problems that they are facing.

For many years, all economists, including myself, used to be somewhat pessimistic about the way things were going on in infrastructure sector in India. From 1991 onwards, the State ceased to invest in infrastructure, but the new policy framework had not fallen into place! So we were stranded between the two stools.

Today, it increasingly looks like the light is at the end of the tunnel on our infrastructure problems.[9] I believe we have made good progress on telecom, roads, ports, electricity and aviation. The big piece where we have yet to obtain real progress is railways.

In *telecom*, we have obtained a revolution by having competition between multiple, private telephone companies. We are now at 40 million mobile phones, and are growing at the rate of 2 million mobile phones every month. Little shops offering internet access are now all over the country. Every visiting card that I encounter has an email address on it. We are one of the world's first countries to shift to a 'unified licensing', where the licensing is neutral to telecom technology. I believe we are the only market in the world where the two major technologies for mobile telephony — GSM and CDMA — are locked in grim competitive battle, with customers reaping the rewards of this competition. Total phone subscribers are at 71 million, and what was once thought to be an ambitious target for teledensity that should be achieved by March 2005 was actually achieved in December 2003. Given the existing pace of hectic growth, it looks rather likely that an additional 100 million lines will be added over 2004–05 and 2005–06. This would take teledensity from 7 per cent today to 17 per cent by March 2006.

In *roads*, we have embarked on an enormous project to build new highways, which will take the sustained mean velocity up from 30 kph to 80 kph. I believe these new roads will generate a new phase of growth in India, by harnessing what I call 'internal gains from trade'. I believe this is the classical gains-from-trade story, being repeated *within* the country, when firms 1000 km apart are able to trade for the first time, thanks to the lowered transactions costs. I think the full impact of these roads on investment, and the geographical distribution of production, will play out in the next five years.

We have yet to make the leap to 8-lane expressways, where we will get sustained mean velocities of 160 kph. But we have a big step forward in terms of learning new institutions, revenue sources, and contracting mechanisms, through which 4-lane highways are now very much in our grasp.

In the area of *ports*, we have made progress by contracting out the operations of ports to international firms who have specialised expertise on this subject. Remarkably enough, we find that when a public sector terminal competes with an international operator in the same port, the performance of this public sector terminal also improves! The turnaround time at ports dropped by half, from 7.5 days in 1996–97 to 3.5 days in 2001–02. These new ideas in contracting are being steadily applied across the country, giving a revolution in how the ports sector works.

These improvements in ports, roads and telecom sound nice. But are they large enough to make a *material* difference? Or are they high rates of growth on a very bad base? It is important to focus on the end-result of better infrastructure, which should be more efficient firms. Using the CMIE Prowess database, we observe the 4000 largest manufacturing companies in India. For these firms, working capital as per cent of sales went down dramatically from 13 per cent in 1996 to a level of 3.5 per cent today. This is a striking change, which reflects both the opportunities of being more efficient using the new infrastructure, and the competitive forces which are pushing firms to think more carefully about how they manage inventories.

In the area of *electricity*, the big change is the Electricity Act, which has setup a path-breaking pro-competitive framework whereby producers and consumers of electricity can interact in an unfettered market. We are already seeing myriad changes in the electricity sector in India as a consequence of this simple fact: that producers and consumers of power are now free to contract with each other across the country. Once again, I see this as a story of going from stifled markets to gains from trade.

Financial Sector Reforms: A Quiet Revolution

A major area of focus in the economic reforms has been the financial sector. Joseph Stiglitz has observed that finance is 'the brain of the economy'. The financial sector controls the efficiency with which incremental capital formation is converted into incremental GDP.

India has made good progress in building a sound regulatory framework for banking, insurance and the securities markets. Many countries, all over the world, have experienced problems with banking. Obtaining safe and sound banking is genuinely difficult, given the extreme leverage of banks, the opacity of their assets, and the moral hazard induced by a safety net. Difficulties in banking escalate into major macroeconomic problems when the banking system is itself large, when compared with GDP. In India today, bank deposits are just 48 per cent of GDP, and net non-performing assets are just 2.3 per cent of assets. Hence, there is little possibility of difficulties in banking derailing the economy.

In recent years, much detailed work has taken place on strengthening the banking system. Banking has become more competitive through a steady pace of entry by domestic and foreign banks, and has been steadily transformed by the introduction of new technology such as Real-time Gross Settlement System (RTGS). Banking has also benefited, as all creditors have, from the strengthening of creditors' rights which began in 2001. This continues to be an active area for new work in developing legal structures and institutional mechanisms.

India's financial system differs from that of many developing countries and it is more in line with the Anglo-Saxon model, with large and liquid public securities markets, and with bank deposits being relatively small when compared with GDP. There has been a particularly remarkable revolution in the stock exchanges in terms of a completely new design replacing traditional notions about how the market should be organised.[10] India's NSE and BSE are the 3rd largest and 6th largest exchanges of the world, measured by the number of trades in 2001 and given the present trends, it is likely that in 2004, NSE will surpass NYSE in terms of the number of trades or transactions. India was a pioneer in shifting to T+2 settlement. India is unique by world standards in the extent to which non-transparent transactions have been proscribed: all trades match on the transparent order-matching screen on the equity market.

Equity derivatives trading was launched in India in June 2000, and now has daily turnover of $4 billion. This was one of the most successful launches of equity derivatives trading in the world.[11] India's success on the stock exchanges is a poster child of our ability to overcome difficult problems of political economy and entrenched interests, to obtain revolutionary change, and rise to the front ranks of the world. These institutions are precious assets today, and will be key building blocks in the next steps of modernising the financial sector, and improving transparency and competition, in the years to come.

In coming decades, enormous flows of savings are going to be intermediated through the financial sector. It is extremely important that the financial sector should be thoughtful and effective in delivering equity and debt capital into those firms in India which convert it into the highest possible GDP growth. This is particularly important because, as we will argue ahead, there is a good likelihood that the savings rate in India will grow significantly in the coming decade. The financial sector is of crucial importance in converting these vast flows of savings into a maximal impact upon GDP growth.

We know, from the experience of other countries, that this process can go wrong. We need to continue to work on carrying through the reforms in the financial sector. We have many strengths in what has taken place in finance, particularly on the equity market, but a lot remains to be done in banking and the debt market.

A new frontier in financial sector development lies in pension sector reforms. From 1998 to 2003, an intensive effort took place in India to think about alternative strategies in pension reforms, and to design an institutional architecture that would be well suited to solve the unique problems of the Indian setting.[12] This led to important cabinet decisions in 2003 which are now being implemented.

The basic thrust of these reforms is to build a defined contribution pension system where workers would get a range of investment choices and fund managers. Centralised recordkeeping infrastructure is envisaged, which gives scale economies, keeps down transactions costs, and maximises the contestability of the market for fund management services. This new pension system has been mandatory for all new recruits to the central government from 1 January 2004 onwards. It marks the dawn of a new breed of sophisticated institutional investors in the country, who will be sources of investment into debt and equity issued by the projects of the future.

Accelerating Privatisation

Privatisation has been a major new theme of reforms in recent years. Major successes, where control of a company has been sold off, include VSNL, BALCO, CMC and Maruti. The true significance of privatisation lies not in the proceeds, but in the impact upon productivity. There are 276 public sector companies at the central level. They contributed Rs.2.28 trillion of 'value added' in 2001–02. Of these, there are 47 companies with *negative* value added; i.e., GDP would go up if these firms ceased to exist. Each 1 per cent of increase in value added by these PSUs amounts to Rs.22.8 billion of additional GDP. The international experience suggests that the value added could go up by 20 per cent to 40 per cent after privatisation. Thus privatisation alone could generate a direct impact worth 2 per cent to 4 per cent increase in GDP. In addition, there would be many positive indirect effects of privatisation. Interestingly enough, considerable privatisation efforts are now taking place at the level of state governments also. Of the 919 companies owned by state governments, 33 have been privatised and 69 have been closed down in recent years.

Link to Productivity Growth

In my discussion about recent themes in reforms, I have highlighted four big areas: globalisation, infrastructure, privatisation, and the financial sector. It is important to reflect on the consequences of success in these four areas: these successes will give improvements in *productivity*. For a given level of labour and capital, progress in each of these areas will give higher output growth.

Areas of Concern

There are two major areas of concern in this happy picture. The first is the problem of successful resolution of fiscal consolidation issues, and the second is that of regional disparities.

Fiscal Consolidation[13]

As you all know, one of the biggest problems faced in India is the fiscal deficit. The consolidated fiscal deficit, of the centre and the states, has been at stubbornly high levels for around twenty years now.

The essence of this problem has been a stagnation in the tax/GDP ratio. From 1990–91 to 2003–04, we did obtain progress on direct taxes, which went up from 1.9 per cent of GDP to 3.5 per cent. The phasing out of customs duties has inevitably given poor growth in indirect taxes, which went from 7.9 per cent of GDP to 5.7 per cent. The fiscal difficulties at the states have given a fresh impetus to state level tax efforts, which have yielded some progress, with growth from 5.3 per cent of GDP to 6.3 per cent of GDP. However, the overall picture has been unchanged, with the tax/GDP ratio being stable at 15.5 per cent of GDP in 2003–04 and in 1990–91. The combination of large fiscal deficits with a stagnant tax/GDP ratio has given sharp growth in the debt/GDP ratio. From 1992 to 1998, the debt/GDP ratio was stable at 60 per cent of GDP, and that might have given some comfort. But after that, it has resumed an extremely rapid climb to the present level of 80 per cent of GDP. This has fuelled concerns about the possibility of India facing the problem of debt trap as interest payments have steadily become a bigger fraction of tax revenues.

Sometimes, India's fiscal problem is seen narrowly in terms of debt sustainability or a debt trap. I think this is a narrow perspective. The fiscal problem can be damaging to growth in coming years, even if it does not come to a debt trap. The reasons for this need to be reiterated:

- The high fiscal deficit has eliminated the room for manoeuvre in terms of counter-cyclical fiscal policy.
- It has sharply circumscribed the ability of the State to initiate new spending programs which could produce highly beneficial public goods.
- It has served to crowd out private investment, and thus reduce GDP growth.
- It has generated incentives for many distorted policies in the financial sector, where it has helped inhibit banking reform and the development of liquid markets for interest rates.

It is important to observe that the fiscal problems would have had an exacerbated impact on growth, by 'crowding out' private investment, if it had not been for the growth in household savings that was discussed earlier. Roughly speaking, Government has taken 10 per cent of GDP in 1990 and in 2003. However, household savings grew from 18 per cent to 23 per cent, thus supplying an *additional* five percentage points of GDP to non-government investment in the country.

In many countries, 'downsizing government', i.e., cutting government *expenses*, has been central to fiscal adjustment. In the case of India, central government expenses dropped from 18.9 per cent of GDP in 1986 to 15.6 per cent of GDP in 2001. These values do not appear to be particularly out of line by international standards, and are broadly consistent with the level of expenses that are required to produce public goods of the required quality and quantity.

Three difficult items of expenditure, i.e., interest payments, defence expenditures and subsidies make up near 100 per cent of tax revenues. In addition, there are highly inflexible expenses such as pensions, transfers to states, etc. Hence, it appears that there is little flexibility in obtaining a fiscal adjustment by compressing expenditures. There is a great deal that can be gained in terms of improving the extent to which existing expenditures are refocused away from subsidies towards providing public goods, and improving the efficiency of provision of public goods. However, it is hard to visualise a drop in expenses which would be large enough to significantly contribute to the required fiscal adjustment.

This leads us to focus on improving tax revenues as the central policy instrument in the required fiscal adjustment. Hence, efforts towards the fiscal consolidation, that have been undertaken, are focused on the following elements:

- Enlarging the tax base by rationalising exemptions and expanding service tax.
- Process engineering of the tax system
- Achieving a simple and rational tax system
- Reduction in transactions costs; improved taxpayer services.
- Reduction in subsidies, with better targeting.

Have these efforts borne fruit? Many observers have pointed out that the tax to GDP ratio is still below the levels found in the late 1980s. This observation, taken in isolation, is sometimes interpreted as implying a failure of tax reforms in India. However, this aggregative fact masks important accomplishments in terms of obtaining change.

	1990		2001	
Source	Collections	%	Collections	%
Income tax (individual)	5,010	9.7	31,764	16.8
Income tax (firms)	4,729	9.2	35,696	18.9
Customs	18,036	34.9	47,542	25.2
Excise	22,406	43.4	68,526	36.3
Service tax			2,613	1.4
Others	1,455	2.8	2,463	1.3
Total tax collections	51636	100.0	188,604	100.0

The table summarises changes in the structure of tax revenues from 1990 to 2001.

The most important accomplishment was in the area of direct taxes, which grew by almost 7 times over these 11 years. Direct taxes hence improved sharply from 18.9 per cent of collections to 35.7 per cent. This may be interpreted as a striking 'Laffer curve' outcome, where a sharp reduction in rates was accompanied by a sharp improvement in tax collections, by influencing incentives towards tax evasion and labour supply. Customs collections have lost ground, and will drop further, as India shifts away from protectionist policies. Taxing the services sector has now begun, in a small way.

These reforms anchor the fiscal consolidation envisaged in the Fiscal Responsibility Act,[14] and the commitments of state governments, which require elimination of the revenue deficit: from 5.83 per cent in 2002–03 to 0 by 2007–08. It is important to envision what the sources of a 5.83 per cent improvement could be. One example of a feasible combination could be as follows:

- An increase in direct taxes to GDP ratio of 1.5 percentage points.
- An increase in union excise duty (including services) to GDP ratio of 2 percentage points.
- State VAT will be implemented in the near future. It will replace many existing taxes, but across the entire transition, it is expected that this will yield an additional 1 percentage point of GDP.
- Reduction in subsidies and enforcement of user charges will yield 1 percentage point of GDP.
- A reduction in interest payments to GDP ratio of 0.5 percentage point is expected, as new debt, at contemporary low interest rates, replaced old, high-cost debt.

The Interim Budget presented in February this year indicates that fiscal consolidation is proceeding on this line, as the revenue deficit for the year 2003–2004 has been projected to decline by 0.5 per cent. This has been due to combination of higher tax/GDP ratio and lower current expenditure.

This fiscal consolidation will assist GDP growth in many indirect ways, including:

- Reduction in the cost of capital,
- Enhanced equity,
- Improved allocative efficiency,
- Increased administrative efficiency,
- Reduced transactions costs, and
- Enhanced transparency and accountability

A successful implementation of this transformation of the tax system, and an elimination of the revenue deficit by 2007–08, is perhaps the most important single issue in public policy in India today. The tax reforms that are currently underway will enable the economy to meet the objective of fiscal consolidation. Successful fiscal consolidation will enable the economy to achieve other important social goals such as better environment protecttion, greater investment in health infrastructure, Research & Development and the agriculture sectors.

Regional Disparities

States	Per-capita SDP 1999–2000 (thousand rupees)	Population 2001 (% of India)
Bihar	6.3	10.7
Orissa	9.2	3.6
Assam	9.6	2.6
Uttar Pradesh	9.8	17.0
Sum of these 4		33.9
India	15.6	100.0

A major problem that India faces is the large cross-sectional dispersion in economic development. There is a roughly 3:1 ratio in the per capita GDP, when we compare the richest states to the poorest states. Much attention has been focused on the 'BIMARU' states (Bihar, Madhya Pradesh, Rajasthan, Uttar Pradesh) which have high population density and low per capita output. The term 'BIMARU' is catchy because the word 'bimaar' means 'sick' in Hindi. The table above identifies the four large states where per capita SDP was over 33 per cent below the national average. These four states make up 33.9 per cent of India's population.

Regional disparities in India have been present for at least a century, if not more. Under normal circumstances, the processes of the market economy should generate 'equalising differences', whereby firms move to low-wage areas in the quest for reduced costs thus equalising differences in wages and land prices. Similarly, individuals migrate to high wage areas, thus equalising wages, and increasing the land per capita in poor areas. These processes are expected to generate convergence of per capita GDP in the normal framework of growth theory.

It is important to emphasise that the forces of convergence depicted here are based on factor mobility. They operate over and above the conventional notions of convergence through trade, which are based on technological catch-up and trade in goods, without factor mobility. This worldview has faced a challenge from the empirical evidence of the 1990s, where there is some evidence of a lack of convergence. Some states, particularly the states of the West and the South, seem to have excelled in harnessing the opportunities of globalisation and the market economy. In other states, weaknesses in human capital and governance have generated reduced growth rates in the post-1990 period.

This has been a source of much concern on the part of many observers, from two points of view. First, it is argued that if the economic reforms of the 1980s and 1990s failed to ignite growth in Bihar, then there is a need to find a new policy mix which can achieve high growth in Bihar. Second, there are fears of mounting political stress that might come about if income disparities between rich and poor states widen further. There is a remarkable similarity between these problems in India and those that have been observed in China, where coastal provinces have progressed enormously compared with the interior.

These problems are undoubtedly important, and are going to be a central issue in Indian economics and politics in the years to come. While the above difficulties are real, there are also many forces at work which are steadily having an ameliorating effect.

Flexibility of the labour market: Factor mobility is a fundamental element of the process of equalising differences. As of today, roughly 90 per cent of India's labour force is in the unorganised sector, which is a classical labour market, undistorted by labour law. In addition, unlike China, India has no government restrictions on inter-state or rural-to-urban migration.

This innate flexibility of the labour market will assist the process of convergence. In the historical data, migration flows do not (as yet) account for substantial movements of the population. The reforms of the 1990s ignited high growth rates in some states. It is likely that migration flows have a lagged response to high wage differentials. By this logic, the 2011 census may be expected to show larger migration flows than were observed in the 2001 census.

Impact of new infrastructure on 'equalising differences': The development economics literature has emphasised the problems of land-locked states, which are unable to harness gains from trade through high costs of transportation.[15]

India's growth experience suggests that geography is important. At the same time, there are exceptions. Coastal states in India have fared well; however, Orissa is a coastal state. Land-locked states have fared poorly; however, Punjab and Haryana are land-locked.

Gains from internal trade are clearly an important mechanism through which poor states can obtain economic growth. This is critically related to costs of transportation. This suggests that the recent successes in infrastructure policy — particularly in roads, ports, airports, and telecom — are highly significant in thinking about regional disparities. The new roads being built by NHAI imply that vegetables produced in Bihar or Orissa can find markets in Calcutta. This constitutes a new impetus for the forces of convergence, as compared with the preceding post-independence experience.

Fiscal transfers: India has a well-developed system of fiscal transfers, through which taxes collected in rich states are transferred to poor states. This constitutes an important channel for convergence — one that is perhaps reminiscent of the 60-year story of North Italy and South Italy.

While these rules have always been with us, the *economic significance* of these transfers improves in line with growth in GDP and in the tax/GDP ratio. Holding the fiscal rules intact, when the size of the pie goes up, larger per-capita flows are being sent into poor states. In the decade of the 1990s, India's GDP was roughly $350 billion and the tax/GDP ratio was roughly 12 per cent. GDP has already risen to $620 billion, giving a quantum leap in the expenditures of government. Looking forward, in a few years, if we envision GDP of $1 trillion and a tax/GDP ratio of 15 per cent, then there will be enormously larger resource flows through existing fiscal institutions, which will generate much larger spending in poor states.

Policy innovations: One important insight derived from the experience of economic growth in East Asia is the importance of 'regional role models'.[16] East Asian countries learned from each other. Across these countries, there was a significant amount of experimentation and real-world trials of alternative ideas, including choices of effective institutions, policies, and technologies. There was a contagion effect within this region with countries learning from each other's success stories.

In the decade of the 1990s, a similar phenomenon has begun with the states of India. States are now increasingly conscious of the importance of local public goods. The political leadership of many states is increasingly conscious of the need to find policy innovations which would improve the quality and quantity of local public goods.

The 1990s began with a certain heterogeneity of governance procedures in the states. The economic reforms of the 1990s have inevitably had a differential impact on various states; some states had policies which were more conducive to harnessing these opportunities. When the gap in per capita income widens, the political system has incentives to search for policy responses which would close the gap. Andhra Pradesh, Madhya Pradesh, West Bengal, and Kerala are all examples of states where there has been a distinct learning from the regional role models, and consequent changes in governance.

In parallel to this learning from regional role models, there are two important policy innovations which are going to fully play out in the coming decade. The first is the move towards smaller states. It is widely conjectured that smaller states are more effective at catering to local variation in preferences and technology, and at ensuring greater accountability for public goods outcomes. Uttaranchal, Bihar, Jharkhand and Chattisgarh are important experiments in this regard. It is, as yet, too early to tell whether the outcomes play out in line with the conjecture. If governance does prove to be superior in smaller states, then (a) it will generate convergence, given that these four states are all below the national average, and (b) it suggests one policy avenue for improving governance in other large states in the future.

The second innovation is the devolution to local governments, as a consequence of the 73rd and 74th constitutional amendment. The underlying premise of Panchayati Raj is that when local citizens control public expenditures, there will be a greater likelihood of obtaining good *outcomes* in terms of producing public goods. There are three key elements of local autonomy: (a) Transfer of functions and schemes, (b) Transfer of staff, and (c) Transfer of funds, and autonomous financial decision making. As of yet, different states have made different degrees of progress on these three fronts. It is, as yet, too early to tell whether the outcomes play out in line with the underlying premise. If we do obtain improvements in governance by empowering local governments, then this would constitute one channel for convergence.

Empirical Evidence

How are we faring? There is some evidence that these effects are already at work and are reshaping the nature of regional inequalities in India. There are two striking illustrations which show the changes which are taking place:

- In a deliciously ironic development, the very phrase 'BIMARU', which symbolised backward states as of 1990, has become out of touch with the location of poverty traps! This symbolises the dynamism of regional economics in India. Rajasthan and Madhya Pradesh have made significant progress in the 1990s. Chattisgarh, Uttaranchal and western parts of Uttar Pradesh have lower poverty. The most difficult areas are now no longer the BIMARU states, but the eastern region comprising Orissa, Jharkhand, Bihar, and eastern parts of Uttar Pradesh. This illustrates the *mutability* of poverty traps in India, and suggests that there *are* forces at work through which poor regions can obtain convergence.

- The second illustration concerns the BPO industry. If the idea of exploiting IT for services exports, in areas like call centres and accounting, had been described to an impartial observer in 1993, the prediction which would have been squarely made is that this would flourish in southern states, owing to the superior quality of local public goods. This would include issues such as education, reliable electricity, law and order and gender issues. Questions of law and order, and empowerment of women, are extremely important in this field, given the need for women to work the night shift. The impartial observer would have solemnly argued that North India was innately and deeply hamstrung when it came to women obtaining high education, participating in the labour force, and working at night.

The actual outcomes, from 1993 to 2003, have been inconsistent with the prediction that IT-enabled services would primarily be located in the peninsula. When we look back at the last ten years, it is an undeniable fact that Gurgaon, Noida and Chandigarh have also emerged as the major centres of IT-enabled services exports. While locations like Bangalore, Madras, Hyderabad, Poona and Bombay have all also succeeded in this area, Gurgaon and Noida are probably the largest centres. This suggests that issues such as low labour cost dominated issues such as poor production of local public goods, which suggests that forces of convergence were effective.

The most interesting evidence about the question of convergence is found in data for investment projects outstanding.[17]

State	4/1995	10/2003	Change (%)
Delhi	313	5966	1804.8
Kerala	991	5579	462.8
Chattisgarh	1097	4525	312.5
Madhya Pradesh	1846	6889	273.3
Tamil Nadu	2491	6941	178.6
Karnataka	3528	8265	134.2
Haryana	3021	6820	125.7
Maharashtra	4409	8957	103.1
Bihar	799	1560	95.3
Andhra Pradesh	3740	7083	89.4
India	**3258**	**5510**	**69.1**
Rajasthan	1852	2771	49.6
Punjab	3662	5148	40.6
Orissa	6073	7432	22.4
Uttar Pradesh	1302	1544	18.6
West Bengal	2408	2686	11.5
Gujarat	12531	11950	-4.6
Jharkhand	3908	3643	-6.8

The table above exploits the CMIE database which tracks investment projects at hand as of a point in time. It juxtaposes the projects under implementation as of April 1995 (the first point in the CMIE database) versus October 2003 (the most-recent date available). All values are expressed as rupees per capita.

This data is interesting from two points of view. Focusing on *levels*, we see states like Gujarat, which have above-mean output and above-mean investment. At the same, there also appear to be equilibrating forces at work. High growth in investment is seen in backward states like Kerala, Madhya Pradesh, Chattisgarh and Bihar. In a striking display of convergence, of the 10 states with above-average growth in per-capita investment, 8 had a below-average *level* of per capita investment as of 1995. In addition, Punjab shows the opposite phenomenon. Low growth in investment is found in high income states like Punjab and Gujarat.

These trends are indicative of the possibility of meeting the objective of regional equity with well defined policies at the Central level and at the State level. Regional equity is going to be perhaps one of the most important issues for the political economy of growth in a federal system like India. We will need to be continuously mindful of this aspect and keep policies under review so as to achieve equity in outcomes across the States of our Union.

III

Growth Outlook: Contributions from Labour, Capital and Productivity

Let me now shift gears considerably. So far I have talked about the reform efforts, repeatedly alluding to the impact of reforms on efficiency, productivity and improved resource allocation.

But what about the perspective for the growth of inputs? Ever since Krugman's 1994 article[18] in *Foreign Affairs*, about the extent to which East Asian growth was 'merely' caused by a high flow of inputs in terms of labour and capital, all of us have had a heightened consciousness about both (a) the power of additional inputs in delivering high growth rates, and (b) the importance of asking whether there is productivity growth over and above this.

Labour

Let me start with labour. It is conventional to focus on citizens between age 15 and 64 as 'the working population'. The fascinating thing about India is that we will be one of the last large countries in the world to experience our demographic transition. Current projections show that from 2010 or so, the fraction of Chinese and of Koreans in the age group of 15–64 will start dropping. In the case of Japan, this fraction has been dropping from 1995 onwards.

In the case of India, we will experience 'demographic dividend' as the ratio of working population to the total population will grow all the way till 2050. In particular, a sharp drop in the dependency ratio from 59 per cent to 50 per cent is projected between 2005 and 2020. The dependency ratio is projected to drop to 47 per cent in 2040. It is only from 2040 onwards that India's dependency ratio is projected to go up. This will give robust fuel to the process of economic growth. This forecast for India reflects the existing young population structure, coupled with a deceleration of fertility, so that a large number of children are not expected to be added.

A second change that is taking place on the labour force is equally significant for economic growth. This concerns the *quality* of the labour force. Every year, the human capital of the stock of labour goes up, through gains in education and gains in experience. Hence, we are likely to obtain improvements in the labour inputs to economic growth from three, distinct directions: (a) Incremental workers, (b) Incremental education and (c) Incremental experience of the existing stock of workers. All this is potent fuel for economic growth. The experience of Asia shows that the 'growth miracles' in Japan or in 'Tiger' economies of South East Asia or in China occurred at the similar stage of demographic transition when the share of working population in total population grew sharply.

Capital

What about capital? One element flows directly from demographics. Children and old people tend to save less; saving is the highest in the working years. Using NCAER survey data,[19] we find that in 1994–95, while the overall savings rate was 20.3 per cent, this dropped to 16.9 per cent when the head of household was below 30. The highest savings rate, of 23 per cent, was found when the head of the household was in the fifties. In the case of urban households, these effects were more pronounced, with a savings rate of just 7.8 per cent when the head of household was below 30.

So the demographic projections which clearly point out that India will have a bigger fraction of the population in the age group from 15 to 64 simultaneously predict a higher savings rate in the future. Further, holding household characteristics identical, a larger number of children would induce higher consumption, so declining fertility is likely to induce higher saving.

A second factor that is at work is the sheer GDP growth. NCAER data shows that there are extremely low savings rates for low income households. Remarkably enough, as of 1994–95, only 1.9 per cent of all saving was done by households with income below the then-prevalent median income. In 1994–95, the poorest 80 per cent of the population accounted for half the income, and this group accounted for 23.9 per cent of total savings. As a rough approximation, we may say that significant savings behaviour only took place in the top quartile of the income distribution of 1994–95. Households in the top decile had a much higher savings rate, of 35.8 per cent, as compared with the general population.

Economic growth steadily pushes households above the absolute income threshold required to be in the top quartile by the income distribution as of 1994–95. Thus, every year, a large number of households graduate into the income group where saving will commence. The bottom 30 per cent of the

1994–95 income distribution has near-zero or negative saving. GDP growth shrinks this set of zero-savings households. The top quartile of the 1994–95 income distribution had high savings rates. GDP growth pushes more households into this set of high-savings households. Through this process, holding other aspects of the stochastic environment of the household constant, the high GDP growth rates that India has been experiencing are likely to generate a steady escalation of the savings rate.

The two arguments suggested above — about the impact of income growth, and about the changing dependency ratio — have been at work for some time. If these arguments are on track, then it should have been the case that the savings rate in India should have been going up in recent years. The empirical evidence is consistent with this prediction, for household savings grew from 18 per cent to 23 per cent over the period after 1990. Looking forward, our arguments suggest that household savings will grow further in the coming 15 years. In addition, growing openness of capital account would mean greater inflow of foreign capital as the country becomes a 'willing globaliser' i.e., more open to trade and investment. This means that in the coming decade, the supply of both domestic and foreign savings are going to sharply increase leading to a much higher rate of capital accumulation compared to the last two decades.

Outlook on Productivity

Paul Krugman noticed that East Asian growth had weak foundations in terms of productivity increases; that the high growth rates were primarily a combination of demographics (an increase in the working population) and capital being brought to bear on production. This is disappointing. The essence of development is improved technology; it is all about new ways of organising production, of injecting new scientific knowledge and new institutions into the economy. We expect that when economic development takes place, *productivity* should be transformed.

It is important to point out that many studies have taken place on productivity in India, and the consensus suggests that there *has* been significant TFP growth in India. The definitive measurement is by Bosworth and Collins in 2003,[20] who find that in the period after 1980, 2 per cent of the growth (out of a total of 5.73 per cent) was accounted for by productivity changes. This suggests that India's reforms process has been able to obtain results in terms of better incentives and competition, coupled with better public goods, inducing improvements in productivity.

The outlook for the acceleration in the TFP growth in the coming decade or two is very promising. This is for several reasons. The first is the impact of information technology. In the coming decade, the rate of diffusion of IT is going to be greater due to increased availability of hardware, telecom infrastructure and human capital. In the US and other countries, the diffusion of IT has had a well documented positive impact on productivity growth. The second reason is the beneficial impact of mesoeconomic reforms and privatisation of the infrastructure sector on productivity. The international experience has been that such meso-economic economic reforms have led to an all-round increase in productivity. The third element is the engines of increasing returns which will be accruing from network industries due to network externalities.[21] The new highway network and telecom networks are two prime examples of new network industries. In the US, both these network industries have had profound impact in accelerating growth in total factor productivity.

When we look back at the experience with growth across various countries over the last 200 years, each experience with rapid growth has been caused by accumulation of capital, coupled with a catching-up of scientific knowledge. Over the years, the technologies of information processing and dissemination have steadily improved. This suggests that the *diffusion of knowledge takes place faster and faster*. This is consistent with the fact that the more-recent growth episodes, like those of China, Korea and Taiwan, have experienced higher growth rates when compared with the older growth episodes, like those of Russia, Japan and the US. Looking forward, India will benefit strongly from the great technological improvements in the diffusion of knowledge which have taken place in the last 25 years. When Korea was integrating into the world economy, and catching up with global scientific knowledge, the process of knowledge acquisition was slower than that found today in India, given the greater extent of information access through the Internet, voice calls, international travel, etc. This suggests that the speed of productivity change in India, in the next 20 years, could be higher than that seen in any experience with rapid economic growth in the last 200 years.

These arguments suggest that in the coming decade, it is not difficult to envisage a sharp increase of more than 50 per cent in the annual TFP growth a doubling of the TFP growth from the present trend of 2 per cent per annum. Such an increase would be in line with the international experience of dynamic economies.

On the Growth Turnpike

This brings me to my main thesis: that India may be about to embark on a new golden age of high economic growth. The key argument runs in these steps:

- There is a near inevitability that there will be a bulge in the working population, particularly till 2020. This effect will be further multiplied due to enhanced levels of skills i.e., accumulation of human capital.

- It is likely that this demographic dividend, coupled with strong GDP growth, will fuel an increase in the savings rate.
- Thus India is likely to fare *better* than it did over the 1980 to 2000 period, in terms of putting factor inputs into the growth process.
- The policies of the recent years — particularly in infrastructure, reductions of protectionism, and building modern securities markets — will continue to fuel TFP growth.
- Being a 'willing globaliser' will attract greater flow of FDI and technology.
- In addition, India has already shown a track record for obtaining TFP growth over the 1980-2000 period. TFP growth will show further acceleration thanks to the impact of information and communication technologies upon the speed of knowledge diffusion and to the network externalities.
- These elements add up to a scenario where GDP growth in India over 2004 to 2024 will be much higher than that seen over 1980 to 2004. In the coming decade or two, growth rate in India may surpass the 'miracle growth' rates achieved by other Asian countries. This is not surprising as India, compared to Japan, China and other high growth economies of Asia, will have advantage of an access to productivity enhancing IT, which was not available in earlier decades. This way, we will be cashing in on the *'late comer's advantage'*.

Concluding Remarks

Now, I would like to sum up. Thanks to painstaking policy reforms initiated over the last two decades by successive Governments, I believe that India is at the threshold of 'a golden age of growth', with India's democratic framework being a key growth fundamental. It seems to me that, over time, India has paid the 'fixed costs' of democracy in terms of the creation of institutional infrastructure, traditions and conventions. Further, India's democratic system has also internalised what Prime Minister Vajpayee calls *Coalition Dharma*, showing that coalitions can provide stable government and push economic reforms. This means that in the future, the economy can reap the dividends from the resultant systemic stability. Thus, India — riding the wave of growth fundamentals such as demographic transition, human capital accumulation, improved incentive structures, diffusion of new technologies such as IT, total factor productivity accelerators through 'network industries', and an improved security environment — will be growing at growth rates which can be above 10 per cent per annum i.e., double digit growth rates. There is an ineffable sense of joy for me personally, and professionally, to see India embark on this growth odyssey, a journey that I call 'India: On the growth turnpike'.

Endnotes

[1] The views in this lecture are mine and not of my employers. It draws heavily upon the collaborative work in progress with Arbind Modi, Ajay Shah and Arvind Subramanian. I am grateful to Centre for

Monitoring Indian Economy (CMIE) and National Council of Applied Economic Research (NCAER) for access to their databases.

[2] Delong, J. Bradford (July 2001) 'India since Independence: An Analytic Growth Narrative'; Rodrik, Dani, and Subramanian, Arvind (2004) 'From Hindu Growth to Productivity Surge: The Mystery of the Indian Growth Transition', NBER Working Paper No.10376.

[3] Easterly, William. (2001). 'The Lost Decades: Developing Countries' Stagnation Inspite of Policy Reform 1980–1998', World Bank, February.

[4] Edwards, Sebastian and Yeyati, Eduardo Levy. (2003). 'Flexible Exchange Rates as Shock Absorbers', NBER Working Paper No. 9867, July.

[5] Reinhart, Carmen and Rogoff, Kenneth S. (2002). 'The Modern History of Exchange Rate Arrangements: A Reinterpretation', NBER Working Paper No.8963, June; Patnaik, Ila. (2003). 'India's Policy stance on reserves and the currency', ICRIER Working Paper No.108, September, 2003; Calvo, A. Guillermo and Reinhart, Carmen M. (2002) 'Fear of Floating', *Quarterly Journal of Economics*, Vol.117, Issue 2, May.

[6] Panagariya, Arvind. (2004). 'India's Trade Reform: Progress, Impact and Future Strategy', India Policy Forum, NCAER, March, 2004.

[7] Rodrik, Dani. (1999) 'Where did all the Growth go? External Shocks, Social Conflict, and Growth Collapses', *Journal of Economic Growth*, 4: 358–412, December.

[8] Bhalla, Surjit S. (2003) *Not as Poor, Nor as Unequal, as you Think — Poverty, Inequality and Growth in India, 1950–2000*, Final Report of a research project undertaken for the Planning Commission, Government of India, December 4.

[9] *Indian Economic Survey* (2003–04), Chapter 9, p. 206.

[10] Shah, Ajay (1999) 'Institutional Change on India's Capital Markets', *Economic and Political Weekly*, XXXIV(3-4): 183–94, January; Shah, Ajay and Thomas, Susan. (2000) 'David and Goliath: Displacing a Primary Market', *Journal of Global Financial Markets*, 1(1): 14–21, Spring.

[11] Thomas, Susan. (2003). 'Derivatives Markets in India 2003', *Invest India*, Tata McGraw-Hill.

[12] Bordia, Anand and Bhardwaj, Gautam (2003) 'Rethinking Pension Provision for India', *Invest India*, Tata McGraw-Hill Series; Shah, Ajay (2005) 'Issues in pension system reform in India' in *India's Financial Sector: Recent reforms, future challenges*, Priya Basu (ed), Macmillan, pp. 205–24.

[13] *Report of the Task Force on Direct Taxes*, Government of India, December, 2002; *Report of the Task Force on Indirect Taxes*, Government of India, December, 2002; Shome, Partho (2002) *India's Fiscal Matters*, Oxford University Press

[14] *Fiscal Responsibility and Budget Management Act* (2003), No. 39 of 2003, *The Gazette of India Extraordinary*, Part II, Section 1, No. 43, August.

[15] Gallup, John Luke., Sachs, Jeffrey D., and Mellinger, Andrew D. (1998) 'Geography and Economic Development', NBER Working Paper No.6849, December.

[16] *The East Asian Miracle: Economic Growth and Public Policy* (1993), World Bank, Oxford University Press, September.

[17] Ahluwalia, Montek S. (2002) 'State Level Performance under Economic Reforms in India' in *Economic Policy Reforms and the Indian Economy*, Anne O. Krueger (ed.).

[18] Krugman, Paul (1994) 'The Myth of Asia's Miracle — A Cautionary Fable', *Foreign Affairs*, November/December.

[19] Pradhan, Basanta K., Roy, P.K., Saluja, M.R., and Shetty, S.L. (2003) 'Household Savings and Investment Behaviour in India', *National Council of Applied Economic Research*, September.

[20] Bosworth, Barry and Collins, Susan (2003) 'The Empirics of Growth: An Update', Brookings Paper on Economic Activity 2: 113–79.

[21] Shy, Oz (2001) 'The Economics of Network Industries', February.

2005 K R Narayanan Oration

Message from the President

I am happy to know that the Australia South Asia Research Centre of The Australian National University is hosting the 2005 Narayanan Oration on the theme 'Science and Shaping our Agricultural Future' on September 27, 2005.

I visualize Village Knowledge Centres (VKCs) in Panchayats, which would empower our rural communities. The VKCs would have computers and connectivity and would be windows to the world of knowledge that would reap the benefits of e-governance, tele-education, tele-medicine, e-commerce and e-judiciary initiatives. VKCs ultimately would be used to access village specific information to shape a prosperous future for these communities. An organisation of farmers by the farmers for agricultural farming and marketing is the need of the hour.

On this occasion, I extend my greetings and felicitations to all those associated with the Australia South Asia Research Centre and wish the Oration all success.

A.P.J. Abdul Kalam
New Delhi 2005

Science and Shaping our Agricultural Future

M S Swaminathan

It is a privilege to deliver a lecture in honour of Dr K R Narayanan, immediate Past President of India. Dr Narayanan represents all that is best in Indian culture and democratic system of governance. He rose from the lowest to the highest position in Indian Society by virtue of his innate human and professional qualities. Dr Narayanan knows the pangs of hunger and has therefore been on the forefront of the hunger free India movement. He encouraged scientists to work on problems relevant to the alleviation of poverty and eradication of hunger. I have therefore chosen the topic, 'Science and Shaping our Agricultural Destiny' for this lecture.

Introduction

From the beginning of time, technology has been a key element in the growth and development of societies. The spread of technologies has however been uneven throughout history. In food production, we have now reached the age of biotechnology and precision farming. Many of the technologies like improved seeds are scale neutral with reference to their relevance to farms of varying sizes but are not resource neutral. Inputs are needed for output and hence those who do not have access to inputs tend to get bypassed by technological transformation. Synergy between technology and public policy has therefore remained a pre-condition for technologies to confer benefit to all sections of the farming community, irrespective of the size of their holdings and their innate capacity to mobilise capital and take risks. Among factors of production, access to irrigation water has been a major determinant of technological change, since without assured irrigation, it is difficult to apply nutrients in quantities essential for high yields, even if genetic strains capable of high productivity are available.

Today, global agriculture is witnessing two opposite trends. In many South Asian countries, farm size is becoming smaller and smaller and farmers suffer serious handicaps with reference to the cost-risk-return structure of agriculture. Farm size in most industrialised countries is becoming larger and larger and farmers are supported by heavy inputs of technology, capital and subsidy. The recent breakdown of the Cancun negotiations of the World Trade Agreement in the field of agriculture reflects the polarisation which has taken place in the basic agrarian structure of industrialised and developing countries.

In India, average yields of major food crops remained well below 1 metric ton per hectare for centuries, until the introduction of high yielding varieties in the 1960s. To produce one metric ton of rice the rice plant needs at least 20kgs of nitrogen and appropriate quantities of phosphorus, potash and micronutrients. The native soil fertility was often below this level and hence yields tended to remain below a ton.

The steps taken after independence to improve the productivity of food crops fall under the following major categories:

- Package of technology
- Package of services in areas such as input supply and extension
- Package of public policies in areas such as land reforms, rural infrastructure development, investment in irrigation, input and output pricing policies and assured and remunerative marketing.

Improvement of agricultural production through the productivity pathway is essential for both resource poor farmers and consumers. Casual agricultural labourers are the largest in number among the chronically poor and cultivators the second largest group. Most of the chronically poor were either landless or near-landless. The smaller the farm, the greater is the need for increasing productivity, so that the farm family has a higher marketable surplus. Productivity improvement also tends to reduce the cost of the commodity, thereby benefiting resource poor consumers. Above all productivity improvement is essential for safeguarding the remaining forests, since otherwise forest land will get converted to produce food. Thus, the productivity pathway of agricultural advance helps in strengthening ecological, livelihood and food security.

What we need is an evergreen revolution, which can help to increase productivity in perpetuity without associated ecological harm (Swaminathan 1996). Exploitative agriculture offers great dangers if carried out with only an immediate profit or production motive. The initiation of exploitative agriculture without a proper understanding of the various consequences of every one of the changes introduced into traditional agriculture, and without first building up a proper scientific and training base to sustain it, may only lead us, in the long run, into an era of agricultural disaster rather than one of agricultural prosperity (Swaminathan 1968). We need ecotechnologies rooted in the principles of ecology, economics, gender and social equity and employment generation. The vulnerable sections need job-led economic growth and not jobless growth.

Inspite of striking agricultural progress and democratic decentralisation, chronic and transient poverty and poverty induced malnutrition are widespread. International and national media refer to this as the co-existence of 'grain mountains and hungry millions' (Swaminathan 2005). Section 2 outlines the issues in the context of food security and access, sections 3 and 4 the transition from the green to gene to evergreen revolution in rice and wheat, section 5 provides case studies that show how we can bridge the technological divide and section 6 concludes.

Food Availability, Access, Absorption and Threats to Food Security

Food security was formerly considered essentially in terms of production. It was assumed that adequate food production would ensure adequate availability of food in the market as well as in the household. In the seventies, it became clear that availability alone does not lead to food security. It is becoming evident that even if availability and access are satisfactory, the biological absorption of food in the body is related to the consumption of clean drinking water as well as to environmental hygiene. Finally even if physical and economic access to food is assured, ecological factors will determine the long-term sustainability of food security systems. We have to define food as physical, economic, social and ecological access to balanced diet and clean drinking water, so as to enable every child, woman and man to lead a healthy and productive life. The needs of each age group must be addressed (see cycle approach described by MSSRF 2001). Such an approach will involve the following steps (Swaminathan 2002a; 2002b).

Food Availability

This is a function of both home production and imports. There is no time to relax on the food production front. The present global surplus of food grains is the result of inadequate consumption on the part of the poor, and should not be mistaken as a sign of over-production.

Food Access

Lack of purchasing power deprives a person from access to food even though food is available. Inadequate livelihood opportunities in rural areas are responsible for household nutrition insecurity. For example, India today has over 30 million tonnes of wheat and rice in government godowns; yet poverty induced hunger affects over 200 million persons. It is endemic in south Asia and sub-Saharan Africa (Ramalingaswami *et al.* 1997; WFP 2001). Macro-economic policies, at the national and global level, should be conducive to fostering job-led economic growth based on micro-enterprises supported by micro-credit. Where poverty is pervasive, suitable measures to provide the needed entitlement to food, should be introduced. The State of Maharashtra introduced, nearly 25 years ago, an Employment Guarantee Scheme to assist the poor to earn their daily bread during seasons when opportunities for wage employment are low.

Food Absorption

Lack of access to clean drinking water, poor environmental hygiene and poor health infrastructure, lead to poor assimilation of the food that is consumed. Nutrition security cannot be achieved without environmental hygiene, primary health care and clean drinking water security. Culinary habits also need careful evaluation as some methods of cooking may lead to the loss of vital nutrients.

Threats to Food Security

The most important among the internal threats to sustainable food security is the damage to the ecological foundations essential for sustained agricultural advance, like land, water, forests and biodiversity. Second, in the areas of farm economics, resource flow to the agriculture sector is declining and indebtedness of small and marginal farm families is rising. Input costs are increasing, while factor productivity is declining. Third, a *technology fatigue* has further aggravated farmers' problems, since the smaller the farm the greater is the need for sustained marketable surplus, in order to have cash income. Linkages between the laboratory and the field have weakened and extension services have often little to extend by way of location, time and farming system specific information and advice (chapter on Wake Up Call in the NCF report).

The external threats include the unequal trade bargain inherent in the WTO agreement of 1994, the rapid expansion of proprietary science and potential adverse changes in temperature, precipitation, sea level and ultra violet ß radiation. Though it is now over ten years since the WTO regime started operating in agriculture, serious attempts are yet to be made to launch in rural areas movements for quality literacy (sanitary and phytosanitary measures and codex alimentarius standards of food safety), trade literacy (likely demand-supply and price situation) legal literacy (IPR, Farmers' Rights) and genetic literacy (genetically modified crops). No wonder the prevailing gap between potential and actual yields even with technologies currently on the shelf is very wide (Table 1).

Table 1: Comparative Crop Productivity (Kg/hectare)

Crop	USA	China	India
Maize	8900	4900	2100
Paddy	7500	6000	3000
Soybeans	2250	1740	1050
Seed Cotton	2060	3500	750
Tomato	6250	2400	1430

Source: Wake Up Call Chapter in NCF Report

In the area of technology, there is also need to bridge the growing digital and genetic divides. Post-harvest technology is poor and there is little value addition particularly in the case of fruits, vegetables and spices including a wife range of tubers and medicinal and aromatic plants. Sustainable intensification, ecologically, economically and nutritionally desirable diversification and value addition to the entire biomass are important for raising small and marginal farm families above subsistence level. All this will call for initiating an era of knowledge intensive agriculture. Modern information communication technologies (ICT) afford an opportunity for launching a knowledge revolution in rural India.

Technological Transformation of Productivity, Profitability and Sustainability: Rice

Asia grows most of the world's rice output and 90 per cent of rice is produced by small farmers who depend on it for their livelihood and food security. The role of rice in national and global food security systems will increase, not only because of increases in population and purchasing power, but also because of likely changes in climate and sea level rise due to global warming. An immediate task is bridging the gap between potential and actual yields, widely prevalent in several rice growing countries and particularly in different parts of India. This is possible even at currently available levels of technology, through mutually reinforcing packages of technology, services and public policies. In the decades ahead, more rice will have to be produced under conditions of shrinking per capita arable land and irrigation water availability and expanding biotic and abiotic stresses. Due to breeding efforts based on an appropriate integration of Mendelian and molecular techniques, the ceiling to yield is being raised continuously (Figure 1).

Figure 1: Progress in the Yield Potential of Rice

Potential yield (t/ha)

8000 BC	1900 Land races	1930 Pureline selection	1950 Cross breds	1965 Semidwarfs (IR8)	1990 (IR72)	1995 Indica/ Indica hybrids	2000 New plant type	2005 Indica/ Tropical japonica hybrids	2010 Biotech-nology

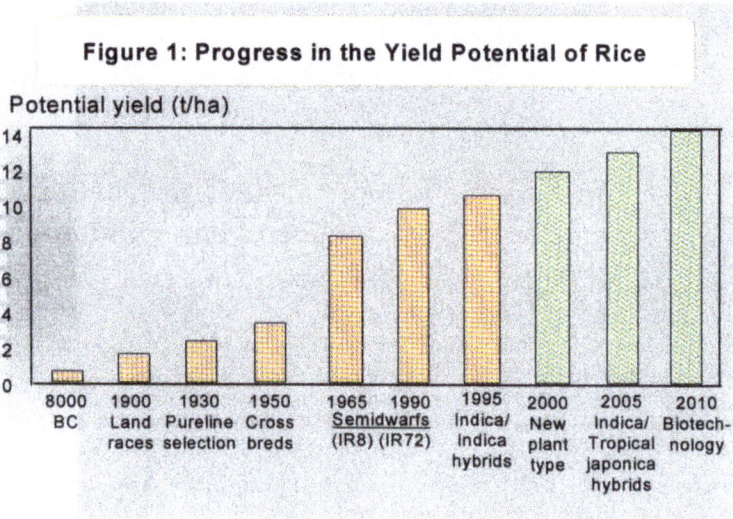

Aided by biotechnology, the greatest potential for productivity gains in yield ceiling in the future lies in rainfed environments (Peacock & Chaudhury 2002). Integrating genetic efficiency with genetic diversity of diverse gene pool through pre-breeding and participatory breeding should be encouraged (Figure 2). Hybrid rice, 'Super rice' and 'Super hybrid rice' are likely to dominate the rice world in the future. What is however important is the initiation of research which can lead to the standardisation of methods of feeding the rice plant for higher yields in an ecologically sustainable manner. Research on breeding and feeding for higher yields should proceed concurrently.

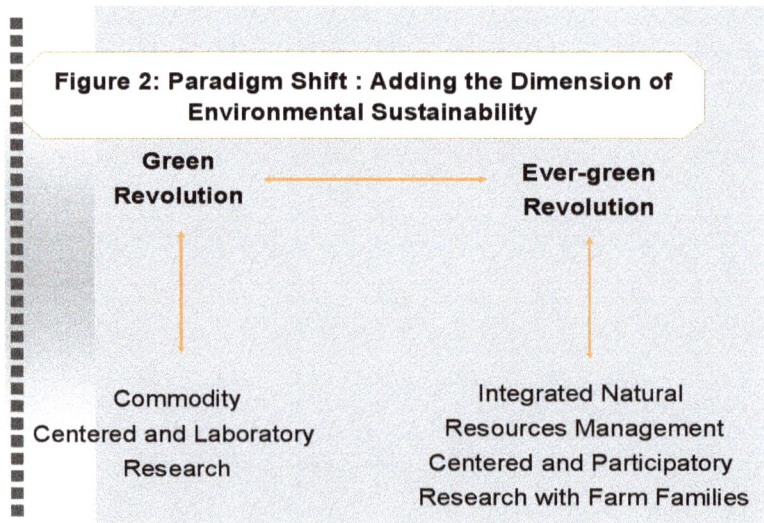

Figure 2: Paradigm Shift : Adding the Dimension of Environmental Sustainability

Green Revolution → Ever-green Revolution

Commodity Centered and Laboratory Research

Integrated Natural Resources Management Centered and Participatory Research with Farm Families

We have several simple and elegant tools that enable us to manipulate the rice genome to elicit desirable responses — tolerance to pests and diseases, moisture stress, salinity-alkalinity, heat, increased photosynthetic efficiency, dry matter accumulation, and source sink partitioning. Rice gene sequence information is widely viewed as an invaluable asset for developing products and technologies. Because of advances in molecular mapping and breeding, there are new opportunities for improving the nutritive qualities of rice, with particular reference to iron, vitamin A and other micronutrients. Under an expanding Intellectual Property Rights (IPR) regime, it is important that research for public good receives the needed support at the national and international levels so that the resource poor can gain from it. Farmers have to achieve revolutionary progress in productivity, quality and value addition. The emerging ecological, economic and social challenges have to be met through partnerships among rice researchers and developmental organizations, committed to the cause of improving the productivity, profitability, sustainability and stability of rice farming systems.

Pingali *et al.* (1997) have described in detail the steps needed to increase rice production in Asia to meet future needs. If global warming and the associated changes in temperature, precipitation and sea level rise do occur, the position of rice in national and global food security systems will increase, since rice has the ability to grow under very diverse environmental conditions. Rice is by far the best-adapted crop to lowland soils that are prone to flooding during wet season. They draw attention to the following challenges facing rice research and development agencies:

- Productivity gains from the exploitation of Green Revolution technologies are close to exhaustion.
- In the absence of further technical change, Asian farmers face increasing costs per tonne of rice produced.
- Adverse agricultural externalities are increasing due to lack of holistic perspective of the farm resource base management.
- Despite an anticipated decline in per capita rice consumption, aggregate Asian demand for rice is expected to increase by 50 to 60 per cent during the 1990–2025 period due to population increase and poverty reduction.
- Economic growth and the commercialization of agricultural systems could reduce the competitiveness of rice relative to other crops and other farm enterprises.
- An upward shift in rice yield frontier is necessary to meet future rice requirements and to sustain farm-level profits.

Compounding these problems, there are potential dangers arising from the diminishing investment in research in institutions devoted entirely to national and international public good and the expanding intellectual property rights (IPR) regime. The question now is how much more improvement can we bring about in productivity without ecological harm? In other words, can we launch an evergreen revolution in rice in the new millennium, marked by sustained advances in productivity, profitability, stability and sustainability of rice farming systems (Swaminathan 1996; 2000; 2002a). How can we also increase the role of rice in the nutritional security of families dependent on it for their dietary energy supply? How can rice production be insulated from the adverse impact of potential changes in precipitation, temperature and rise in sea level? Above all, how can we maintain and strengthen international cooperation in rice improvement?

Increasing Production and Productivity

Bridging the yield gap

Due to imperfect adaptation to local environments, insufficient provision of nutrients and water, and incomplete control of pests, diseases and weeds the present average rice yield is just 40 per cent of what can be achieved even with technologies currently on the shelf. There is considerable scope for further investment in land improvement through drainage, terracing, control of acidification, etc. in areas where these have not already been introduced. While irrigated areas are making good progress, there is need for more attention on intensive research and development in rainfed, low land and upland areas. Ensuring that benefits from technology accrue to resource poor or marginal farmers will require special efforts as outlined in the case studies in section 5.

An integrated approach is necessary to remove the technological, infrastructure and social and policy constraints responsible for the productivity gap and in some cases, productivity decline. Reducing the cost of production through eco-technologies and improving income through efficient production and post-harvest technologies will help to enhance opportunities for both skilled employment and farm income. Public policies should not only pay attention to agrarian reform and input and output pricing, but also to reaching the unreached in technology dissemination through training, techno-infrastructure and trade. A constraints analysis of the type shown in Figure 3 should be undertaken. Public policy on anticipating and avoiding production constrains research on facilitating adoption of new technology by small farmers should receive as much attention as agronomic research.

Future agricultural production programmes will have to be based on a three-pronged strategy designed to foster an evergreen revolution, which leads to increased production without associated ecological and social harm. These strategies include defending the gains already achieved, extending the gains to rainfed areas and making new gains through farming systems diversification and value addition.

Defending the gains already achieved

There is need for stepping up maintenance research for ensuring that new strains of pests and pathogens do not cause crop losses and prevent the introduction of invasive alien species. Water harvesting, watershed development and economic and efficient water use can help to enhance productivity and income considerably. Where water is scarce, high value but low water requiring crops should be promoted. As pulses and oilseeds are important income earning and soil enriching crops, they should be included in rice farming systems.

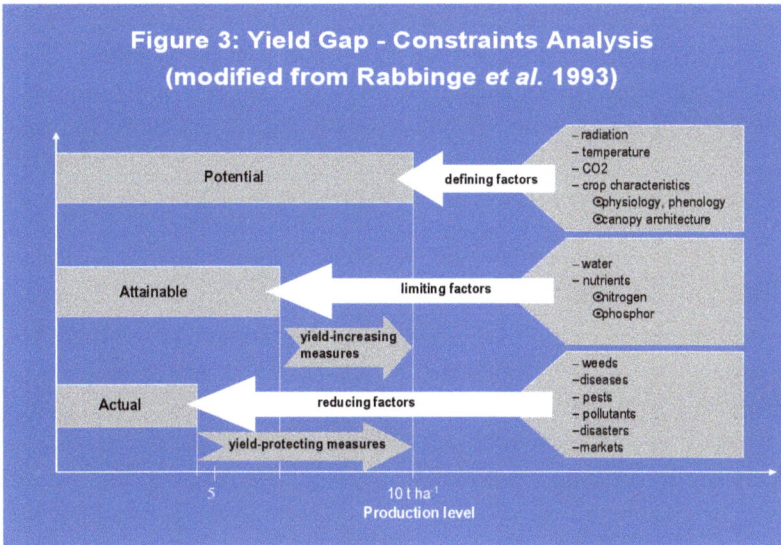

Figure 3: Yield Gap - Constraints Analysis (modified from Rabbinge *et al.* 1993)

Extending the gains

There is need to develop and disseminate eco-technologies for rain-fed and semi-arid, hill and island areas, which have so far been bypassed by modern yield enhancement technologies. Regional imbalances in agricultural development are growing based largely on the availability of assured irrigation on the one hand and assured and remunerative marketing opportunities on the other. The introduction of eco-regional technology missions that look at all the links in the chain and work towards the stipulated goal, aimed at providing appropriate packages of technology, the specific farm infrastructure services required by the techonology (techno-infrastructure), and input and output pricing and marketing policies, will help to include the excluded in agricultural progress. Technologies for elevating and stabilizing yields are available for semi-arid and dry farming areas (Ryan & Spencer 2001). Therefore the emphasis should be on farming systems that can optimize the benefits of natural resources in a sustainable manner and not merely on cropping systems. Dry farming areas are also ideal for the cultivation of low water requiring but high value pulses and oilseeds.

Making new gains

Farming systems intensification, diversification and value-addition should be promoted. Watershed and wasteland atlases should be used for developing improved farming systems, and designing what crops to grow based on soil structure so as to provide more income and jobs. Value addition to primary products should be done at the village itself. This will call for appropriate institutional structures which can help provide key centralized services to small and marginal farm families and provide them with the power of scale in eco-farming involving techniques like integrated pest management, integrated nutrient supply, scientific water management, precision farming, etc. as well as in marketing. A quantum leap in sophistication of management of all production factors will be required to sustain yield gains from the present levels to the commercially feasible threshold of about 80 per cent yield potential (Swaminathan 2001).

Small farm management

Institutional structures, which will confer upon farm families with small holdings, the advantages of scale at both the production and post-harvest phases of agriculture, are urgently needed. For example, thanks to the cooperative method of organisation of milk processing and marketing, India now occupies the first position in the world in milk production. Strategic partnerships with the private sector will help farmers' organisations to have access to assured and remunerative marketing opportunities.

Vital Areas for Sustainable Advances in Rice Productivity

There are great opportunities for achieving higher yields per unit of land; provision of water at the right time to rice farmers enabled them to shift to precision farming methods. The five vital areas of research, development and extension, which need attention from the point of view of achieving environmentally sustainable advances in rice productivity, are soil health and fertility management; water management; integrated plant health management; energy management; and post-harvest management (for more details see Swaminathan 2004).

Evergreen revolution

As earlier mentioned, this implies improvement of productivity in perpetuity without associated ecological harm. Rice scientists should foster an evergreen revolution in rice through partnerships for the development and dissemination of precision farming technologies. The major goals that were proposed for the FAO sponsored International Network for an Evergreen Revolution in Rice by Swaminathan (2002b) are as follows:

- Initiate an Integrated Gene Management programme.
- Improve productivity per unit of input, particularly of nutrients and water and thereby reduce the cost of production.
- Substitute to the extent possible knowledge and farm produced inputs for capital and market-purchased chemicals.
- Enhance the ecological and social sustainability of high-yield technologies.
- Increase farmers' income and opportunities for skilled employment.
- Establish an information grid and farmer-participatory knowledge system for empowering women and men engaged in rice farming with new knowledge and skills, thereby conferring on rice farmers the strengths of Knowledge Societies.

Research Strategies and Priorities

These Strategies include Integrated Gene Management (IGM), integrated efforts in feeding and breeding rice for high productivity, information empowerment, overcoming hidden hunger caused by micronutrient deficiencies and promoting rice as a substrate for oral vaccines.

The IGM programme in rice should be based on conservation, sustainable use and equity in sharing benefits. The over 100,000 strains available today in rice is the result of the conservation ethics of farm and tribal families. Most of them are from Asian countries. India is the largest contributor to this collection followed by Laos (Appa Rao *et al.* 2002).

Overcoming hidden hunger caused by micronutrient deficiencies

The challenge of micronutrient deficiencies in diet is becoming great especially for the chronically poor. Iodine, Vitamin A and iron deficiencies are serious in many parts of the developing world. Worldwide, iron deficiency affects over one billion children and adults. Recent analyses from the United States Institute of Medicine (Earl & Woteki 1998; Potrykus 1997; Swaminathan 2002a) highlight the effect of severe anaemia in accounting for up to one in five maternal deaths. Maternal anaemia is pandemic and is associated with high MMR; anaemia during infancy, compounded by maternal under-nutrition, leads to poor brain development. Iron deficiency is also a major cause of permanent brain damage and death in children and limits the work capacity of adults (Smith & Haddad 2000; Swaminathan 2002b). There is not enough appreciation of the serious adverse implications to future generations arising from the high incidence of low birth weight (LBW) among newborn babies. LBW is a major contributor to stunting and affects brain development in the child. The new millennium will be a knowledge century, with agriculture and industry becoming more knowledge intensive. Denial of opportunities for the full expression of the innate genetic potential for mental development even at birth is the cruelest form of inequity that can prevail in any society (Smith & Haddad 2000). We must take steps to eliminate as soon as possible such inequity at birth leading to a denial of opportunities to nearly one out of every three children born in South Asia, for performing their legitimate role in the emerging knowledge century.

Wherever rice is the staple, a multi-pronged strategy for the elimination of hidden hunger should be developed by rice scientists. IRRI has undertaken research on enriching rice genetically with iron and other micronutrients. Fortification, promotion of balanced diets, new semi-processed foods involving an appropriate blend of rice and micro-nutrient rich millets as well as genetic improvement, could all form part of an integrated strategy to combat the following major nutritional problems in predominantly rice eating families:

- Protein-energy Malnutrition
- Nutritional anaemia (Iron deficiency)
- Vitamin A deficiency
- Iodine deficiency
- Dietary deficiencies of thiamin, riboflavin, fat, calcium, vitamin C and zinc

Swaminathan (2002a) suggested that the International Rice Commission could include nutrition security aspect as an integral part of the International Network. We must fight the serious threat to the intellectual capital of developing countries caused by low birth weight children and hidden hunger (UN Commission on Nutrition). Some of the research areas worthy of attention in this context are described below.

Breeding for nutritional quality

Nutritive quality is as important as cooking quality for countries in tropical Asia, where rice is the principal source of dietary protein, vitamin (B_1) and minerals (Fe, Ca) (Juliano & Villareal 1993). Rice provides about 40 per cent of the protein in the Asian diet. Among the cereal proteins, rice protein is considered to be biologically the richest by virtue of its high digestibility (88 per cent), high lysine content (+ 4 per cent) and relatively better net protein utilization. Yet, it is nutritionally handicapped on account of two factors *viz*: (i) its inherently low protein content (6–8 per cent) and (ii) inevitable milling loss of as much as 15–20 per cent. Unlike in other cereals, increased protein content in rice does not result in decreased protein quality as all of its fractions (glutelin 65 per cent, globulin and albumin 15 per cent and lysine-cysteine rich prolamin 14 per cent) are rich in lysine and other essential amino acids. Even a marginal increase of 2 percentage points of protein, therefore, would mean 10–15 per cent increase in the nutritionally rich protein intake in our diet.

Genetic engineering approaches for correcting micronutrient deficiencies

Breeding for Nutritional Improvement was recommended at the 19th Session of the International Rice Commission, which called for an increase in focus on strategies to combat malnutrition (Philip *et al.* 2000; Gopalan 2001). There are four categories of direct interventions believed to be successful in reducing micronutrients malnutrition; supplementation, fortification, dietary diversification and genetic enhancement. Nutritional status of populations will focus on the potential for improving malnutrition, primarily micronutrient malnutrition through genetic improvement.

Golden rice

About 250 million people worldwide are deficient in vitamin A. Over five million children in South and South-east Asia are reported to suffer from the serious eye disease 'xerophthalmia' every year and about 5,00,000 of them eventually become partially or totally blind due to deficiency of vitamin-A. Besides affecting vision, vitamin-A deficiency predisposes children to varied respiratory and intestinal diseases resulting in high mortality. Researchers from Swiss Federal Institute of Technology inserted these genes from daffodil and a bacterium into temperate rice plants to produce a modified grain, which has sufficient β carotene (precursor of vitamin A) to meet total vitamin A requirements in a typical Asian diet (Ye *et al.* 2000). Golden rice technology was made available to developing nations for research. If this technology can be moved to the production stage, it could represent an important contribution to improved human nutrition. In particular, rice fortified genetically with vitamin A and iron will be very useful to improve the nutritional status of pregnant and nursing women.

Iron deficiency

Iron deficiency anaemia (IDA) is the world's most common nutritional deficiency. It affects pregnant and nursing women and young children most commonly. IDA in mothers predisposes to still births, neonatal mortality, anaemia and low birth weight in infants, and increases the risk of maternal mortality (Swaminathan 2002; Earl & Woteki 1994). Regular intake of iron or administration of iron prevents anaemia. Daily supplementation with iron-folic acid tablets is a low-cost and effective intervention.

Technological Transformation of Productivity, Profitability and Sustainability: Wheat

The rediscovery of Mendel's laws of genetics in 1900 opened up a new era in crop breeding in general, and wheat breeding in particular. Although the art of plant breeding is as old as the beginning of agriculture nearly 12,000 years ago, systematic research in the areas of genetics and cytogenetics, which commenced in the early part of the 20th century, created uncommon opportunities for improving the productivity, profitability, stability and sustainability of wheat production. Even before Mendel (1822–1884), plant hybridizers like Kolreuter, Knight, Gartner and Burbank were able to produce improved varieties of crops through careful observation and selection. The concept of sustainability to which we now attach great importance was recognised long ago as essential for sustained agricultural progress.

During the past 100 years, Mendelian genetics has helped not only to exploit naturally occurring genetic variability but has also accelerated the process of generation, manipulation and combination of new variability. We are now in a state of transition from Mendelian to Molecular breeding. Breeder's eye for selection and for spotting the winner will continue to play an important part in successful plant breeding.

It is projected that global demand for wheat will increase by 40 per cent by the year 2020. Also, 67 per cent of the world's wheat consumption will be in developing countries. Between 1961 and 1990, yield increases accounted for 92 per cent of the additional cereal production in developing countries. In the years ahead, there is no option except to produce more from less per capita land and water resources. Can we sustain the yield revolution in wheat? It will be useful to consider this issue in the context of the genetic pathways which led to the wheat revolution of the 20th century.

Progress in Yield Improvement

Wheat is a crop of great antiquity. We can identify at least 4 major phases in the evolution of wheat breeding during the 20th century.

Phase I (1900–1930): Early days of Mendelian genetics

Soon after the re-discovery of Mendel's laws of genetics in 1900, systematic work on the genetics of resistance to stem, leaf and stripe rusts started. Selection from naturally occurring genetic variability also began.

During the early part of the 20th century, the major breeding challenges were in the area of resistance to rusts and grain quality improvement. A study of the yield improvement achieved between 1900 to 1930 in USA shows only limited progress. The emphasis was more on stability of production through disease resistance than on achieving quantum jumps in yield.

Phase II (1930–1960): Enlarging the base of theory and its application

This period was marked by the introduction of cytogenetic knowledge and tools in wheat improvement. This phase of wheat improvement was characterised by widening the gene pool used by breeders, incorporation of genes for the semi-dwarf plant type, shuttle breeding and breeding to meet the challenge of physiologic specialisation in pathogens.

Phase III (1960–1980): The green revolution phase

This phase is also generally referred to as the *green revolution* era. It was characterised by revolutionary progress in improving wheat production and productivity in several developing countries like India and Pakistan. The introduction of the semi-dwarf plant type enabled the wheat plant to yield well under conditions of good soil fertility and irrigation water management. Farmers who were used to harvesting 1 to 2 tonnes of wheat per hectare started harvesting over 5 tonnes/ha (Swaminathan 1993). In view of the widespread interest in this remarkable transformation in India's agricultural destiny, it will be useful to summarise some of the highlights.

During 1942–43, the Indian sub-continent witnessed a severe famine in Bengal resulting in the death of nearly three million children, women and men. This prompted Jawaharlal Nehru, the first Prime Minister of Independent India to remark in 1948, 'everything else can wait, but not agriculture'.

In 1964, a National Demonstration Programme was started in farmers' fields, both to verify the results obtained in research plots and to introduce farmers to the new opportunities opened up by semi-dwarf varieties for improving very considerably the productivity of wheat. When small farmers, with the help of scientists, harvested over five tonnes of wheat per hectare, its impact on the minds of other farmers was electric. The clamour for seeds began and the area under high yielding varieties of wheat rose from four hectares in 1963-64 to over four million hectares in 1971–72. A small Government programme became a mass movement (Swaminathan 1993). Wheat production in India rose from 10 million tonnes in 1964 to 17 million tonnes in 1968. In 1999, Indian farmers harvested about 72 million tonnes of wheat, taking India to the second position in the world in wheat production.

Greater interdisciplinary collaboration among breeders, plant pathologists, agronomists, physiologists, soil scientists, entomologists, nemotalogists, economists and other social scientists, climatologists and policy makers was the principal factor responsible for the success of the green revolution. The green revolution era can also be termed *the golden age in interdisciplinary and international collaboration* in wheat improvement for sustainable food security. The concept of shuttle breeding transcended continental boundaries and a global college of wheat scientists emerged. Above all, the green revolution showed how to generate synergy between technology and public policy.

Phase IV (1980–2000): Transition from Mendelian to molecular breeding

The last 20 years have witnessed great progress in using sophisticated approaches to wheat breeding. Hybrid wheat is reaching the possibility of large scale commercial cultivation. The use of genetic-cytoplasmic male sterility and of chemical hybridizing agents (CBA) are responsible for progress in the commercial exploitation of hybrid wheat. Different management practices such as lower seed rate, raised bed planting, split nitrogen application and different row width are being tried to enhance the expression of hybrid superiority. The cultivation of hybrid wheat is slowly gaining in momentum in South Africa, Australia (New South Wales), China, Argentina and France. The use of wild relatives in genetic engineering is growing (Khush & Baenziger 1998). The global average yield of wheat is 2.5 t/ha; the low average yield of wheat is because of large areas of wheat being under rainfed conditions. Progress in improving yield is however steady. So far, advances in yield improvement have been associated with increases in harvest index (i.e., grain-straw ratio). Further advances will depend upon greater biomass production and not merely on partitioning the phytosynthates.

Challenges Ahead

At the dawn of the 21st century, we can look back with pride and satisfaction on the revolution, which farm men and women have brought about in our agricultural history during the 20th century. The Punjab farmer, hardworking, skilled and determined, has been the backbone of the revolution.

While we can and should rejoice about the past achievements of farmers, scientists, extension workers and policy makers, there is no room for complacency. We will face several new problems, of which the following are important.

- First, increasing population leads to increased demand for food and reduced per capita availability of arable land and irrigation water.
- Second, improved purchasing power and increased urbanisation lead to higher per capita food grain requirements due to an increased consumption of animal products.
- Third, marine fish production is tending to become stagnant and coastal aquaculture has resulted in ecological and social problems.

- Fourth, there is increasing damage to the ecological foundations of agriculture, such as land, water, forests, biodiversity and the atmosphere and there are distinct possibilities for adverse changes in climate and sea level.
- Fifth, while dramatic new technological developments are taking place, particularly in the field of biotechnology, their environmental, food safety and social implications are still being debated.
- Finally, gross capital formation in agriculture is tending to decline in both public and private sectors during the present decade. The rate of growth in rural non-farm employment has been poor.

Since land and water will be shrinking resources for agriculture, there is no option in the future except to produce more food and other agricultural commodities from less per capita arable land and irrigation water. In other words, the need for more food has to be met through higher yields per unit of land, water, energy and time. It would therefore be useful to examine how science can be mobilised for raising further the ceiling to biological productivity without associated ecological harm. It will be appropriate to refer to the emerging scientific progress on the farms as an evergreen revolution, to emphasise that the productivity advance is sustainable over time since it is rooted in the principles of ecology, economics, social and gender equity and employment generation.

The green revolution based on Mendelian genetics has so far helped to keep the rate of growth in food production above population growth rate. The green revolution was however, the result of public good research supported by public funds. The technologies of the emerging gene revolution based on molecular genetics in contrast, are spearheaded by proprietary science and can come under monopolistic control. How can we take the fruits of the gene revolution to the unreached? This is a challenge, which we need to address.

I would like to list 5 major challenges, which will confront the wheat scientists during this century.

Equity

The Convention on Biological Diversity (CBD) stipulates that plant exploration, collection and introduction should be based on the principles of prior informed consent and equity in benefit sharing. Therefore exchange of wheat genetic resources in the future will be possible only on the basis of Material and Knowledge Transfer Agreements.

Ecology

Ecological sustainability of high productivity will be an important determinant in relation to the choice of technologies. For example, if hybrid wheat can enable us to produce 8 to 10 t/ha, over 300 kg. of nitrogen will be needed by the crop. It is obvious that if the nutrient needs of hybrid or other high-yielding wheat varieties are to be met entirely through mineral fertilizers, there will be serious environmental problems including nitrate pollution of ground water. Hence, success in achieving high productivity on a sustained basis will depend upon our ability to develop new methods of feeding the plant. Research on breeding and feeding should be carried out concurrently by a team of breeders, physiologists, agronomists and soil scientists.

Concerns relating to genetically modified organisms (GMOs)

There are growing public and political concerns relating to GMOs. The concerns relate to food and environmental safety and bioethics. It is essential that these concerns are carefully addressed through a mechanism for risk-benefit analysis, which inspires public confidence. An integrated disease management strategy should be developed to ensure that GMO's with novel genetic combinations for disease resistance do not break down due to the emergence of new physiological strains of pathogens. Also, regulatory procedures should be transparent and should inspire public confidence. There is also need for integrating molecular breeding with organic farming methods.

Expansion of proprietary science

The world is witnessing an expansion of proprietary science governed by Intellectual Property Rights (IPR). Public good research supported from public funds, in contrast, is shrinking. What will be the impact of such a situation on international varietal or other trials organised by CIMMYT? Is the golden age of cooperative research coming to an end? How can we find a balance between public good and private profit?

Climate change and safeguarding genetic diversity

Will molecular breeding resulting in 'super wheats' lead to a high degree of genetic homogeneity in farmers' fields? We know that genetic homogeneity will enhance genetic vulnerability to biotic and abiotic stresses. Hence, we should foster an integrated programme of pre-breeding and participatory breeding. Pre-breeding will help to generate novel genetic combinations, while participatory breeding with farm families will help to combine genetic efficiency with genetic diversity. Numerous location specific varieties can be developed in this manner. This will be the most effective way of meeting challenges arising from potential changes in temperature, precipitation and sea level as a result of global warming arising from the growing imbalance between carbon emissions and absorption.

Sustaining and Strengthening Agricultural Progress

In a predominantly agricultural country like ours, agricultural progress serves as the most effective safety net against hunger and deprivation. There is need for intensifying our efforts to improve agricultural productivity, quality and income. An urgent need in this area is the strengthening of institutional structures, which can help to confer on small and marginal farmers, the ecological and economic benefits of scale at both the production and post-harvest phases of farming. The following are some of the institutional structures whose reach has to be extended.

Without socially relevant and beneficial institutional structures, the extrapolation domain of successful experiences and development efforts will remain limited.

S. No	Sector	Institutional Mechanism
1.	Dairy	Cooperatives
2.	Poultry	Egg Coordination Council
3.	Integrated on-farm and off-farm employment	Biovillages
4.	Power of scale to small producers	Small Farmers' Agri-business Consortium
5.	Technological upgrading of production and post-harvest sectors	Agri-Clinics Agri-business Centres
6.	Group action for micro-enterprises supported by micro-credit	Market-driven Self-help Groups
7.	Timely and affordable credit	Kisan Credit Cards, Integrated Informal and Formal banking systems
8.	Operation of minimum support price	Food corporation of India and State Food Corporations, as well as assured buy-back arrangement and contract farming by the private sector

Dr K R Narayanan inaugurated the JRD Tata Ecotechnology Centre at the M S Swaminathan Research Foundation (MSSRF) in 1998. In the second part of my lecture, I shall briefly summarise the work done in MSSRF on issues relating to linking ecological security with food and livelihood security in a mutually reinforcing manner.

In 2005, MSSRF whose work has always received encouragement and support from Dr K R Narayanan will be completing 15 years of work in the areas of research, education, capacity building, mentoring, policy advocacy and networking. In retrospect, the decision made in 1990 to choose integrated coastal zone management for priority attention with a view to linking the ecological security of coastal areas and the livelihood security of coastal communities (both fisher and farming families) in a mutually reinforcing manner has proved to be a wise one. The Coastal System Research (CSR) programme of MSSRF was designed to give concurrent scientific attention to sea and land surfaces along the shoreline. The CSR programme was initiated in anticipation of potential adverse changes in sea level as a result of global warming. An early scientific step in this process was the conservation of mangrove genetic resources and the rehabilitation of degraded mangrove wetlands in Tamil Nadu, Andhra Pradesh, Orissa and West Bengal. Such mangrove forests served as 'bio-shields' during the Tsunami attack on 26 December 2004. They had also served a similar purpose during the super cyclone in Orissa in 1999. These observations have helped to generate at both the political and public levels interest in the development of bio-shields along the shoreline.

The following are among the major contributions of the CSR programme during 1990–2005.

- Restoration of degraded mangrove wetlands along the east coast of India: the area restored by MSSRF scientists alone comes to 1475 ha of degraded area restored with the help of 5240 families organized in 33 village mangrove councils. Nearly 7 million saplings were planted.
- Conservation strategy for mangrove genetic resources in the Asia–Pacific Region and the establishment of a Genetic Garden for meeting the challenge of sea level rise at Pichavaram, Tamil Nadu
- Genome mapping of mangrove species (*Avecinnia marina*) and the identification and transfer of genes for sea water tolerance from *A.marina* to rice, mustard and pulses.
- Development of a trusteeship mode of management of the Gulf of Mannar Biosphere and helping to create the first Biosphere Trust in the world, with the support of the Global Environment Facility and the Governments of Tamil Nadu and India
- Development of integrated Bio-shield — Biovillage — Village Knowledge Centre Programmes in coastal areas.
- Development of a Code for the participatory management of mangrove ecosystems, involving cooperative action among fisher and farm communities and Forest and Fisheries departments.
- Development of a comprehensive strategy for the rehabilitation of Tsunami ravaged coastal areas in Tamil Nadu, Pondicherry, Andhra Pradesh, Kerala and the Andaman and Nicobar Islands
- Drawing national and international attention to the urgent need for conserving mangrove wetlands and promoting the adoption of a *Charter for Mangroves* .
- Organising national and international training programmes for creating a cadre of well trained Mangrove forest managers.
- Preparation of comprehensive Atlases of the Mangrove forests of Tamil Nadu, Andhra Pradesh and Orissa

- Standardisation and popularization of mangrove propagation methods based on both vegetative and micro-propagation techniques; and helping local communities to undertake the raising and planting of mangrove forests.
- Preparation of a Tool Kit for raising bio-shields in coastal areas.
- Establishment of the first community developed and managed artificial reef in the Gulf of Mannar area based on the technology developed by the Central Marine Fisheries Research Institute
- Developing eco-agriculture strategies for coastal drylands through participatory evaluation and propagation of varieties of pulses developed at the Bhabha Atomic Research Centre through mutation breeding, and the establishment of green belts and genetic garden of horticultural crops for sustainable food and livelihood security.
- Launching a Fish for All movement at Kolkata in December, 2003 in association with the World Fish Centre (ICLARM) located in Penang, Malaysia, to promote sustainable capture and culture fisheries movements.
- Advocacy for the adoption of aquarian reform measures designed to promote harmony between artisenal and mechanized fisheries as well as aquaculture and agriculture.

The CSR approach helped MSSRF to propose a comprehensive and integrated strategy for launching a 'Beyond Tsunami' programme based on concurrent attention to ecological, livelihood, agronomic, psychological and educational rehabilitation. The experience gained by MSSRF in developing integrated coastal zone management procedures helped a National Committee set up by the Ministry of Environment and Forests under my Chairmanship to review the Coastal Regulation Zone Notification of 1991, to propose 12 basic guiding principles for the sustainable and scientific management of the Coastal Zone. Some of these are:

- Ecological and cultural security, livelihood security and national security should be the cornerstones of an integrated coastal zone management policy.
- The coastal zone would include an area from territorial limits (12 nautical miles), including its sea-bed to the administrative boundaries or the biological boundaries demarcated on the landward side of the sea coast. The coastal zone management should also include the inland tidal water bodies influenced by tidal action and the land area along such water bodies. This area should be taken up for an integrated, cohesive, multi-disciplinary and multi-sectoral coastal area management and regulatory system
- Regulation, education and social mobilization should be the three major components of a participatory and sustainable Coastal Zone Management strategy. Panchayati Raj institutions in coastal areas should be fully involved in the educational and social mobilization programmes.

- Coastal regulation needs to be based on sound scientific and ecological principles and should safeguard both natural and cultural heritage. Heritage sites need particular care and should be conserved in their pristine purity. These include areas of environmental significance, rich in biodiversity and scenic beauty. Bird sanctuaries, parks and breeding grounds of migratory birds should be protected.

- The precautionary approach should be used where there are potential threats of serious or irreversible damage to ecologically fragile critical coastal systems and to living aquatic resources. Scientific uncertainty should not be used as an excuse for the unsustainable exploitation of coastal resources — both living and non-living.

- Ecological economics should underpin economic activities, so that present day interests and future prospects are not antagonistic. Significant biological, cultural and natural assets should be considered incomparable, invaluable and irreplaceable and should receive overriding priority in the allocation of resources for coastal area protection and conservation

- Coastal policy and regulations should be guided by the principles of gender and social equity as well as intra-generational and inter-generational equity, (i.e., the interests of future generations). They should be based on Mahatma Gandhi's dictum, 'Nature provides for everyone's needs, but not for anyone's greed'. All stakeholders should be involved in decision making. Precious biological wealth, coming under Marine Biosphere Reserves, should be managed in a Trusteeship mode, with all the stakeholders protecting the unique natural wealth of biosphere reserves as Trustees and not as owners. A case study should be made on how the Gulf of Mannar Biosphere Trust is functioning, so that the Trusteeship pattern of sustainable management by the principal stakeholders can be replicated.

- The regeneration of mangrove wetlands, coral reefs and sea grass beds as well as the promotion of coastal forestry and agro-forestry will confer both short and long term ecological and livelihood benefits. Carbon sequestration through coastal bio-shields will make an important contribution to promoting a balance between carbon emission and absorption, in addition to offering protection during coastal storms and calamities like tsunami. An important lesson taught by the tsunami disaster is that the rehabilitation of degraded mangrove forests and the raising of coastal plantations of salicornia, casuarinas, Vetiver and appropriate species of halophytes will represent a 'win-win' situation both for nature and coastal human habitations. No further time should be lost in initiating a national coastal bio-shield movement along the coasts of the mainland of India as well as islands. This can be a priority task under the National Rural Employment Guarantee and Food for Work Programmes.

- The severe loss of life and livelihoods as well as property caused by tsunami in Andaman & Nicobar Islands and in the coastal regions of Tamil Nadu, Kerala, Andhra Pradesh and Pondicherry teaches us that short term commercial interests should not be allowed to undermine the ecological security of our coastal areas. Human memory tends to be short and neglecting the lessons of tsunami will be equivalent to writing off the future of coastal communities.

Based on the experience gained during the last 15 years, it is proposed to establish in Chidambaram a Resource Centre for Integrated Coastal Zone Management, for the purpose of imparting training in the erection of bio-shields, the development of biovillages and the establishment of Village Knowledge Centres. Tool Kits for these purposes have already been prepared.

In addition to the above, steps have been taken in association with the Tata Relief Committee and the World Fish Centre (ICLARM) to establish a Fish for All Training and Resource Centre at Akkarapettai village near Nagapattinam for imparting training in all aspects of capture and culture fisheries through the principle of learning by doing. The Centre will give attention to capacity building of fisher women and men in every step in the chain of capture / culture to consumption.

During 2004–05, MSSRF's strategic and participatory research to meet the challenges of climate change, which has been so far confined to the coastal zone, was extended to the arid and semi-arid areas of Andhra Pradesh and Rajasthan with financial and technical help of the Swiss Agency for Development Cooperation (SDC) and in partnership with Action for Food Production (AFPRO) and the National Institute of Agricultural Extension Management (MANAGE). This project will help to study vulnerability to adverse changes in temperature and precipitation and develop mitigation and adaptation strategies. Such proactive measures are essential to prevent human suffering resulting from agricultural collapse during drought and flood. The climate change programme will take into account the impact of radiation, carbon dioxide concentration in the atmosphere, temperature and precipitation. It will also help to understand and chronicle traditional coping mechanisms, so that these can be conserved and strengthened. Computer simulation models on the impact of variations in temperature and precipitation will be developed and contingency plans to mitigate the adverse impact of climate change will be introduced.

Besides developing a methodology for conserving the Gulf of Mannar Biosphere Reserve for posterity through a multi-stakeholder trusteeship system of management, MSSRF has evolved during the last 15 years three other major institutional innovations in areas of significance to sustainable food and livelihood security and poverty eradication. These are described briefly below.

Community Nutrition and Water Security System

This system introduced in the Koraput district of Orissa consists of organizing field gene banks (*insitu* on-farm conservation), seed banks, genetic enhancement through participatory breeding, water banks (i.e., water harvesting and saving in farm ponds), and Grain Banks, as shown in Fig. 4.

This system helps to enlarge the food basket by facilitating the inclusion of millets and other under-utilised but nutritious crops in the Community Grain Bank. Such a decentralised Community managed Nutrition Security system helps to foster concurrent attention to conservation, cultivation, consumption and commerce. The tribal community of Koraput pioneering this system was given the Equator Initiative Award by UNDP at the World Summit on Sustainable Development held at Johannesburg in 2002.

Currently there are 2,34,676 village Panchayats in 31 States and Union Territories. In addition, there are traditional councils in Meghalaya, Mizoram and Nagaland. Each of these Panchayats/local bodies can spearhead the Community Food and Water Security movement. This will be the fastest and a sustainable method of making hunger history.

Fostering Job-Led Economic Growth

The most serious challenge facing India is overcoming the famine of jobs or sustainable livelihood opportunities in rural India. MSSRF, whose mandate is imparting a pro-poor, pro-nature and pro-woman orientation to technology development and dissemination, designed and developed the biovillage model of sustainable human well being for this purpose in 1992. The biovillage concept involves the technological upgradation of agriculture and agro-based enterprises in villages through ecotechnologies developed by blending frontier technologies like information and biotechnologies as well as space, nuclear and renewable energy technologies with traditional ecological prudence. Thus, the biovillage based on the economics of human dignity, capitalizes on the benefits conferred by ecotechnology to both the environment and the rural economy. By giving simultaneous attention to on-farm and non-farm employment, the biovillage promotes job-led economic growth and helps to transfer poor families from the primary to the secondary and tertiary sectors of economic activity. This model is now being adopted both in other parts of India and other countries like Bangladesh and Mozambique.

The principal features of the biovillage model of sustainable and equitable rural development are shown in Fig.5

With the help of the Technology Information Forecasting and Assessment (TIFAC) programme of the Govt. of India, a Business Plan was prepared for establishing Rice BioParks. A wide range of economically viable business activities were identified for producing value-added products from rice straw, husk, bran and grain. Business plans were prepared for nearly 28 different enterprises.

Thus, the biomass of cultivated plants can provide opportunities for new enterprises. Similarly, the production and marketing of the biological software essential for sustainable agriculture such as, biofertilizers, biopesticides, vermiculture etc., could help self help groups (SHG) of women and men to enhance their income. MSSRF organized a workshop for sharing experiences on SHGs. It became clear at the workshop that SHGs can become economically sustainable only if they have backward linkages to technology and credit, and forward linkages to markets and management. MSSRF has developed an accounting software for helping SHGs to maintain both accuracy and transparency in accounting.

With the help of the Central Food Technology Research Institute, Mysore, training in post-harvest processing was given to trainees from Ladakh to help them prepare value-added products from apricot and seabuckthorn. Similarly, technical advice was given to the Sher-E-Kashmir University of Agricultural Science and Technology of Kashmir in Srinagar for establishing a Womens' Biotechnology Park at Srinagar on the lines of the one functioning in Chennai.

Under the International Year of Rice Year Programme, consultations were held at Koraput in Orissa, Pattambi in Kerala and Shillong in Meghalaya for reviewing the current status of research on medicinal and aromatic rices. Detailed scientific strategies were developed for the improvement of the *Navara* rice of Kerala and *Kalajeera* rice of Koraput through participatory breeding and knowledge management. In all such programmes the role of women in conservation and enhancement of genetic resources was given specific attention.

Centre

The third major institutional innovation developed by MSSRF for transforming the rural economy is the computer-aided and internet connected Village Knowledge Centre.

The work undertaken by MSSRF in setting up community centered and managed Village Knowledge Centres (VKC) in Pondicherry villages since 1998 based on modern information and communication technologies (ICT) with financial support from IDRC of Canada has shown that ICT helps to improve the timeliness and efficiency of farm operations and enhances income through producer-oriented markets. Also, experience has shown that bridging the digital divide is a powerful method of bridging the gender divide. Knowledge connectivity therefore confers multiple economic and social benefits. The VKC operates on the principles of social inclusion and giving voice to the voiceless.

The information provided, which includes location-specific data on entitlements to different Government schemes, is demand-driven and is in the local language. For example, in Union Territory of Pondicherry there are over 150 schemes designed to help the poor; yet nearly 20 per cent of families are below the poverty line. After the onset of the digital age, knowledge on entitlements and how to access them has grown rapidly. The VKC will be a powerful instrument for operationalising the provisions of the Right to Information Act (2005).

Encouraged by the ability of rural women and men to take to ICT like fish to water, MSSRF initiated in 2003, two major steps to take ICT to every one of the over 600,000 villages in India by 15 august, 2007, which marks the 60th anniversary of 'our tryst with destiny', to quote Jawaharlal Nehru. The first is the organization of a National Alliance for Mission 2007: Every Village a Knowledge Centre which provides a platform for partnership to all committed to the cause of extending the power of ICT to rural India. The National Alliance has now over 150 members comprising Central and State Government agencies, business and industry, academia and non-governmental and mass media organizations.

The second is the establishment of the Jamsetji Tata National Virtual Academy for Rural Prosperity with generous support from the Tata Education Trust. The Internet — community radio combination is a powerful method of reaching the unreached in terms of delivery of dynamic information. Public policy in promoting the use of community radio should be based on the following principle enunciated by the Supreme Court in its judgment delivered in December1995, 'Air waves constitute public property and must be used for advancing public good'. This is the same principle enshrined in the Dandi March movement of Mahatma Gandhi in relation to sea water, which is the basis of MSSRF's programme on sea water farming for coastal area prosperity.

At a recent meeting held at MSSRF, Panchayati Raj leaders have assured that they will provide space, electricity and telephone connection for establishing VKCs in the Panchayat premises. Thus, all the 234676 Village Panchayats in 31 States and Union Territories as well as Traditional Councils in the N.E. States can be brought together under the umbrella of the National Alliance. A hub-spokes model will help to reach all villages from Panchayat VKCs. Such Centres can be operated by ICT-Self-help Groups of rural women and men. MSSRF is assisting NABARD to organize about 10000 ICT — SHGs in 10 States of the country during 2005-06,

Besides connectivity and content, capacity building is essential for ensuring local ownership of VKCs. This is where the Jamsetji Tata National Virtual Academy (NVA) of MSSRF hopes to play a key role. The President of India, Dr APJ Abdul Kalam inducted the first 137 Fellows of the NVA drawn from 15

States on 11 July 2005 at New Delhi. Microsoft is providing generous support for capacity building under its Unlimited Potential programme.

The Fellows of NVA are rural women and men who have studied up to the tenth class or up to the first degree. They serve as Master Trainers and undertake the training of other rural women and men as well as children. These grassroots academicians will be the torchbearers of the rural knowledge revolution. Another significant development in taking the benefits of the space age to the rural poor was the inauguration by the Prime Minister of India, Dr Manmohan Singh on 18 October 2004 of an ISRO–MSSRF joint initiative in setting up Village Resource Centres (VRCs) which can link rural families to the best available sources of knowledge in medicine and health care, education, agriculture, markets and government programmes. This programme which initially linked MSSRF (Chennai) to VRCs in Thiruvayaru, Sempatti and Thangachimadam in Tamil Nadu is being extended to Chidambaram, Pudukottai, Pondicherry, Nagapattinam and Kanyakumari during this year. With the help of the Indian Space Research Organisation, additional centers are being opened in Tsunami affected areas and in Farmers' 'distress hotspots' in Kerala, Andhra Pradesh, Maharashtra and Karnataka. These are areas where suicides by farmers occur. Those operating the computer aided knowledge system at such Centres will be either wives or daughters or sons of those who were driven to take their lives. This will help to provide a sense of realism and urgency in achieving a match between content and the need to save livelihoods and lives. While VKC operates at the village level, the VRC is designed to cover a Block and thereby serve as a resource center for all the villages in the Block. The design of a VKC is on the lines shown in Fig. 6.

The Prime Minister of India has announced a well-funded Bharat Nirman programme to accelerate progress in providing urban amenities in rural areas and to bring an additional ten million hectares under assured irrigation. Knowledge connectivity should be the backbone of the Bharat Nirman programme, since it is fundamental to deriving maximum benefit, in terms of a better quality of life in villages, from the investment on roads, telephone connectivity and other forms of physical connectivity. The involvement of Panchayats and Gram Sabhas in providing the needed logistic and policy support will ensure the efficient functioning of VKCs. To begin with VKC should be tools of information, knowledge and skill empowerment of rural families, particularly of the economically and socially under privileged sections of the society. This is a fundamental responsibility of Government. Hence, the initial expenses should be met from the Bharat Nirman Programme and the Universal Service Obligation (USO) Fund. By the end of this decade (i.e., by 2010), the VKCs will become vibrant centers of economic activity and will provide opportunities for outsourcing of assignments from urban to rural areas. They will then become not only economically self-reliant but will help to create a wide range of skilled jobs for youth in villages. A VKC centred Bharat Nirman will be the most effective method of fostering rural and agrarian prosperity and arresting the unplanned migration of the rural poor to urban areas resulting in the proliferation of urban slums. Therefore, knowledge connectivity through VKCs should be the corner stone of a New Deal for Rural India.

What motivates the scientists and scholars of MSSRF are the words of the Poet Rabindranath Tagore

> With your mind intent, cross this sea of chaos
> And sail to that shore of new creation

References

Appa Rao, S., Bounphanousay, C., Schiller, J.M. and Jackson, M.T. 2002a. 'Collection, classification, and conservation of cultivated and wild rices of the Lao PDR', *Genetic Resources and Crop Evolution*, 49, 75–81.

Earl, R. and Woteki, C.E. (eds) 1994. *Iron deficiency anemia: recommended guidelines for the prevention, detection and management among US children and women of childbearing age*. Institute of Medicine.

Food and Nutrition Bulletin, 21(3), September 2000, Supplement, Ending Malnutrition by 2020: An Agenda for Change in the Millennium, Final Report to the ACC/SCN by the Commission on the Nutrition Challenges of the 21st Century, United Nations University Press

Gopalan, C. 2001. Combating Vitamin A Deficiency and Micronutrient Malnutrition through dietary improvement, MSSRF, Chennai (mimeographed).

Juliano, B.O. and Villareal, C.P. 1993. *Grain quality evaluation of world rices*. IRRI: Manila.

Khush, Gurdev S. and Baenziger, P. Stephen 1998. 'Crop improvement: emerging trends in rice and wheat', in V.L. Chopra, R.B. Singh and A. Varma (eds), *Crop Productivity and Sustainability — Shaping the Future*, Proceedings of the 2nd International Crop Science Congress, pp. 113–25.

MSSRF (M.S. Swaminathan Research Foundation). 2001. *Community Grain Bank: An Instrument for Local Food Security*. MSSRF, Chennai.

Peacock, K. and Chaudhury, A. 2002. 'The impact of gene technologies on the use of genetic resources', in J. M. M. Engels, V. Ramanatha Rao, A.H.D. Brown and M.T. Jackson (eds), *Managing Plant Genetic Diversity*, 23–31. IPGRI.

Philip, James et al. 2000. 'Ending malnutrition by 2020: an agenda for change in the millennium', *Food and Nutrition Bulletin*, 21(13): 88.

Pingali, P.L., Hossain, H., and Gerpacio, R.V. 1997. *Asian Rice Bowls: The Returning Crisis*, CAB International in association with IRRI, p. 341.

Potrykus, I. 1997. Transgenic rice (Oryza sativa) endosperm expressing daffodil (Narcissus pseudonarcissus) phytoene synthase.

Ramalingaswami, V., Johnson, U. and Rohde, J. 1997. 'Malnutrition: A South Asian Enigma', in Stuart Gillespie (ed.), *Malnutrition in South Asia*, Rosa Publication 5. Nepal: UNICEF.

Ryan, J.G. and Spencer, D.C. 2001. *Future Challenges and Opportunities for Agricultural R&D in the Semi-Arid Tropics*. Patancheru: ICRISAT.

Smith, L.C. and Haddad, L. 2000. *Overcoming Child Malnutrition in Developing Countries: Past Achievements and Future Choices*. Washington D.C.: International Food policy Research Institute.

Swaminathan, M.S. 1968. 'The Age of Algeny, Genetic Destruction of Yield Barriers and Agricultural Transformation', Presidential Address, Agricultural Science Section, Fifty-fifth Indian Science Congress, Varanasi, January.

Swaminathan, M.S. (ed.) 1993. *Wheat Revolution: A Dialogue*, Madras: Macmillan India Ltd, pp. 164.

Swaminathan, M.S. 1996. *Sustainable Agriculture: Towards an Evergreen Revolution*, pp. 232. Delhi: Konark Publishers Pvt. Ltd.

Swaminathan, M.S. 2000. 'Bridging the nutritional divide', *The little magazine*, II(6), available at http://www.littlemag.com/hunger/swami.html.

Swaminathan, M.S. 2000. 'An evergreen revolution', *Biologist*, 47(2): 85–9.

Swaminathan, M.S. 2001. 'Food Security and sustainable development', Current Science, 81, 948–54.

Swaminathan, M.S. 2002a. 'Building a National Nutrition Security System', paper presented at India-ASEAN Eminent Persons Lecture Series 11, Jan 2002, FAO, Bangkok.

Swaminathan, M.S. 2002b. 'Nutrition in the Third Millennium: Countries in Transition', Plenary Lecture 17th International Congress on Nutrition Vienna, 27–31 August 2002.

Swaminathan, M.S. 2004. 'Technological change and food production: implications for vulnerable sections', Working Paper 20, CPRC-IIPA, New Delhi.

Swaminathan, M.S. 2005. *India's Greatest Living Industry: Hundred Years Later*, IARI New Delhi, IARI Centenary Lecture. 16 March.

WFP 2001. *Enabling Development: Food Assistance in South Asia*, New Delhi: Oxford University Press, pp. 316.

Ye, X., Al-Babili, S., Kloti, A., Zhang, J., Lucca, P., Beyer, P. and Potrykus, I. 2000. 'Engineering provitamin A (ß-carotene) biosynthetic pathway into (carotenoid-free) rice endosperm', *Science*, 287: 303–305.

2006 K R Narayanan Oration

Message from the President

I am delighted to find that The Australian National University, Canberra is organizing the K R Narayanan Oration with the theme 'India's Space Enterprise: A case study in Strategic Thinking and Planning'. I am happy that this Oration is being delivered by Dr K. Kasturirangan, one of the foremost space scientists in India. Former President of India K R Narayanan was a noted statesman and strategic thinker who has contributed to the development of India in different spheres.

Indian space programme has its origin with the unveiling of the vision by Dr Vikram Sarabhai as early as 1962. He visualized the importance of space application for societal upliftment through communication and remote sensing satellites for a country like India with six hundred thousand villages spread in remote corners of the nation. Now seven hundred million people 70 per cent of our population live in the rural areas. Dr Vikram Sarabhai gave a roadmap to build expertise to achieve the ultimate goal of building India's own launch vehicles and satellites and ability to launch them from Indian launch station by Indian scientists in partnership with academic institutions and industry.

Over the last four decades, the vision of Dr Sarabhai has been translated into mission mode programmes by Prof. Satish Dhawan and his nurtured leaders like Dr U R Rao and Dr K. Kasturirangan and now Dr G. Madhavan Nair. Today India is self reliant in space technology with its own satellite for remote sensing and communication applications.

The benefits of space programme are now reaching the society through tele-education, tele-medicine, e-governance, meteorology, communication and broadcasting, resource assessment and disaster management. This has been realized through strategic thinking and meticulous planning. Further, India is poised to send a probe for lunar exploration and develop reusable launch vehicles. This will lead to manned missions and mining in planets through international collaborations. The leadership attributes and qualities developed through India's space programme have found significant applications in many socio-economic programmes of the country.

Considering that half of the world population is yet to experience the excitement of space programme, I am sure this Oration will generate a renewed interest by these countries in space missions through international co-operation drawing the benefits of expertise and experience available with countries like India.

I greet the organizers of K R Narayanan Oration and wish the participants success in the mission of promoting science and technology for societal upliftment.

A.P.J. Abdul Kalam
New Delhi 2006

India's Space Enterprise — A Case Study in Strategic Thinking and Planning

K. Kasturirangan

It is a matter of proud privilege and honour for me to be invited to deliver the 2006 Narayanan Oration at the Australia South Asia Research Centre (ASARC) of The Australian National University (ANU). It is with profound regret and sorrow that we had to confront Mr. K R Narayanan's demise recently on 9th November 2005. Whenever I met him, he left in me an indelible impression of his awe inspiring and deep erudition and his extraordinary passion and commitment to uplift underprivileged segments of the society. Nonetheless, he also pursued relentless efforts to achieve excellence in all walks of life. His holistic approach to science and technology has been candidly revealed in his speech on the eve of Golden Jubilee celebrations of the Indian Republic

> We cannot and ought not halt movement in the trajectories of our modern progress. Factories will and must rise, satellites must and will soar to the heavens, and dams over rivers will rise to prevent floods, generate electricity and irrigate dry lands for cultivation. But that should not cause ecological and environmental devastation and the uprooting of human settlements, especially of tribals and the poor. Ways and methods can be found for countering the harmful impact of modern technology on the lives of the common people. I believe that the answer to the ill-effects of science and technology is not to turn our back on technology, but to have more science and technology that is directed to human needs and for the betterment of the human condition.

It is my good fortune that I could pay my own humble tribute to this noble soul through this oration instituted in his honour. I also thank the ASARC of ANU and its Executive Director, Professor Raghbendra Jha for this invitation.

2. Early History

Modern Space science had its beginnings around 1946 when scientists started the deployment of instruments to the outer fringes of the earth's atmosphere using balloons and rockets to study radiations from outer space as well as geophysical phenomena. In spite of the professed scientific goals for the first earth satellite missions, the launch of SPUTNIK on 4 October, 1957 by the then Soviet Union added a new dimension (Logsdon 2001) to the cold war between the US and the Soviet Union. The early scientific satellite missions of the US also had implicit goals of pursuing US interest in establishing the international legal principle that national sovereignty did not extend to the altitudes at which the satellite would orbit. Thus there was no obstacle in international law to the over flight of a reconnaissance satellite over Soviet territory. Against this back drop, it is significant to note that the early inspiration for the Indian space program came not from any military objectives, but from the interests of a large scientific community who have been actively engaged in research programs related to geophysics and astrophysics. When Vikram Sarabhai and Homi Bhabha suggested support to space science and technology for possible application to Indian problems, in 1962, the Sputnik era was just five years old. Pandit Nehru's approval for the application of space technology in India was an act of extraordinary foresight and courage. This decision in the absence of experience with operational systems, the newness and complexity of the technology and the high risks involved, could have only been based on a vision of the future and an abiding faith and confidence in the Indian scientists and people.

3. The Vision

The vision of space that Dr Vikram Sarabhai gave for India is extra-ordinary for its realism and pragmatism, unique for its deep insights into the socio-economic context of the country, extensive in the level of details and identification of different dimensions and remarkable for the display of his own conviction. In the annals of our Science and Technology endeavour, very rarely has one come across such a vision that has withstood the test of time — in this case over more than four decades. Some glimpses of his vision (Sarabhai 1979) are in order at this juncture, as an early example in strategic thinking.

The vision recognized that promotion of space research, besides contributing to societal benefits and enrichment also results in intangible benefits coming out of the need to develop high technologies for economic development and security. The vision also identified space's unique ability to create leadership and the benefits of international collaborations. Further, it could help develop the nucleus of a new culture where a large group of persons in diverse activities learn to work together for the accomplishment of a single objective. Establishing a synchronous satellite over the Indian Ocean to improve meteorological forecasting, critical to agricultural operations and evolving national plans using space technologies for resource survey were also visualized as important for India. The vision called for an exciting development of a synchronous direct television broadcasting satellite that could serve as the most powerful means of mass communication to reach a large segment of the population in an economically depressed region of the world. Early in the conceptualization of a satellite based communication and broadcasting system, issues of system choice including the financial implications and the economic benefit were recognized as important. The establishment of strong linkages with key user agencies was central to this vision. Dr Sarabhai's emphasis on self-reliance made it the life current of the Indian space program and enabled the program to overcome numerous challenges in the course of its journey towards operational applications of space. His vision was not merely restricted to technology and application, but also to the attendant needs of new organizational structures on one side, and the fundamental issue of the role of humans in space on the other (Sarabhai 1966).

Development of this vision itself was spread over a decade from 1961. This period was characterized by consultation among the various stakeholders (ISRO Report 1972) — using professionals across the world as sounding boards — for detailed assessments of the different dimensions of the envisaged program through experimentation, analysis and simulation that factored in the socio-economic context of the country. In retrospect, it is gratifying to note that such an elaborate and carefully formulated vision helped to grow the program, in a directed manner over the next three decades without any major deviations, except for small midcourse corrections on some specific parts of the program. It is also of interest to note that this entire decade accounted for an expenditure, that is less than 1 per cent of the total investment in the space program up to 2006 (constant price basis)

4. Present Dimensions of Indian Space Program

The Indian space program today is a large integrated program, which is self-reliant and applications driven, maintaining vital links to the user community and committed to excellence in scientific endeavours.

The program developed capabilities to produce world-class satellites and launch vehicles and to apply them in diverse areas relevant to national development. India has established two operational space systems. The Indian National Satellite (INSAT) system, currently made up of nine satellites in orbit is one of the largest domestic satellite communication system in the world. The Indian Remote Sensing satellite (IRS) system, with a constellation of seven satellites, comprises some of the best satellites in the world for generating information on natural resources. Space launch vehicles developed by India are aimed towards providing autonomous launch capability to orbit these classes of satellites. India's Polar Satellite Launch Vehicle (PSLV) is well proven through eight successive successful flights and it provides the capability to orbit remote sensing satellites of the 1.4 tone class in polar sun synchronous orbits. The Geo synchronous Satellite Launch Vehicle (GSLV), capable of launching 2 to 2.5 tone class of INSAT satellites, has been operationalised with three successful flights in a row, making India one of the six countries in the world to demonstrate capabilities for geo-stationary satellite launch.

Both IRS and INSAT satellites have benefited the country in various areas of national development. INSAT satellites are the main stay for the Television broadcasting and provide connectivity to more than 1100 TV transmitters. They also network radio stations, provide rural area communications, business communications and Tele-education and Tele-medicine services. They are also used to relay cyclone warnings, gather meteorological data, assist weather forecasting for emergency communication support during disasters and providing search and rescue support. The imageries and data from the IRS satellites are used for vital applications such as locating zones for availability of ground water in habitations having no access to drinking water, monitoring agricultural crops, providing advisories to coastal fishermen on potential zones for fishing, planning water shed, rural development and waste land management programs as well as disaster management support.

Front ranking scientific investigations are being carried out in the fields of astronomy, atmospheric sciences and long-term climatic research using satellites, balloons, sounding rockets and ground instruments. India has also embarked on an ambitious planetary exploration program, the flagship mission of which is Chandrayaan-1. This mission aims to place a satellite around the Moon for physical and chemical mapping of the lunar surface.

India has forged bilateral co-operative arrangements with more than 20 countries including Australia, China, France, Germany, Russia and USA. The scope of the international co-operation is multi-dimensional in nature, which includes conduct of joint missions, offering opportunity for flight of instruments onboard Indian satellites, exchange of meteorological data and offering education and training in the area of Space. It is worth noting that six scientific instruments from the USA and Europe are being flown in India's Lunar Mission Chandrayaan-1. India has established a Centre for Space Science, Technology and Application Education for Asia and Pacific, affiliated to the UN and is offering well-structured educational programs.

An entity called Antrix Corporation has been established to promote commercial use of the space assets of ISRO and to help Indian space industries achieve global competitiveness. Global marketing of IRS data, launching of four foreign small satellites by PSLV, leasing of INSAT transponder capacity to commercial operators including INTELSAT, supply of spacecraft subsystems and mission support services of Indian ground stations are some of the highlights of the Antrix space business. It has also recently established an alliance with Europe's leading satellite manufacturer, EADS Astrium, to jointly manufacture communication satellites using the INSAT bus for selling in global markets.

India piloted a satellite communication policy in 1997 paving the way for use of INSAT capacity by private users and for private ownership of communications satellite assets. Further, a comprehensive remote sensing data policy on acquisition and distribution of remote sensing data for civilian users is also in place. Remote sensing data from satellites have been accepted as legal evidence in many States of the country for purposes such as environment impact assessment for site clearances, forest encroachment and infrastructure development.

Linkages with academia have also been an important aspect of Indian space program. More than 80 universities and academic institutions of higher learning are involved in a variety of research projects related to space science, technology and applications.

In a nutshell, these multifaceted contributions from the Indian Space program, which has been developed and run with modest budgets, make it particularly significant in the modern context.

5. Evolving Strategies

The evolution of the Indian space program over the past four decades represents a systematic and phased approach to building knowledge, technological capacity and an organizational system to ensure effective application of sophisticated technologies to national development (Dhawan 1985; Kasturirangan 2001).

Beyond the first decade of vision and initiation, the space program evolution can be broadly categorized under three distinct phases. The first phase related to proof of concept demonstration, the second dealt with the realization of end-to-end systems at an experimental level that then led into the current operational phase. In what follows, we discuss briefly some of the examples of strategic thinking and planning while progressing through these phases.

5.1. Proof of Concept Phase

The proof of concept phase of the Indian space program was characterized by the use of foreign space systems, configuring the ground system to suit national needs and conditions as well as working closely with the potential user community. We illustrate the nature of the activities in this phase through three examples.

The first is an experiment to develop, test and manage a satellite based instructional television system, to demonstrate the utility of satellite television for mass communication with a specific emphasis on remote rural areas communications. Known as the Satellite Instructional Television Experiment (SITE), it used the American Satellite, ATS-6 specially moved over Indian Ocean to conduct this experiment in 1975–76. The responsibility of design, development, deployment, operation and maintenance of ground equipment was entirely that of India and it involved nearly 2400 direct reception television stations in six clusters. India also undertook development of instructional programs, in the areas of family planning, agriculture, national integration, primary education, and teacher training. While departmental boundaries are often difficult to cross in a bureaucratic system, in a multi-disciplinary project such as SITE, it often became necessary to work across conventional boundaries and sort out the interface problems. SITE gave very valuable inputs as to how TV, a new extension tool can be integrated into the existing organization of the user agencies. Social research and evaluation design was also carried out for impact survey of target populations. Further, the experiment helped arriving at cost estimates for a national operational satellite system.

The second example related to the Satellite Telecommunication Experimental Project (STEP). This project, undertaken primarily to understand the issues of interfaces between space and ground systems for communication, was conducted with a Franco-German satellite, Symphonie. STEP helped in concretizing our initial thinking on 'Disaster Warning Systems', radio networking concepts and transporatable terminal developments, and provided vital inputs to the planning of INSAT.

The third example relates to space based earth observation system. Landsat, launched by USA in 1972 provided an unique opportunity to test out the utility of a satellite based earth observation system for obtaining timely, accurate and precise information of earth resources. The exercise of establishing ground systems, integrating space based data with conventional aerial and ground based data and working closely with user community, such as the Geological Survey of India, Agriculture, Forestry and Water resources users provided several crucial insights for planning the future operational remote sensing systems.

In summary, the proof of concept demonstrations enabled evaluating the potential of the vantage point of Space for addressing the country's developmental needs and issues of scalability at the national level. An important outcome was the evaluation of uniqueness of space in providing new services, or for assessment of their superiority vis-à-vis conventional approaches. Further, this phase enabled a short turn around time and a low cost strategy for evaluating the concepts, the systemic issues including technologies, the institutional frameworks and the user interfaces.

5.2. Experimental Phase

The experimental phase was identified with a strategy to derive an end-to-end experience in the realization of space systems where the potential of its use at the national level had already been clearly demonstrated in the proof of concept phase. Here the strategy took due cognizance of the fact that space systems are inherently complex, carry high risks and are investment intensive. Further the creation of a heritage in hardware, human resource and methods are critical to develop confidence for operational systems. There was also a need to minimize the impact of probable early failures in the public mind and the political system. This phase additionally facilitated competence building at the core level, helped in the detailed evaluation of issues for scaling the effort to the national level and set the rules relating to the overall practices in system engineering. The overall demonstration of the systemic approach in this phase paved the way for the country to create national systems at a much larger scale with bigger and more sustained investments. We briefly discuss the nature of two satellite missions, Bhaskara and Apple, that were accomplished based on these considerations.

The Bhaskara Satellites (two of which were built and launched in 1979 and 1981), were earth observation satellites with a low resolution of 1 Km operating in two spectral bands. The Bhaskara program at a cost of Rs.60 million, and spread over six years gave valuable experience of building imaging camera systems, realizing satellite platform to take pictures from space, receiving the image information and processing these on the ground through appropriate ground infrastructure. Further, the mission enabled evaluating application interface methodologies with users in resource areas such as vegetative cover, geology and hydrology.

The Ariane Passenger Payload Experiment (APPLE) conducted in 1981, provided experience in satellite communications, including building of a body stabilized geosynchronous satellite. The involvement of the user agencies early in the program, had a very significant influence on the adoption of the satellite communication technology in operational communication systems of India in the subsequent years.

The experimental phase also saw some very significant progress in the design and development of launch vehicles. Systematic efforts in building capabilities, studies of configurational options, issues of phasing the program, development of relevant infrastructure were all part of both the proof of concept and the experimental phases. The strategy for developing the launch vehicle was dictated by the country's decision to have autonomy in accessing space. Before going for the realization of a full-fledged launch capability, the need to have a phased development was recognized as necessary both for building competence and for developing the needed confidence. Successful realization of India's first launch vehicle SLV-3, with a modest payload capability of 40 kg and initiation of the augmented capability version ASLV with 150 kg payload capability took place in this phase. Valuable experience and inputs from both SLV-3 and ASLV, provided the basis for planning, configuring and implementing strategies for the current operational launch vehicles, the PSLV and GSLV (Gupta 2006).

The proof of concept and experimental phases together accounted for an expenditure of 8 per cent of the total expenditure as on 2006 (constant price basis).

5.3. Operational Phase

The operational phase, as described in section-4 called for certain unique strategies and decision making. Let me give a couple of examples in this connection. Encouraged by the lessons of the SITE experiment and recognizing the potential of a space-based communication and broadcasting system for meeting the developmental needs of the country (Kale et al. 1971), India decided to go for a space-based communication and broadcasting system. Taking into account, the time frame for indigenous design and development of an operational Indian National Satellite (INSAT) and recognizing the urgency to initiate services in this area, India decided to go for a bought out option for the first generation INSAT systems, even as we embarked on the design and development of the second generation systems. The four satellites of the first generation were thus procured, launched and operated for providing space based communication and broadcasting services for meeting national needs. The subsequent three generations of satellites, many of which are currently in service, were all designed and built indigenously. The strategy adopted was different in the case of earth observations. Although the then operating foreign satellites were used for developing the remote sensing applications in the country, the special requirements of earth observations, peculiar to our country as well as cost and strategic considerations called for an indigenous design and development route for the realization of operational remote sensing satellite systems. 'Bhaskara' missions provided the necessary confidence to undertake such an effort. The implementation of this strategy has resulted in India's own world class IRS series of satellites.

Another example is about the decision, in the early phase itself, to de-couple the time frame for the development of the launch vehicles from their role in providing operational support for satellite launches. Considering the complexities and the longer time frames for the development of launch vehicles, India consciously decided to seek launch support services for operational satellites from outside agencies. Such a strategy enabled the timely establishment of space services and also provided specific inputs for sizing the launch systems for these classes of satellites. The present capabilities of PSLV and GSLV and their future versions are based on the evolutionary requirements coming out of the IRS and INSAT programs.

The above considerations, relating to the introduction of high technology systems for meeting developmental and other innovative service goals, therefore called for pragmatic strategies. This in turn required understanding and analyzing the complex interplay of several issues. First was a detailed assessment and evaluation of alternate approaches to arrive at the most optimal solutions. The second was to decide on exercising buy or build options taking into account the time frame for the introduction of services. In the case of buy options, a parallel indigenous development plan was created to achieve self-reliance goals.

Coming to the organizational systems (Kasturirangan 2001; Narasimha and Kalam (eds) 1988), experience from earlier experiments involving broadcasting, communication and remote sensing, and dealing with the user communities, provided valuable inputs for the creation of innovative formal institutional frameworks. In the case of remote sensing, the institutional framework involved setting up of the Planning Committee of the National Natural Resources Management System (NNRMS), which at the overall level is mandated to provide directions for the creation of space based remote sensing capabilities for the country. NNRMS consists of Secretaries of the line departments of the Government of India dealing with natural resources and is headed by a Member of Planning Commission. Such a structure enables the involvement of major user communities to address issues of ensuring the use of such systems in their own areas of thematic applications, while at the same time facilitating the incorporation of this new and powerful technique into conventional approaches. Similarly the INSAT Coordination Committee, with the Secretaries of the user departments (Information and Broadcasting, Communication, Information Technology and Science & Technology) working along with the Secretary of the Space Department, was created as an apex body to address the development of space communication, broadcasting and meteorology and planning their utilization. In the context of Space Science, the Advisory Committee On Space Sciences (ADCOS) represented by some of the leading space scientists in the country provides directions for space science research. The three structures identified above have no parallel, anywhere else in the world and have played a crucial role in sustaining the various space endeavours. Being user driven also means the beginning of a culture of accountability and transparency. Another important aspect is that the overall space program in India is overseen by a high level body, known as the Space Commission, chaired by the Head of the Space organization and reporting directly to the Prime Minister. This structure ensures that the space program derives strength from the highest level and that the policy directions are duly integrated by different government agencies.

Another aspect of the organisational strategy was to create an industrial base for supporting the space program (Dhawan 1983 and 1988) and for carrying out relatively routine operations, while the space agency concentrated on pushing the internal output up the value chain by enhancing the quality and content of research and development output. This also enabled us to progressively increase the strength of highly qualified professionals without increasing the overall size of the organization. Also, in successive five-year plan periods, the organization could deliver increasingly larger number of complex missions, as illustrated in the Fig. 1.

Fig. 1

DEPARTMENT OF SPACE

GROWTH OF BUDGET, MANPOWER & MISSIONS

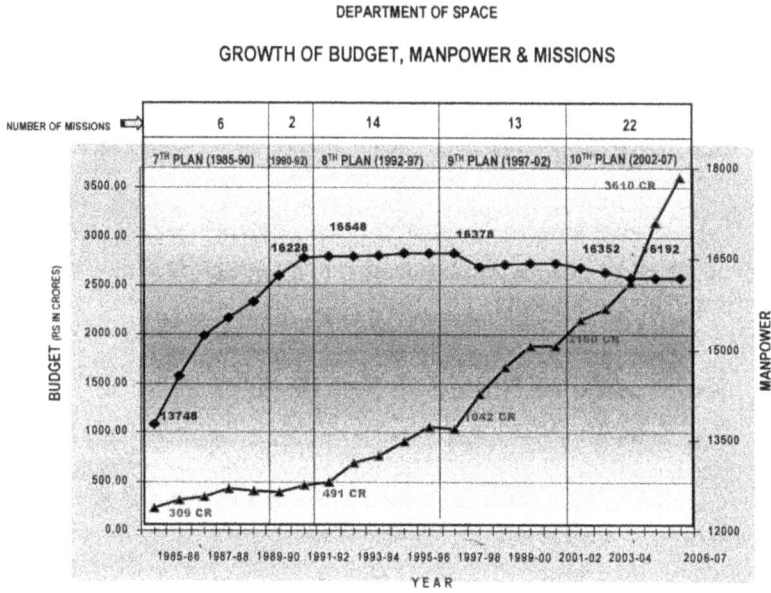

There have also been instances where the justification for initiating a new activity based on measurable direct benefits is lacking. At the same time the intangible benefits that could come from some of these programs could be convincing or not so convincing. An interesting case in point is the recent Indian initiative for planetary exploration Chandrayaan-I (Kasturirangan 2004a). We had to go through an elaborate process of consultation and justification with the scientific community, academics, the political system and the public media before this mission was given the go ahead. The steps that were taken are shown in Fig. 2.

Fig. 2

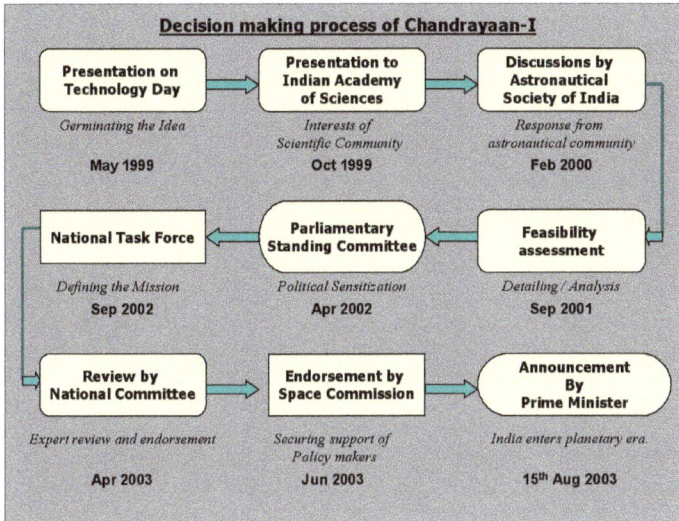

This process, spread out over four years, culminated in the announcement by the Prime Minister of India on August 15, 2003 (India's independence day) on the nation's decision to enter the new era of planetary exploration. This is also a good example of a practice of ethics of decision making in science involving consultation of a large cross-section of society and ensuring transparency.

6. Relevance of Space to South Asia

Although applications of space technology have taken deep roots in society and practiced for well over four decades, many countries in the developing world are yet to fully experience the excitement and take full advantage of space systems. In this context, the experience of India could be relevant for a developing country wanting to realize a cost effective and socially relevant program.

Turning to the development needs and priorities in South Asia, it is not difficult to realize that an appropriate application of space technology and creation of services based on space technology are highly relevant. South Asia comprising Afghanistan, Bangladesh, Bhutan, India, Maldives, Nepal, Pakistan and Sri Lanka have a combined population of 1.45 billion, which is about 22 per cent of the global population. Because of the agrarian focus of a predominant proportion of their populations, efficient use of natural resources such as land and water assumes great importance. The high population density places tremendous pressure on environment, requiring sound strategies for sustainable management (Rao 1995). There is also the issue of a divide between urban and rural areas in terms of access to health and education facilities. Common to all these countries, there is the major issue of response to natural disasters that are adversely impacting their economic growth. For ensuring equity-oriented development in such situations, there is a need to adopt high technologies such as space.

Some of the Space technology inputs that relate to the needs of South Asia in terms of providing solutions are highlighted below (Kasturirangan et al. 2004).

Needs	Areas where Space Technology can help
Improving Food Security	• Water shed management • Optimal Land use strategy plan • Control of Land degradation • Drought mitigation and proofing • Recovery of irrigation systems • Monitoring of crops and cropping systems • Ground water targeting • Siting water harvesting structures • Fisheries forecasting
Infrastructure development	• Road connectivity analysis • Selection of site • Land use mapping / monitoring • Urban mapping • Community Information Kiosks • VSAT communications network
Health and Education – bridging gaps and improving quality	• Tele Medicine Network • Tele Education Network
Disaster Management and Response	• Cyclone warning (Land falls) • Flood damage assessments • Flood plain GIS/Flood zoning analysis • Drought monitoring • Land slide zoning
Environment management	• Vegetation monitoring • Forest mapping, a forestation plans • Coastal zone regulation monitoring • Mining impacts • Urban sprawl and Land use monitoring • Monitoring desertification. • Weather watch • Water conservation and management • Atmospheric pollution monitoring

It is pertinent to note that information inputs from space technology lead to better decision-making and interventions. Both long term and short term goals are to be set in order to realize practical solutions in the shortest possible time and to build capacity for sustaining the programs. An appropriate organizational nucleus has to be created to plan and implement space activities.

A conceptual framework for use of space for development is shown in Fig. 3.

Use of space technology, with an accent on capacity building, is sine qua non for its progress. The conceptual framework given above is based on the experience of India, and the relevant strategies described in the earlier sections are quite relevant for wider application in the region as well as other developing parts of the world.

Fig. 3

A CONCEPTUAL MODEL FOR USE OF SPACE FOR DEVELOPMENT

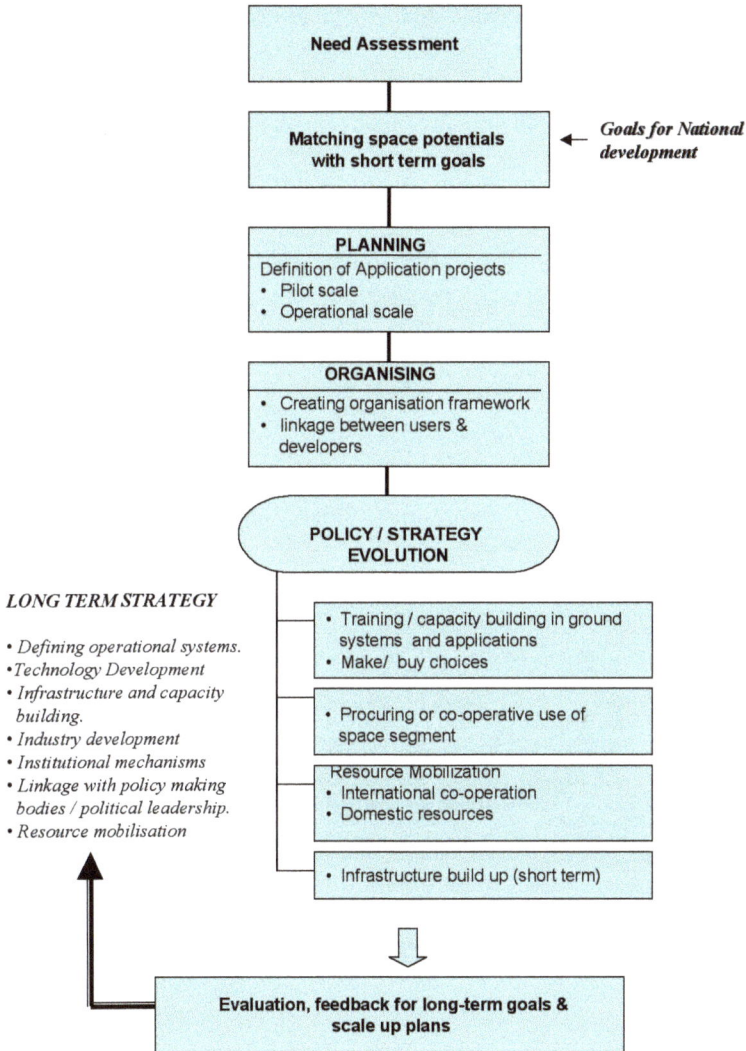

7. Economic Aspects of India's Space Program

By the early nineties, all the four major components of the space programe, namely, Satellite Communications, Meteorology, Earth Observations and Launch Vehicles had entered the operational stage.

The Satellite-based Communication Services (SATCOM) Policy of 1997 and the Remote Sensing based value added services envisaged opening of the space industry to the private sector. Therefore it was considered timely and appropriate to commission a study on the economic aspects of the Indian space program through the Madras School of Economics (Sankar 2006a; 2006b; Sankar et al. 2003).

7.1. Space Expenditures

Accumulated space expenditures since inception to the last fiscal year ending on March 31, 2006 amounted to US$ 7 billion. These expenditures category-wise are given in Fig. 4.

Fig. 4

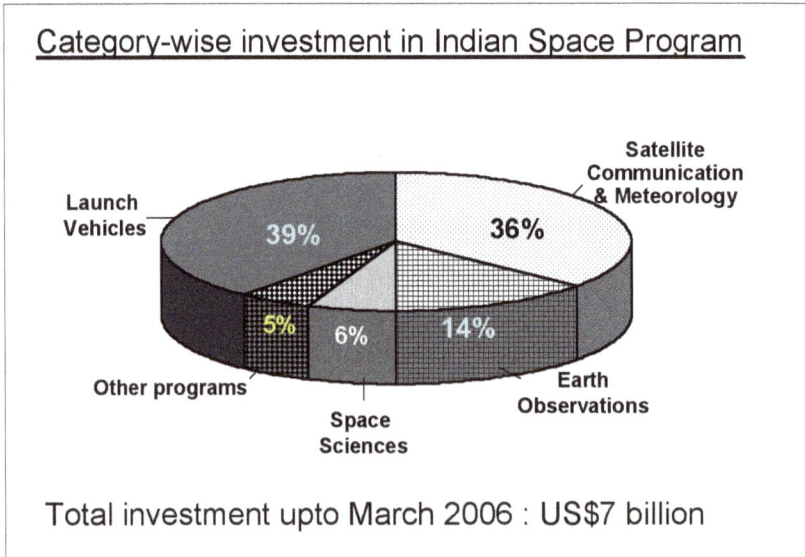

Category-wise investment in Indian Space Program

Launch Vehicles 39%

Satellite Communication & Meteorology 36%

Other programs 5%

Space Sciences 6%

Earth Observations 14%

Total investment upto March 2006 : US$7 billion

As is obvious from the figure, 39 per cent investment is on launch vehicles, 36 per cent on Satellite communications and meteorology, 14 per cent on earth observations, 6 per cent on space sciences and the balance on other items. About three-fourth of the total expenditure was incurred towards development of technology in the case of launch vehicles, whereas in the case of satellite communications, meteorology and earth observations, three-fourth of the investment is for building operational systems based on service needs of the country.

The space expenditure of India as a percentage of gross domestic product (GDP) today stands at 0.09 per cent. Compared with the current annual government space budgets of US $2.5 billion for Japan, and US$1.5 billion for France, India's space budget is US$0.60 billion.

7.2. Methodology

For the purposes of economic analysis, it is useful to classify space activities into two stages, namely, (i) design, development, testing, manufacturing and launch of spacecrafts into desired orbital slots (construction stage), and (ii) applications of satellite services to different uses (exploitation stage). The output basket of the space program contains a mix of private goods, public goods, social goods and strategic/incommensurable goods. Research in space sciences, most meteorological services and information are public goods. Equity considerations are important in provision of certain goods e.g. access to public telephone, access to radio and TV. The social goals dominate in public sector radio and TV programs. Use of the space program as an instrument for guaranteeing strategic, political, scientific and economic leadership yields strategic and incommensurable benefits. The methodology adopted for the two stages, category-wise, is given in Fig. 5.

Fig. 5

Framework of Economic Analysis

Indian Space Programme

Construction Stage
Creating infrastructure & Technological capabilities

- Launch Vehicles
- Satellites
- Ground Segment

OBJECTIVE & EVALUATION CRITERIA

- *Self reliance*
- *Cost effectiveness*
- *Spin-off benefits*

Exploitation Stage
Application of Space Systems for National Development

Broadcasting	Tele-communications	Meteorology	Earth Observations
Private / Social goods	*Private / Social goods*	*Public goods*	*Public goods*

B E N E F I T S

Broadcasting
- *Cost Savings*
- *Social Benefits*
- *Commercial benefits*

Tele-communications
- *Cost Savings*
- *Social Benefits*
- *Commercial benefits*

Meteorology
- *New / improved services*
- *Value of information*
- *Social benefits*

Earth Observations
- *Cost and time savings*
- *New / improved services*
- *Value of information*
- *Strategic edge*

Contributions to Economic development

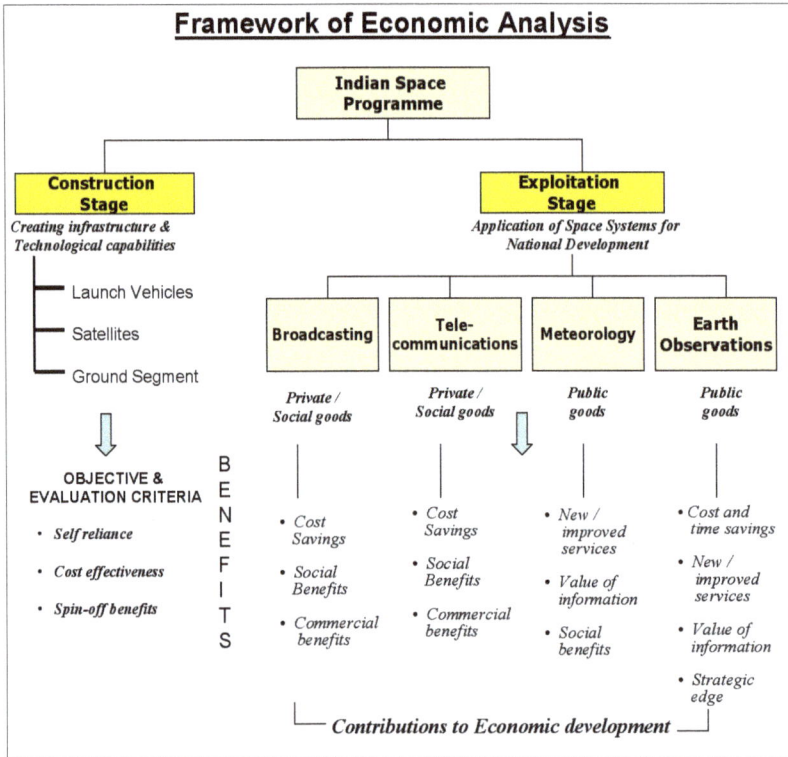

7.3. Construction Stage

Regardless of the nature of goods / services provided and whether it is produced by a public firm or private firm, cost minimization is a valid criterion. The economic costing methodology requires (i) a rational basis for allocation of costs among the payloads of a multi-purpose satellite (ii) apportionment of common and joint costs amongst various ongoing programs of the organization / institution (iii) investment expenditure, their time pattern and cost of capital and (iv) output streams, their time pattern and discount rates for present value.

The global market for communication transponders is generally competitive with many private and public suppliers and many customers buying the transponders. Government induced market distortions are relatively less in this market. Hence, the international market prices can serve as a benchmark for assessing the cost effectiveness of INSAT transponders. A detailed study on economic costing of INSAT transponders with 10 per cent cost of capital on investments and 5.5 per cent discount factor on future returns has brought out the cost advantage of INSAT transponders by at least 25 per cent of the prevailing international prices. The cost performance of INSAT system has been considered to be commendable keeping in view the relatively high capital cost in India and the dependence on some foreign components in the production of the satellites.

A comparative analysis of remote sensing satellites and launch vehicles is rather difficult due to non-availability of reliable estimates of the costs of foreign systems and also due to differences in capabilities. However, preliminary estimates show that the costs of Indian Remote Sensing Satellite (IRS-1D) is very much lower than the reported costs of similar LANDSAT and SPOT satellites. Similarly, the development cost of India's PSLV and GSLV is US $1.3 billion as compared to about US $ 4 billion for the European Ariane 1 to 4, though there are some capacity variations in these systems.

7.4. Exploitation Stage

For measurement of the benefits, the role of satellite technology is considered under three different categories: (a) where the technology is unique, (b) where the technology is a substitute to existing technologies, and (c) where the technology is complementary to existing technologies. In the second case, one can measure cost savings due to satellite technology compared with the existing technology. If the technology is superior to the existing one, one has to estimate the incremental value of the improvement. Where the space technology is used in conjunction with many other technologies, one has to rely on a cost allocation procedure or a benefit sharing method or on expert opinion to estimate the benefit attributable to the space technology.

The INSAT system has played a key role in augmenting Broadcasting, Telecommunications and Meteorological services in the country and has contributed immensely to economic and social development. Satellite communication technologies are terrain and distance independent and they enable governments to achieve goals such as the development of backward and remote areas at low costs and in a short time and thereby achieve technological leapfrogging.

7.4.1. Television

The Major benefits of the INSAT system to Doordarshan (public TV) are expansion in area coverage from 14 per cent in 1983 to 78 per cent in 2005, population coverage from 26 per cent in 1983 to 90 per cent in 2005, increase in the number of channels from 2 to 32, remote area coverage, satellite news gathering, dissemination of weather and cyclone warning and use of TV as a media for training and education.

A detailed analysis show that for enhancing the population coverage further from 90 to 100 per cent with the distribution of a bouquet of 20 DD channels by the public broadcaster Doordarshan, the capital cost and annual operating cost through terrestrial technology is Rs.34560 million and Rs.5184 million respectively while a satellite based solution with direct reception at homes, would involve a capital cost of Rs.6380 million and annual operating cost of Rs.357 million. Thus, given the unique physiographical feature of India, the satellite communications is the least-cost option for achieving 100 per cent population coverage.

The growth of satellite TV has also aided in the emergence of new economic activities. The advent of satellite TV contributed to the growth of several industries like the manufacturing of TV sets, cables, receiving antenna and other equipment and program production. There are about 100,000 cable TV operators and about 35 million cable TV households in the country. The gross earnings of cable TV operators is nearing Rs. 10 billion.

7.4.2. Telecommunications

Remote area communication is an important objective of public policy. There is considerable cost savings due to use of satellite technology compared with the alternative of optical fiber cable network in remote area communication. The cost of connecting 393 remote areas, currently served by INSAT, by optical fibre cable would be Rs.23580 million while the comparable cost for satellite technology would be Rs.10460 million. It may be noted that there are 30,000 remote villages of similar nature needing connectivity. The other uses of satellite technology are: alternative media back up for terrestrial services, business communications, portable terminals for disaster management, Tele-medicine and Satellite Aided Search and Rescue.

Apart from the cost saving, there are many external benefits which are diffused economy-wide. In case of Andaman and Nicobar (AN), rapid expansion of telecom since the mid-nineties facilitated the integration of AN with the mainland thereby boosting the growth of industry, trade and tourism and raising the growth rate of gross state domestic product to more than 8 per cent.

7.4.3. Meterology

Satellites have made significant contributions to the generation of meteorological information by extending observation to oceans and remote areas on land, enabling generation of new types of observations, facilitating new concepts of data assimilation into models, reducing costs of a few types of observations and enhancing the reliability of certain types of data.

Meteorological services are recognized as public goods. The major contributions of satellite technology are in the areas of weather technology (cloud motion vector, wind-sea surface temperature and outgoing long wave radiation) and tropical cyclone (identification of genesis and current position, intensity of change and transmission of cyclone warnings). A comparative study of 1977 (before INSAT) and 1990 (after INSAT) cyclones which hit Andhra Pradesh, shows that even though the two cyclones are similar, due to the successful tracking of the cyclone in 1990 with the INSAT imaging instrument (VHRR) and the success of preparatory steps taken by the government, the loss of lives in 1990 was only 817 compared with 10,000 in 1977. This is an important incommensurable benefit of satellite technology.

7.4.4. Remote Sensing

The advantages of remote sensing are synoptic coverage, multi-spectral capability, multi-temporal capability and digital capture of data. Remote sensing technology is being used in three different situations. It is an exclusive tool for estimation of snow melt run-off, rapid assessment of areas affected by natural disasters, identification of potential fishing zones in offshore areas and mapping of inaccessible areas. It is a substitute tool to conventional methods in mapping of land use, waste lands, and urban land use; preparing ground water prospect maps, watershed development plan, coastal zone management plan etc; and in monitoring forest cover, urban sprawl, status of environment etc. It is a complement in cases like area and crop forecasting and urban development plans. Its advantage is that it yields unbiased, timely and enhanced information. Based on case studies of applications of remote sensing in India's development programs, Table 3 provides estimates of investments, direct returns, and economic benefits.

Apart from the major benefits enumerated above, the policy of self-reliance has also enabled internal competence building and technology development and spin-offs to non-space sectors. For example, the spin-off outputs till 2005 include 224 Technology Transfers, 165 patents, 10 trademarks and 17 copyrights. ISRO has nurtured a symbiotic partnership with more than 500 Indian firms. The flow of funds to industry currently is about 40 per cent of the space budget. This partnership has generated significant spin-off effects to the industries in terms of improved manufacturing processes, quality control and management practices.

Table 3: Investments and Benefits in Remote Sensing

A	Investments	Rs. Millions
	Operational Missions	10,080
	Data Reception, Processing and Applications	5,540

B	Direct Returns	
1.	Returns from sale of Satellite Data and Value Added Products by NDC	1,600
2.	Returns from ANTRIX through access fees and royalty	600
3.	Opportunity cost (cost of foreign satellite data equivalent to IRS data used).	~ 5,000
4.	Cost saving due to value addition	~ 12,000
5.	Cost saving due to mapping using RS data	~ 11,000

C	Economic Benefits		Rs. Millions	
	Program	Nature of Benefit	Estimate from Case Studies	Potential Benefit to the country in the Long-run
1.	National Drinking Water Technology Mission	Cost saving due to increase in success rate	2,560 (5 States)	5,000 – 8,000
2.	Urban Area Perspective / Development / Zonal / Amenities Plan for Cities / Towns	Cost saving in mapping	50.4 (6 Cities)	16,000 – 20,000
3.	Forest Working Plan	Cost saving in mapping	2,000 (200 Divisions)	11,860
4.	Potential Fishing Zone Advisories	Cost saving due to avoidance of trips in non-PFZ advisories	5,450	16,350
5.	Wasteland Mapping: Solid Land Reclamation	Productivity gain	990 (UP)	24,690
6.	Integrated Mission for Sustainable Development: Horticultural Development in Land With and Without Shrub	Gross income	Rs.0.20 to 0.40 (per hectare)	13,000 – 26,000
7.	Bio-prospecting for Medicinal Herbs	Value of Indian life saving drugs		800

Note: 1US $ = Rs. 45.

8. Concluding Remarks

Space, in India, has become deeply intertwined with many facets of the national developmental endeavour. As we continue into the 21st Century, the relevance of space as demonstrated by India is becoming even more applicable to a large number of countries across the world, faced with the daunting problems of development and improving the quality of life. Further, the growing role of space in addressing issues of environment and sustainability of development as well as in the formulation of the related policies, treaties and conventions adds to the importance of this endeavour on a global scale (Kasturirangan 2004b). It is in this context that I thought it worthwhile to provide a model for organizing space research activities addressing particularly the peculiar problems of a developing country. Our approach to growing a world class space program highlights the fact that bold and imaginative adoption of new technologies to accelerate the process of development is realistic even with modest investment. Space, thus is well within the reach of the developing world, and even more important could be a sustainable endeavour. What is needed is a vision, forward looking leadership and above all the political will. I hope the pragmatic approaches, elucidated here, will serve to inspire embarking on such an exciting and meaningful venture by countries not touched by its innovative consequences.

Turning the spotlight again on India and her dreams to transform herself into a developed nation in the very early part of 21st century, it is pertinent to note that the mix of strategies and planned approaches evolved so far by Indian space program have the potency to fire a powerful vision of future space endeavours. In its core part, this vision will continue to orient space activities towards societal needs such as education, health services, sustainable management of resources and environment, disaster management support and so on, possibly with new generations of thematic satellite constellations. Further, it could embrace new steps for expanding the horizons of knowledge through front ranking missions for space exploration in a way that strengthens international cooperation. Future space missions will also be strong instruments for new advances in technology bringing in new synergies such as those between air and space, energy and matter, and living and nonliving objects. Our vision has to cater to younger generation, whose population will be over one half of a billion, for technological leadership, environmental stewardship and economic prosperity (Kasturirangan 2004c). While the strategic framework of the Indian space endeavour will evolve further in response to the changing environment India could even leverage space capabilities in bringing greater global integration in many other human endeavours. It is important to recognize the values that gave those strategies potency and vitality. Striving always to keep Space relevant to the public, transparency, accountability, drive for excellence, cost-effectiveness and team culture are the backbones of the strategy. They are responsible for the success of the Indian Space Enterprise and indeed for effectiveness of its strategic thinking and planning.

Before I conclude, it is appropriate to recall the extraordinary directions provided by the successive leaderships of the organization; M.G.K. Menon, Satish Dhawan and U.R. Rao; scientists with vision and deep understanding of the role of technology in national development. The culture of team spirit is a special attribute of the space program. We recall with pride the yeoman contributions made by our present President H.E. Dr A.P.J. Abdul Kalam in creating and nurturing this culture when he headed the India's prestigious first launch vehicle project SLV3. The success story of space program is also a tribute to the sustained enthusiasm, dedication and hard work of men and women of ISRO/DOS and other cooperating agencies.

To all of them and to the political system symbolized by the late Shri K R Narayanan, we owe the credit for touching the lives of millions of people towards a sustainable improved quality of life.

References

Dhawan, S., 1983, 'Space and Industry', Shri Ram Memorial Lecture, New Delhi, February 7.

Dhawan, S., 1985, 'Application of Space Technology in India', Aryabhatta Lecture, Indian National Science Academy, August 2.

Dhawan, S., 1988, 'Prospects for a Space Industry in India', Lala Karamchand Thapar Memorial Lecture, New Delhi, February 26.

Gupta, S.C., 2006, *Growing rocket Systems and the Team*, Prism Books Private Limited, Bangalore.

ISRO Report, 1972, Seminar on 'Indian Program for Space Research and Applications', August 7–12.

Kale, P.P., and William, F., Sarlez (Jr), Cochairs, 1971, 'INSAT Satellite Systems' study by MIT and ISRO, published by ISRO.

Kasturirangan, K., 2001, 'Space: An Innovative Route to Development', 4th JRD Tata Memorial Lecture, Assocham, August 31.

Kasturirangan, K., 2004, 'Environment from Vantage Point of Space', Third Darbari Seth Memorial Lecture, New Delhi, August 19.

Kasturirangan, K., 2004, 'Space — A Vision for the Next 25 years', 40th Founder Memorial Lecture, Sriram Institute for Industrial Research, New Delhi.

Kasturirangan, K., 2004, 'Space Science in India — Two Recent Initiatives', Sir Jagdish Chandra Bose Memorial Lecture, delivered at the Royal Society, London, December 14.

Kasturirangan, K., and Fracois Becker, Cochairs, 2004, 'Space to Promote Peace', IAA Commission — V Study' Group Report, Paris, September.

Logsdon, John M. (ed.), 2001, 'Exploring the Unknown', selected Documents in the History of US Civil Space Program *Vol. V: Exploring the Cosmos*, the NASA History Series.

Narasimha, R., and Kalam A.P.J. (eds) 1988, *Developments in Fluid Mechanics and Space Technology*, Dedicated to Satish Dhawan, Indian Academy of Sciences, Bangalore.

Sankar, U., 2006, 'The Indian Space Program: An Exploratory Analysis', to be published by Oxford University Press, New Delhi.

Sankar, U., 2006, Private Communication.

Sankar, U., et al., 2003, 'Economic Analysis of Indian Space Program: An exploratory study', Madras School of Economics, Chennai, November.

Sarabhai, V.A., 1966, Sources of Mans Knowledge, National Program of Talks Series, 'Exploration in Space'.

Sarabhai, V.A., 1979, *Sarabhai on Space*, A collection of writings and speeches, ISRO, Bangalore.

U.R. Rao., 1995, *Space Technology for Sustainable Development*, Tata McGraw Hill Co., New Delhi.

www.ingramcontent.com/pod-product-compliance
Lightning Source LLC
Chambersburg PA
CBHW051656210326
41518CB00030B/2596